SCRAPBOOK TIPS
& TECHNIQUES
BOOK 2

Feb 2009 7mo

that daddy's heart because of how cute you are!!

today YOU

emily-jane... or daddy's little heartsweet... he loves you so!!

one of a kind

so happy

little

Creating Keepsakes

Editor-in-Chief
Jennafer Martin

Founding Editor
Lisa Bearnson

Managing Editor
Lara Penrod

Creative Editor
Megan Hoeppner

Senior Editor
Kim Jackson

Editors
Lori Fairbanks, Joannie McBride

Senior Online Editor
Amber Ellis

Online Editor
Erin Weed

Associate Editors
Dorathy Gilchrist

Contributing Writers
Lori Anderson, Brittany Beattie, Mandy Douglass,
Ali Edwards, Becky Higgins, Jen Jockisch,
Elizabeth Kartchner, Jana Lillie, Jennifer McGuire,
Amanda Probst, Jessica Sprague, Kim Watson

Art Director
Erin Bayless

Senior Designers
Neko Carillo, Maren Ingles

Contributing Designer
Gaige Redd

Photography
American Color, Symoni Johnson, Vertis
Communications

Library of Congress Control Number: 2010941392
ISBN-13/EAN: 978-1-60900-163-6

Creative Crafts Group, LLC.

President and CEO
Stephen J. Kent

VP/Group Publisher
Tina Battock

Chief Financial Officer
Mark F. Arnett

Corporate Controller
Jordan Bohrer

VP/Publishing Director
Joel P. Toner

VP/Director of Events
Paula Kraemer

VP/Production & Technology
Derek W. Corson

VP/Consumer Marketing
Dennis O'Brien

Leisure Arts

Editor-in-Chief
Susan White Sullivan

Director of Designer Relations
Cheryl Johnson

Special Projects Director
Susan Frantz Wiles

Senior Prepress Director
Mark Hawkins

Imaging Technician
Stephanie Johnson

Publishing Systems Administrator
Becky Riddle

Mac Information Technology Specialist
Robert Young

President and Chief Executive Officer
Rick Barton

Vice President and Chief Operations Officer
Tom Siebenmorgen

Vice President of Sales
Mike Behar

Director of Finance and Administration
Laticia Mull Dittrich

National Sales Director
Martha Adams

Creative Services
Chaska Lucas

Information Technology Director
Hermine Linz

Controller
Francis Caple

Vice President, Operations
Jim Dittrich

Retail Customer Service Manager
Stan Raynor

Print Production Manager
Fred F. Pruss

Scrapbooking is a fantastic hobby—it not only connects you and your life stories with future generations later on, it connects you with your creative spirit now. And with all of the fun supplies and tools out there to play with, the creative possibilities are endless. That's why the staff at *Creating Keepsakes* scrapbook magazine have put together some of the best of our tips and techniques for you to try.

You'll have a marvelous time trying the

• budget-friendly ideas
• easy techniques for all scrapbook skill levels
• simple supply tricks
• quick ideas for supply leftovers and scraps
• easy-to-follow tips for fun page accents

and much, much more throughout this book. With a few supplies and a little time, you can unleash the creative artist in you to create beautiful, creative scrapbooks that you—and future generations—will love to look at over and over again.

Enjoy!

JENNAFER MARTIN
Editor-in-Chief
Creating Keepsakes magazine

Scrapbook Tips and Techniques, Book 2

CONTENTS

Computer Tricks

Tools & Techniques

Planning the Year

quick-start icons

Find the tips and layouts throughout the book that fit your needs—just use these icons for quick reference.

BUDGET-FRIENDLY   DESIGN   FRESH FACE   JOURNALING   ONLINE CONTENT

PHOTO   QUICK PAGE   SOLUTIONS   SKETCH   TECHNIQUE

fast, frugal & fabulous!

You won't need to take a lot of time or break the bank to create these stunning effects.

Is completing more scrapbook pages one of your goals for the new year? If so, we've got suggestions for you to meet that goal quickly and inexpensively. From creative ways to help further stretch your dollar to quick and simple solutions for creating pages in less time, these ideas will add personal and handmade touches to your layouts. You'll see that being fast and frugal doesn't have to mean your page is any less fabulous or your creative freedom is restricted.

BY JOANNIE McBRIDE

Flare

Favorites
1. watching the snow
2. flakes accumulate
3. driving on a freshly plowed road
4. pure whiteness all around me
5. around me
6. the contrast of
7. blue skies & snow
8. knowing i can look
9. forward to next time
10.

all around our little valley · december 2008

Winterland *by Wendy Sue Anderson.* **Supplies** *Cardstock:* American Crafts; *Patterned paper:* Cosmo Cricket (ledger) and October Afternoon (pink); *Ribbon:* Making Memories; *Ink:* Clearsnap; *Paper snowflakes and scallop tag:* Making Memories; *Letter stickers, brads and pen:* American Crafts; *Adhesive:* Glue Dots International and Tombow; *Other:* Thread.

use local postcards

Most of us have incorporated postcards on layouts about vacations and trips to faraway places. Consider, though, using a *local* postcard for a great, inexpensive addition to your pages about activities around home. Wendy Sue Anderson included two postcards from a local store to highlight some great views of places around her valley. The winter scenes provide a fun complement to her snow photos. She added ribbon to cover the city names on the postcards, and the result is terrific.

 BUDGET TIP: Ink your chipboard or foam letters to coordinate with your layout. Wendy's "Winterland" letters were originally white, and she colored them with a pink inkpad.

 JOURNALING TIP: Use numbered journaling spots to add fun facts or memories about your home town.

think border strips over ribbon

Decorative border strips are often less expensive than spools of ribbon. Rather than layering several ribbon strips on your page, consider using only one ribbon strip and adding paper strips in the remaining areas you'd planned for ribbon.

 BUDGET TIP: You don't even need to buy decorative border strips—you can make your own with decorative-edge scissors and leftover strips of paper.

 TECHNIQUE TIP: Give a paper border strip a bit of charm and dimension by adding shaped ribbon or decorative trim over the top, like Suzy Plantamura did with her snowflake trim over the pink strip.

Hoping for Snow! *by Suzy Plantamura.* **Supplies** *Cardstock:* Bazzill Basics Paper; *Patterned paper:* My Little Shoebox (green), My Mind's Eye (snowflake) and October Afternoon (stripe); *Journaling sticker:* Sassafras; *Cardstock borders:* My Little Shoebox; *Snowflake trim and staples:* Making Memories; *Chipboard snowman and snowflakes:* My Mind's Eye; *Letter stickers:* American Crafts (coral) and Making Memories (white); *Rub-ons:* Cosmo Cricket; *Journaling spot:* me & my EIG ideas; *Pen:* Newell Rubbermaid; *Adhesive:* EK Success and Glue Dots International; *Other:* Ribbon.

Frosty Fun *by Allison Davis.* **Supplies** *Cardstock:* Bazzill Basics Paper; *Patterned paper and transparency frame:* My Mind's Eye; *Chipboard and foam letters:* American Crafts; *Snowflake punch:* Martha Stewart Crafts; *Ink:* ColorBox, Clearsnap; *Rhinestones:* Kaisercraft; *Embroidery floss:* DMC; *Pen:* EK Success; *Adhesive:* Glue Dots International, Scrapbook Adhesives by 3L and All Night Media, Plaid Enterprises.

punch within a square shape

Square punches are fabulous, especially when another shape is punched in the center of the square. That's just what Allison Davis did on her layout using a snowflake punch. She used both the negative space (the square with the snowflake punched out) as well as the punched snowflake shapes to create a grid pattern to use as her background. She also included rhinestones on some of her punched snowflakes to add sparkle to her pages. Most of her layout design consists of photos and paper scraps—now that's economical.

PHOTO TIP: Use a square punch to crop accent photos as well as paper. Adhere the photos to your layout using dimensional adhesive to help them stand out from the paper squares.

TECHNIQUE TIP: Ink the edges of punched shapes to add subtle depth to your pages.

accent with clothing tags

Tags are definitely a fun addition to a layout, and these days you can find some unique and stylish tags on almost any piece of clothing you purchase. It's like getting a free page embellishment when you purchase a new pair of jeans or a cute blouse. Brigid Gonzalez accented her pages using three clothing tags, which she cut in half for six separate accents. The design fits perfectly with the theme of her layout—the swirl patterns even replicate the look of steam rising from a hot cup of cocoa.

 TECHNIQUE TIP: Brigid used a silver-leafing pen to outline the edges of all six tag pieces to complement the foil stamp already printed on the top half of the clothing tags. This little addition adds great unity to the layout and its accents.

DESIGN TIP: Tuck part of your clothing tags behind a photo to hide the store name.

HOT chocolate

There's nothing like it on a cold, wet wintry day, except maybe the microwave s'mores that go along with it. Mmmmmm! All of that chocolatey, marshmallowy goodness is enough to chase away even the worst winter doldrums. God bless the folks from Swiss Miss and Jet-Puffed. Sometimes I don't know what we'd do without them!

Hot Chocolate by Brigid Gonzalez. **Supplies** *Cardstock:* Die Cuts With a View; *Border punch:* Fiskars Americas; *Silver-leafing pen:* Krylon; *Software:* Adobe Photoshop CS3; *Fonts:* Benny Blanco ("Hot") and Vegur ("Chocolate" and journaling); *Adhesive:* Scrapbook Adhesives by 3L; *Other:* Clothing tags.

make "snowballs" from felt

It may be cold outside, but Kim Watson's "Mr. Freeze" layout is definitely melting my winter blues away! Could a snowman get any cuter than the one in Kim's photos? He's almost as delightful as the snowballs Kim created using a piece of felt from a local craft store. A simple hand-stitched design in the center of each felt circle adds extra snowflake appeal. I love the imperfection of each hand-cut circle and how Kim continued the snowball theme by using circular journaling spots.

 TECHNIQUE VARIATION: If stitching is not for you, try using rub-on borders or a pen to create your own stitching effect.

Mr. Freeze by Kim Watson. **Supplies** *Cardstock:* American Crafts and Bazzill Basics Paper; *Patterned paper:* Pink Paislee; *Stamps and buttons:* Autumn Leaves; *Embroidery floss:* Scrapper's Floss, Karen Foster Design; *Letter stickers:* American Crafts (red) and Making Memories (white); *Ink:* Clearsnap; *Corner-rounder punch:* EK Success; *Software:* Adobe Photoshop CS3; *Brads and pen:* American Crafts; *Adhesive:* Scrapbook Adhesives by 3L and Tombow; *Other:* Thread.

Downtown *by Kelly Purkey.* **Supplies** *Cardstock and rub-ons:* American Crafts; *Patterned paper:* American Crafts (silver) and Making Memories (ledger); *Rhinestones:* Queen & Co.; *Punches:* Fiskars Americas; *Fonts:* Filosofia and Rosewood; *Other:* Thread.

add a little hand stitching

Stitching is one of the least expensive ways to add a perfect finishing touch to a layout. To create a fresh title with stitching, Kelly Purkey first printed her title onto cardstock, and then she hand-stitched around most of the letters. She added a simple cross-stitch on her snowflakes and "O" letters to tie in the stitched look.

TIME-SAVING TECHNIQUE: Use a variety of punches in different shapes, sizes and themes to create your own accents for a few hours one evening. Store the finished creations so they're ready for future layouts.

Hoeppner Home by Megan Hoeppner. **Supplies** *Cardstock:* American Crafts, Core'dinations, Die Cuts With a View and Stampin' Up!; *Patterned paper:* Bella Blvd and October Afternoon; *Flocking:* Doodlebug Design; *Ribbon:* American Crafts; *Letter stickers:* October Afternoon; *Stickers:* Bella Blvd; *Square punch:* Fiskars Americas; *Pen:* Marvy Uchida; *Adhesive:* Scrapbook Adhesives by 3L.

create flower blossoms from adhesive squares

Game nights are a definite must during the winter, and here's a fun twist that's sure to be a crowd-pleaser. Use a favorite family board game as inspiration for your design, like Megan Hoeppner did with a crossword theme. To create the flowers, Megan used ribbon for the stems and foam squares dipped in flocking for the blooms. It's super easy and budget friendly!

BUDGET TIP: Use small scraps of paper to create a border or frame around a photo block.

TECHNIQUE VARIATION: Add glitter or micro beads to adhesive squares to create your flower accents.

HOW-TO: CREATE FLOWER BLOSSOMS FROM ADHESIVE SQUARES

❶ Remove the backing from one side of your adhesive square; dip it into flocking.

❷ Rub the flocking into the adhesive with your finger.

❸ Use a brush to remove the excess flocking so you can save it for future use. **ck**

10 Ways to Make the Most of LEFTOVERS

Appetizing tips for getting more from your stash.

Beyond the time spent with family and the big turkey dinner, my favorite part of Thanksgiving is the leftovers! I love that I can use leftovers for the next few meals without having to buy something new. The same principle applies to scrapbooking. Just as you wouldn't toss that last bit of stuffing, hold onto your bits and pieces after finishing layouts. They can be used on later layouts, saving you the cost of buying something new. Now that's cause for giving thanks! I'll share six layouts to show you what I mean.

BY AMANDA PROBST

3 Years Later by Amanda Probst. **Supplies** Cardstock: Prism Papers; Chipboard: Junkitz, Making Memories, Rusty Pickle, Scenic Route and Target; Paint: Making Memories; Pen: American Crafts; Pastel pencil: Koh-I-Noor; Fonts: Typist and VNI-HLThuphap; Adhesive: 3D Foam Squares and E-Z Runner, Scrapbook Adhesives by 3L.

Tip 1: Use the insides of chipboard letters to create a border.

Save the insides of your e's, b's and other letters. On this layout, I gathered a bunch of the insides of chipboard e's, painted them all black and grouped them to create scallop borders. I can envision using the insides of o's to make a polka-dot background.

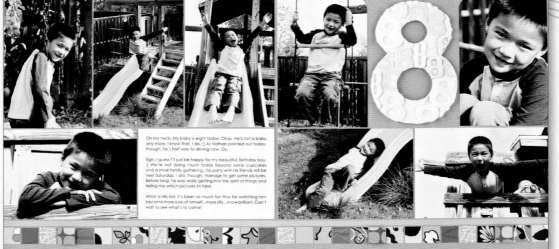

8 by Amanda Probst. **Supplies** Cardstock: Prism Papers; Patterned paper: American Crafts, Imaginisce, Junkitz and SEI; Letters and numbers: American Crafts; Font: Century Gothic; Adhesive: 3D Foam Squares and E-Z Runner, Scrapbook Adhesives by 3L.

Tip 2: Group stickers of the same number and then cut them out to form the number.

I don't know about you, but I rarely use the numbers in my letter sets. Rather than letting them go to waste, though, I used them here to create a more visually interesting title—placing them all together and then hand-cutting the numeral "8" shape. I happened to have this many in white, but if you had mixed colors you could always paint them all to match.

a leaf hunt

The boys and I decided to take advantage of the sunshine yesterday and headed out on a "leaf hunt." I brought the wagon and our little kid rake, though of course Micah refused to ride in the wagon and of course they all fought over the "one" rake I had. Sigh. But, it was heaps (and piles) of fun! We ventured all around our neighborhood, walking to the common areas and raking up piles of leaves for the boys to jump in... and bury each other in... and roll in...and throw at each other. Of the 206 pictures I took, here are just a few... 10.15.2007

 A Leaf Hunt *by Amanda Probst.* **Supplies** *Cardstock:* Prism Papers; *Patterned paper:* My Mind's Eye and October Afternoon; *Felt paper:* Creative Café; *Border punch:* Fiskars Americas; *Foam letters:* American Crafts; *Font:* Rockwell; *Adhesive:* 3D Foam Squares and E-Z Runner, Scrapbook Adhesives by 3L; Glossy Accents, Ranger Industries.

Tip 3:

Use index prints from your photo developer to accentuate the centers of embellishments.

On this layout, I simply punched circles from the index prints I received with my printed photos. I added a layer of Glossy Accents to the top to give them an epoxy feel, and then I affixed them to my hand-cut leaf accents.

Tip 4:

Save punched scraps to create personalized journaling cards.

Before you trash the leftovers after using a border punch, think again! Save those pieces to create quick little borders for hand-made journaling spots, like I used with the orange scraps that border the top and bottom of my journaling block.

Anatomy of a Soccer Season *by Amanda Probst.* **Supplies** *Cardstock:* Prism Papers; *Vinyl letters:* American Crafts; *Letter stickers:* EK Success; *Pen:* American Crafts; *Chipboard letter negatives:* Rusty Pickle; *Paint:* Making Memories; *Fonts:* DB Soccer Doodles and Rockwell; *Adhesive:* E-Z Runner, Scrapbook Adhesives by 3L; Glue Dots, Glue Dots International.

Tip 5:

Turn the negative shape of a chipboard "O" into a frame.

After you remove a chipboard "O" letter from its backing, paint the left-over chipboard piece to make a handy frame. Another letter's leftovers could make for an even more interesting accent.

Tip 6:

Use long sections of trimmed paper strips as accents on your layout.

The next time you need to trim ¼" from your cardstock to fit your design, hang onto the trimmed-away section. One day's trash is another day's treasure. Hey, every little bit makes a difference. I used thin strips of orange cardstock to create a grid design.

CHANGE of place

I thought about making a list of things I'm thankful for yesterday. I didn't quite get to it. :) Yesterday, we went down to my brother's new house about 45 minutes away...the first time we've ever spent Thanksgiving with family without being in Washington with a LOT of family. It was a quiet but nice change in tradition. We had a delicious meal with Zach, Marcy, Melissa and all the kids, and ended up with the inevitable leftovers. The kids had a seemingly good time without incident (which is saying something for having had an 8 year old, two 6.5 year olds, three 3 year olds and an almost 3 year old, lol). Sadly, we're going to have to thank the Wii for that one. That's pretty much how the older kids spent the entire day. The two little boys (Micah and Aaron) spent much of their time watching their big brothers. The two little girls watched Strawberry Shortcake and played with the dollhouse in the other room. :) I'm sure if we'd turned off the Wii and involved them in some other activity, they'd have done finer. But we let them have their fun for the day...and were simply thankful for the quiet and the break.

Change of Place *by Amanda Probst.* **Supplies** *Cardstock:* Prism Papers; *Patterned paper:* Jillibean Soup and Prima; *Rub-on:* Fancy Pants Designs; *Letters:* American Crafts; *Pens:* American Crafts and Copic; *Font:* Rockwell; *Adhesive:* E-Z Runner, Scrapbook Adhesives by 3L.

Tip 7:

Combine paper strips with a twist.
If you need a patterned paper with just the right colors to coordinate with the rest of your layout, create your own from cardstock scraps. As a new twist for this old trick, use different widths for each strip and add a rub-on design over the top to unify them together.

Tip 8:

Glam up dot-patterned papers with gems.
If you have leftover gems in a variety of colors, then use them to accentuate a dot-patterned paper that already features a multicolor design.

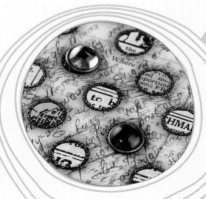

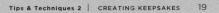

Tip 9:

Combine journaling cards from different collections.
Use leftover journaling tags together to create a larger writing space, running your text across all three journaling cards.

Walk in the Clouds by Amanda Probst. **Supplies** *Metallic cardstock and Mirri paper:* Prism Papers; *Ribbon:* Creative Café and Little Yellow Bicycle; *Monograms:* My Mind's Eye; *Letter stickers:* American Crafts (fabric) and Making Memories; *Journaling tags:* October Afternoon; *Pen:* American Crafts; *Adhesive:* E-Z Runner, Scrapbook Adhesives by 3L; *Other:* Staples.

Tip 10:

Use portions of monogram letters to form a decorative border.
Fancy borders and edges are popular these days. Make your own with letters like J, K and X that don't get used much anyhow. They look great in the red and cream border design on my "Walk in the Clouds" layout.

HOW-TO: Turn monograms into borders.

① Trim the base off giant monogram letters.

② Align the cutoff sections to create a border. **ck**

make the most of leftovers

BY KIM WATSON

"REUSE, RECYCLE, REINVENT" has become a mantra in most households these days. So it goes without saying that we have to take the same approach in our scrap rooms. Luckily, many manufacturers are spending as much time on their packaging as they do their products—making our job of reinventing easier.

reuse, recycle, reinvent

Last Days of Summer *by Kim Watson.* **Supplies:** *Cardstock:* American Crafts and Bazzill Basics Paper; *Patterned paper:* American Crafts and Sassafras; *Packaging:* Prima; *Die cuts and rub-ons:* American Crafts; *Brads:* We R Memory Keepers; *Ribbon:* 7gypsies; *Stickers:* American Crafts and Jenni Bowlin Studio; *Button:* Fancy Pants Designs; *Punches:* Fiskars Americas, Martha Stewart Crafts, and Paper Shapers; *Software:* Adobe; *Pen:* Sakura; *Adhesive:* Scrapbook Adhesives by 3L, Therm O Web, and Tombow; *Other:* Thread and typewriter.

Seeing all of my die-cut Prima flower backing cards stacked in neat piles sparked the idea of including them on my layout as a mini album. To reuse your backing cards as mini albums, thereby including more photos on your layout, simply tie a few together, embellish, and add to your page.

ALBUM SHOWN OPEN

Stolen Moments by Kim Watson. **Supplies:** Cardstock: American Crafts, Bazzill Basics Paper, and Core'dinations; Patterned paper: American Crafts and Adornit-Carolee's Creations; Packaging: Prima; Buttons: BasicGrey and Fancy Pants Designs; Stickers: American Crafts, Bella Blvd, Jenni Bowlin Studio, Making Memories, and October Afternoon; Felt accents: American Crafts and Making Memories; Button, chipboard, and rub-on: American Crafts; Punches: EK Success, Fiskars Americas, and Stampin' Up!; Software: Adobe; Font: Myriad Pro; Adhesive: American Crafts, Scrapbook Adhesives by 3L, and Tombow; Other: Thread.

Backing cards aren't the only packaging you can put to good use. Recycle the clear acetate inserts from your packaging to create fabulous flowers. Simply draw flowers on the acetate, cut out, ink the edges, and finish each with a brad, button, or rhinestone. Or use a flower punch or die-cutting machine to make the work go that much faster.

DESIGN TIP:
Use leftover rub-ons to add fun words, images, or color to your acetate flowers.

 Ferris Ride *by Kim Watson.* **Supplies:** *Cardstock:* American Crafts and Bazzill Basics Paper; *Patterned paper:* American Crafts and Hambly Screen Prints; *Ribbon and twill tape:* Making Memories; *Stickers:* American Crafts; *Brads:* American Crafts, Bazzill Basics Paper, and Bella Blvd; *Die cuts:* Cosmo Cricket and Doodlebug Design; *Flower:* Bella Blvd; *Lace:* Cocoa Daisy kit; *Punch:* Stampin' Up!; *Stamp:* Michaels; *Glitter glue:* Ranger Industries; *Ink:* Close to My Heart; *Adhesive:* American Crafts, Scrapbook Adhesives by 3L, and Tombow; *Software:* Adobe; *Other:* Lace.

If you're looking around your scrap room, noticing that you always seem to be left with the plain ribbons and twill tape from a package, try this idea to make them fun enough to use on any layout:

Try painting or inking your plain ribbons, and allow them to dry. Then embellish them with jewels, buttons, brads, rub-ons, or a little glitter. For a little added texture, you can also stitch on them before adding them to your layout. **ck**

make the most of leftovers

BY JEN JOCKISCH

PATTERNED PAPER is my go-to supply. I love to layer, distress, paint, and sew it. So I always have a ton of small paper scraps lying around. To use them up, I make these paper flowers using only what I have near me. It saves time because I don't have to dig for just the right paper, and in the process, I've found that certain patterns that I would never have thought worked well together, actually make for a great mix.

turn *leftovers* into something amazing

Playing Outside *by Jen Jockisch.* **Supplies:** *Cardstock, pens, and ribbon:* American Crafts; *Patterned paper:* BasicGrey, Jillibean Soup, October Afternoon, Pink Paislee, Prima, Sassafras, Scenic Route, 7gypsies; *Buttons:* American Crafts, BasicGrey, and Fancy Pants Designs; *Alphabet stickers:* American Crafts and Making Memories; *Punches:* EK Success, Martha Stewart, and We R Memory Keepers; *Adhesive:* 3M; *Other:* Tags.

MAKE FLOWERS USING PATTERNED PAPER SCRAPS

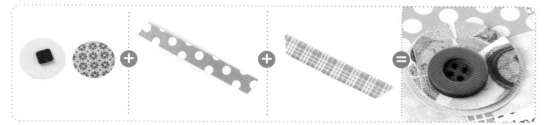

Goofy Drawers *by Maggie Holmes.* **Supplies:** *Patterned paper:* Sassafras and Studio Calico; *Chipboard letters:* Scrap Within Reach; *Buttons:* Making Memories; *Fabric and stamps:* Studio Calico; *Metal charm:* Making Memories; *Die cut:* Jenni Bowlin Studio; *Rub-ons:* Hambly Screen Prints; *Pen and punch:* EK Success; *Ink:* Clearsnap; *Mist:* Maya Road; *Scissors:* Fiskars Americas; *Adhesive:* Making Memories and Tombow; *Other:* Cardstock.

MAGGIE'S LEFTOVERS

Using just some spray mist and the backing leftover from chipboard letters, Maggie Holmes created this amazing background for her page. This is a great way to use items we would normally just throw away. Plus, it adds a unique design to the page.

Simply lay the negative on your page, holding it firmly with your hand, and then mist over it. Let the ink dry for a moment, then remove the negative. That easily, you have a fun, interesting, and inexpensive addition to your page.

MAKE BACKGROUNDS USING CHIPBOARD LETTERS

DESIGN TIP:
Try out different negative shapes for lots of creative possibilities

Sweet by Andrea Friebus.
Supplies: *Cardstock:* American Crafts; *Patterned paper:* Fancy Pants Designs, Masterpiece Studios, and Melissa Frances; *Chipboard:* Cherry Arte and K&Company; *Letter stickers:* Creative Memories; *Acrylic paint:* Michaels; *Ink:* Clearsnap; *Embroidery floss:* DMC; *Adhesive:* Therm O Web; *Other:* Buttons, date stamp, and pen.

ANDREA'S LEFTOVERS

Who doesn't have tons of left-over letter stickers lying around? Most of them just end up in the trash or sit collecting dust. Why not do something creative with them? I love how Andrea Friebus mimicked the design of her patterned paper with just cardstock and some leftover alphabet stickers.

How to: Create Sticker Flowers

1. Place leftover stickers on a piece of cardstock, forming a circular pattern.

2. Carefully tear around the stickers to create rough circle.

3. Ink edges of circle, and sew button in center.

MAKE FLOWERS USING LETTER STICKERS

DESIGN TIP:
Use different colors or fonts for vibrant embellishments, or try using rub-ons or stamps to create a different look. To see the step-by-step instructions for making these amazing flowers, visit us online at *creatingkeepsakes.com/issues/may_june_2010*. **ck**

make the most
of leftovers

BY MANDY DOUGLASS

NONE OF US like to throw out perfectly good leftovers—whether it's food or scrapbooking supplies. The only difference is with scrapbooking supplies, you can also put the product packaging to good use. But what to do with it? Join me and Stacy Cohen as we challenge ourselves to use our packaging to create unique embellishments, and we'll show you how to turn what was once trash into scrapbooking treasure.

create unique *accents* with your leftover supplies

Spring Favorites *by Mandy Douglass.* **Supplies** *Cardstock:* American Crafts; *Letter stickers:* Doodlebug Design; *Patterned paper:* Pebbles Inc.; *Brads and buttons:* American Crafts; *Ink:* Clearsnap; *Circle punch:* Marvy Uchida; *Font:* Gotham; *Adhesive:* Scrapbook Adhesives by 3L and Therm O Web; *Other:* Sticker packaging.

HOW TO: MAKE FLOWERS

 Morning Fix *by Stacy Cohen.* **Supplies** *Patterned paper:* Little Yellow Bicycle; *Letters:* Adornit-Carolee's Creations ("day" and "until"), BasicGrey ("Morning Fix") and Making Memories (tiny black and white letter stickers); *Flowers:* Prima (white); *Buttons:* Favorite Findings (small pearl); *Brad:* Autumn Leaves, *Rhinestone:* K&Company for Target; *Paint:* Shimmerz; *Pearls:* KaiserCraft; *Glitter glue and liquid pearls:* Ranger Industries; *Ink:* Ranger Industries and Tsukineko; *Gesso:* Golden; *Adhesive:* Beacon Adhesives, EK Success and Tombow; *Other:* Buttons, cheesecloth, coffee filters, and twine.

STACY'S LEFTOVERS

For this fantastic page, Stacy used more than just her scrapbooking leftovers; she also incorporated her kitchen leftovers. She used a coffee filter for the flowers, cheesecloth to cut out additional flower shapes to embellish the coffee filter flowers, a plastic coffee can lid to punch out even more flowers and leaves, instant coffee mixed with gesso to paint along the edges of the photos, and twine from her kitchen junk drawer for the hand stitching around the border of the layout. Not only were the leftover components from her coffee products useful, they also tie right into the theme of her page!

HOW TO: MAKE BUTTERFLIES

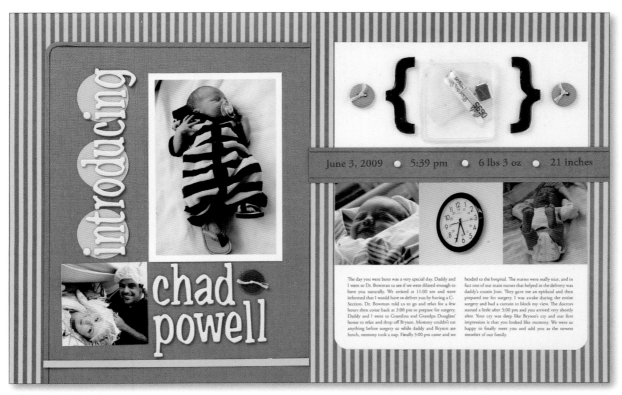

Introducing Chad Powell *by Mandy Douglass.* **Supplies** *Patterned paper:* K&Company; *Brads, button, cardstock, pen and stickers:* American Crafts; *Font:* Garamond; *Other:* Brad packaging.

MY LEFTOVERS

I chose to use the leftover packaging from my brads to create a keepsake bubble for my son's hospital bracelets. I also turned leftover brown cardstock scraps from another project to cover my bracket stickers. Then I made them stand out and shine using dimensional glue, like the letter stickers on the opposite page.

HOW TO: MAKE A KEEPSAKE HOLDER

6 *quick* helps

ADHERE BUTTONS THE ARTSY WAY

Here's a cool trick from Kristi Hellyer: Squeeze paint onto the back of a button, turn it over, and press the button onto your project. The thicker-consistency paint seeps out the sides for a seal effect. Adheres beautifully!

use these solutions to **simplify** *your scrapbooking*

Cards *by Jana Lillie.* **Supplies** *Paint:* Heidi Swapp for Advantus; *Buttons:* Buttons Galore; *Patterned paper:* SEI; *Heart brads:* Queen & Co.; *Ribbon:* American Crafts; *Other:* Heart card.

BY JANA LILLIE

SOLVE YOUR ALBUM AND JOURNALING WOES

Ever feel overwhelmed by the need to gather photos, journal *and* design pages before you can move on? Help is here! With Kim McCrary's no-stress album approach, you simply use the left-hand page for journaling and the right-hand page for photos and embellishments. Journaling is a cinch with ready-made questionnaires, and you can embellish the right-hand pages at your leisure.

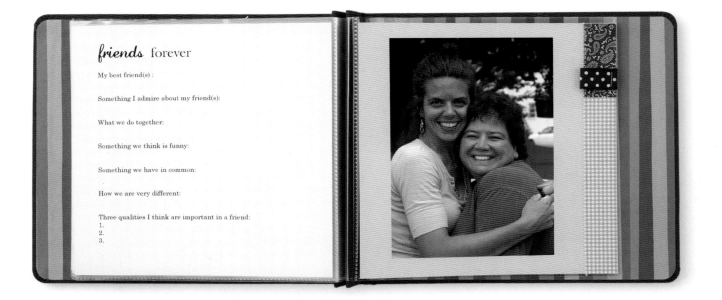

friends forever

My best friend(s) :

Something I admire about my friend(s):

What we do together:

Something we think is funny:

Something we have in common:

How we are very different:

Three qualities I think are important in a friend:
1.
2.
3.

TUNE UP YOUR DIGITAL CAMERA

To get your camera in prime condition for the new year:

- Turn off your camera, then hold it upside-down and blow off any loose dust particles.

- Clean the lens and body gently with a soft, dry cloth (microfiber is best) or lens tissue paper. *Avoid* canned air (it can blow dust *into* your lens).

- Own a DSLR? Sprinkle a few drops of lens cleaning fluid on lens cleaning paper and clean off any fingerprints and grime. *Avoid* paper towels or tissues.

- Recharge your batteries. Buy a second battery for peace of mind.

- Store your camera in a camera bag. *Avoid* dust, dirt, humidity, high-traffic areas, extra cold or hot temperatures.

- Ever shoot pictures under snowy or rainy conditions? Chuck Delaney, columnist with the New York Institute of Photography (*nyip.com*), recommends packing a plastic bag and rubber bands in your camera bag. During inclement weather, simply slip the plastic bag over your camera and secure it with rubber bands.

INK A WHITE "CORE"

Charin Reed loves the look of distressed, white-cored cardstock, but not all of her cardstock has a white core. Her solution? Just swipe the paper edges with white ink!

That's what Close To My Heart artist Katie Tippets did here.

Envelope *by Katie Tippets for Close To My Heart.* **Supplies** *White ink, cardstock, stamps, embossing powder, buttons, ribbon, hemp, texture tools, dimensional elements, embroidery floss and Originals Card Confidence Program:* Close To My Heart; *Ink:* VersaMark, Tsukineko.

Display a new design each month!

DANGLE A PRETTY DESIGN

You've got supplies galore—why not create a snowflake to hang in January? Rita Shimniok did—and it was so much fun that she's creating a themed ornament for each month of the year. Invite family and friends to join you!

Snowflake Ornament *by Rita Shimniok.* **Supplies** *Chipboard snowflake:* Magistical Memories; *Ghost snowflake:* Heidi Swapp for Advantus; *Bling snowflake stickers:* me & my BIG ideas; *Jewel:* Imaginisce; *Paint:* Delta Creative; *Pearlescent medium:* Liquitex; *Punch tool:* We R Memory Keepers; *Other:* Pearls.

COLOR-CODE YOUR INKS

Beth Wolfgang stores her inkpads upside-down (to keep the dye inks "juicy") but found herself repeatedly turning the pads over to check the color. When she did, the names were tricky to read and the sample colors were often "off."

Her solution? White office labels! Beth inks a small portion with an inkpad's color and attaches the results to the back of the pad. No office labels around? Beth has also cut the excess from Bazzill chip toppers. **ck**

6 *fast,* fun *ideas*

1

SPIN A COOL PAGE

Shannon Taylor took the spinner from an old game and used it on a scrapbook page! (You can find old board games at thrift stores.) A spinner works for all kinds of "choice" pages—favorite foods, best friends, what a child wants to be when grown up.

wow with these solutions and secrets

BY JANA LILLIE

Wanna Play? *by Shannon Taylor.* **Supplies** *Software:* Adobe Photoshop CS, Adobe Systems; *Title:* Shannon's own writing, cut from actual game box; *Font:* Mostlios, Internet; *Black paint pen:* EK Success; *Adhesive:* Therm O Web; *Other:* Spinner from old game.

REVIEW FAST WITH PHOTO TAGS

Can't remember which camera mode works best for a certain shot? Download our CK Camera Mode Teach Sheets at *creatingkeepsakes.com* for a quick reference. Laminate the finished sheets if desired and tuck them in your camera bag. Or, create a cute tag version like Jennifer Gallacher's for your camera strap!

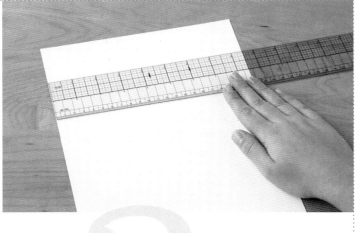

Photo Tags *by Jennifer Gallacher.* **Supplies** *Cardstock:* Provo Craft; *Patterned paper:* Déjà Views by The C-Thru Ruler Co.; *Corner-rounder and circle punches:* McGill; *Beaded chain:* Making Memories; *Ribbon:* Li'l Davis Designs; *Font:* Century Gothic, Microsoft.

FIND THE CENTER—FAST!

Often wonder where the center of your page is? Kelly Lautenbach used to—until she took her C-Thru ruler and added two marks with a fine-tipped permanent pen. The first mark is at 4¼" (the center of an 8½" page), while the second is at 6" (the center of a 12" x 12" page). "Centering items is *so* much easier," says Kelly.

Another smart idea? To evenly space unmounted letter stamps for a title, Bernadette Henderson positions them on a strip of double-sided tape on a ruler. The tape stays on the ruler.

TRY THIS TWIST ON RESIST

To create Jennifer McGuire's cool resist look, first select chipboard or stickers with a semigloss or glossy white finish. Stamp the surface with the Clear Resist Pad by Ranger Industries (or VersaMark by Tsukineko) and let dry. Generously rub dye or chalk ink over the piece and buff away the excess. Your image will "pop" visually!

Stars *by Jennifer McGuire.* **Supplies** *Chipboard:* Creative Imaginations; *Stamp:* Hero Arts; *Ink:* Clear Resist Pad, Ranger Industries; ColorBox Fluid Chalk, Clearsnap.

❶ Cut desired shape from vinyl with cutter. Remove positive image and save for future project.

❷ Attach negative image of die cut to your piece of paper or project. Paint over openings with a foam brush and let dry.

❸ Peel off the mask and enjoy your cool, custom shape!

Good Tunes by Elizabeth Kartchner. **Supplies** *Die-cut machine:* Cricut, Provo Craft; *Patterned paper:* KI Memories (stripe and music notes) and My Mind's Eye (polka dot); *Paint:* Sea Breeze, Delta Creative; *Transparency:* Hambly Studios; *Letter stickers:* American Crafts; *Buttons:* BasicGrey; *Paper frills:* Doodlebug Design; *Font:* 2Peas Lighthouse, "15 Essential Fonts" CD, Autumn Leaves; *Other:* Thread and self-adhesive vinyl.

CUT A QUICK VINYL MASK

To add a fun shape to her page, Elizabeth Kartchner die cut a design from self-adhesive vinyl. Next, using the negative portion as a "mask," she painted over it. *Note:* To avoid little "globs" of paint, position the mask so it's completely flush with the paper surface before painting.

Swirl Accent by April Massad. **Supplies** *Cardstock:* Bazzill Basics Paper; *Stamp:* Autumn Leaves; *Embossing ink:* Stampabilities; *White embossing powder:* Ranger Industries; *Other:* Cornstarch.

MINIMIZE STRAY POWDER WITH CORNSTARCH

The next time you want to emboss light-colored powder on dark cardstock, try April Massad's surprising solution. First, rub an ultra-thin layer of cornstarch on the cardstock image area. (Cover a little beyond where you'll be embossing.)

Next, stamp on top of the cornstarch. Sprinkle on embossing powder, tap off excess, and apply heat with a heat gun. The cornstarch will prevent embossing powder from sticking where there's no ink. After the image has cooled, lightly brush off any cornstarch or stray embossing powder with a paintbrush. Works like a charm to prevent stray embossing powder from sticking to your design! **ck**

4 *artsy* ideas

1

PRINT PHOTOS ON PAPER BAGS

Tracey Locher wanted worn, rustic-looking pictures for a mini book, so she printed her photos directly on brown paper bags from her local grocery store that she'd treated with deacidification spray. "The pictures came out so soft and antiqued . . . I loved it!" says Tracey. For quick instructions and a peek at the entire mini book, turn the page.

Try these
clever
tricks today

E Is for Easter *by Tracey Locher.* **Supplies** *4" x 6" accordion album,* patterned paper, chipboard, trim, letter stickers and quote stickers: Rusty Pickle; *Cardstock:* Bazzill Basics Paper; *Buttons:* foof-a-La, Autumn Leaves; Rusty Pickle; *Ink:* Tim Holtz Distress Ink, Ranger Industries; *Pens:* Uni-Ball Signo (white), Newell Rubbermaid; Artist and Le Plume, Marvy Uchida; *Embroidery floss:* DMC; *Finish:* Mod Podge, Plaid Enterprises; *Deacidification spray:* Archival Mist, Preservation Technologies; *Other:* Brown paper bags, string, mini wooden clothespins, copper wire, straight pins and Velcro.

BY JANA LILLIE

1 continued

HOW TO CREATE TRACEY'S "PAPER BAG" PHOTO LOOK

While you may have seen paper-bag albums before, it's likely you've never seen photos printed on paper bags. Here's how to accomplish the look:

1 Select a digital photo, then cut a piece of paper (several inches larger than the photo) from a grocery bag.

2 Treat the paper with a deacidification spray.

3 Position the paper in the middle of a letter-sized sheet of copy paper. Tape it in place.

4 On your computer, change the photo's color saturation to 50–70% in Adobe Photoshop Elements or other photo-editing software.

5 Print the photo, making sure the ink is dry before removing the piece of paper from the copy paper.

6 For added visual interest and dimension, crumple or tear your photo.

2 PAINT BEFORE YOU PUNCH

Do your fingers get messy while painting raw chipboard letters or shapes? Noel Culbertson has a solution! Simply paint the letters or shapes while they're still attached to the sheet they came on. When they're dry, punch the items out and attach them to your layout. The unpainted sides add a sense of dimension.

Celebrate Spring *by Noel Culbertson.* **Supplies** *Cardstock:* Bazzill Basics Paper; *Patterned paper and journaling card:* My Mind's Eye; *Chipboard letters:* Heidi Swapp for Advantus; *Flowers:* American Crafts (purple and blue), Making Memories (pink) and Prima (white); *Rickrack and brads:* Stampin' Up!; *Rub-on:* Creative Imaginations.

TRY OUR EGG-SHELL TRICK

The next time you boil and peel an egg, save the egg-shell. Carefully peel off any membrane inside and let the shell dry completely. Next, use a hard object (cup bottom, ice-cream scoop, etc.) to grind the shell into coarse or fine pieces in a bowl. Alter with mediums as desired. Here, April Massad sprinkled crushed eggshell on a painted butterfly, let it dry, then applied a coat of glitter paint on top.

Happy B-Day by April Massad. **Supplies** *Letter tag:* Bazzill Basics Paper; *Patterned paper:* BasicGrey; *Chipboard butterfly:* Technique Tuesday; *Swirl stamp:* Fancy Pants Designs; *Transparency:* Hambly Studios; *Letter stamps:* The Paper Studio; *Paint:* Apple Barrel, Plaid Enterprises; *Ink:* ColorBox, Clearsnap (pink); StazOn, Tsukineko (black); *Embossing pen and holographic embossing powder:* Ranger Industries.

MAKE POP DOTS IN A PINCH

Nothing "elevates" a 3-D embellishment like an adhesive dot below it. Add a 3-D Pop Dot from EK Success, for example, and you've got instant lift.

What if the need is urgent and you don't have any dots on hand? Make your own! Michelle Novella runs a strip of fun foam through her Xyron 150 sticker maker. She then flips the foam over and runs it through the machine again so both sides are sticky. Next, she takes a hole punch and punches as many "dots" as needed. Michelle likes to color the sides black with a permanent marker for a shadowed, dimensional look. For the same look, you could also run black fun foam through the Xyron 150 instead. **ck**

{ 6 tricks you *gotta* try }

1

A POCKET PAGE WITH "PUNCH"

Michelle McClung quickly caught our eye with a cute pocket page that incorporates punches from baby cards. Clever! We invited Samantha Walker to do something similar with sweet Carlton Cards samples we'd received from American Greetings. Who could resist this page and mailbox?

Get *more* from your supplies

Colin McKay Walker *by Samantha Walker.* **Supplies** *Cardstock:* Bazzill Basics Paper; *Mailbox:* Creative Imaginations; *Die-cut cardstock:* Holey Cardstock, Samantha Walker Collection by Creative Imaginations; *Cards:* Baby line (sold exclusively at Target), Carlton Cards; *Jumbo square punch:* Marvy Uchida; *Letter stickers:* Chatterbox; *Large bracket sticker and corner rub-ons:* Karen Russell Collection by Creative Imaginations; *Adhesive:* Krylon (spray) and Plaid Enterprises(dots); *Ink:* Stampin' Up!.

BY JANA LILLIE

Original Tinkering Ink paper sheet   >>

CREATE A QUICK 3-D EFFECT

Want to help a lovely patterned paper come "alive" like Betsy Veldman did here? Partially or completely cut shapes from the design and use them to create a layered effect! Simply adhere the page they're cut from to another sheet of paper, then add a foam square or adhesive dot below each cut-out piece for instant life and lift!

Summer Swing by Betsy Veldman for *Tinkering Ink.* **Supplies** *Cardstock:* Die Cuts With a View; *Patterned paper:* Al Fresco, Tinkering Ink; *Chipboard letters:* Pressed Petals (large "S"), Provo Craft (white with green polka dot) and Scenic Route (blue); *Frame stamp:* Inque Boutique; *Foam squares:* Therm O Web.

GET IN FRONT OF THE ACTION

For the best, most expressive shots of your child playing a team sport, zoom in from the front during practice. Your child won't mind (it's not the "real" game), and you'll both love the concentration and effort reflected in his or her face in the photographs! Don't forget: Setting your camera on sports or action mode (⚡) will help "freeze" the action and keep details sharp.

PHOTO BY SUMMER FULLERTON

APPLY LARGE RUB-ONS WITH EASE

Find it tricky or tedious to apply large rub-ons evenly? Use a pan or craft scraper! CK editor Lori Fairbanks swears by her Pampered Chef Nylon Pan Scraper shown here (a set of three is only $2.75). Or, pick up the popular Inkssentials Craft Scraper (retail $1.00) offered by Ranger Industries.

5

DAZZLE WITH DOUBLE EMBOSSING

April Massad surprised us with a new discovery: embossing dies can be used to heat emboss! Called "double embossing," the technique lets you create a heat-embossed design within a die-embossed design. Here's how to create the look in minutes:

Hi *by April Massad.* **Supplies** *Embossing machine:* Revolution, QuicKutz; *Cardstock:* Bazzill Basics Paper; *Patterned paper:* Fancy Pants Designs; *Rhinestone brads and flowers:* Making Memories; *Self-adhesive rhinestones:* Junkitz; *Stamps:* Imaginisce (bird) and KI Memories ("hi"); *Embossing powder:* Ranger Industries; *Embossing ink:* Stampabilities; *Other:* Cornstarch.

1. Rub a little cornstarch lightly over the paper you are going to emboss (this helps keep embossing powder from sticking where you don't want it). Ink the raised-image side of your embossing die with VersaMark or embossing ink.

2. Lay your paper (cornstarch side up) on the side of the die that is NOT inked. Close the die shut. Emboss paper, then remove it from the die.

3. Pour embossing powder on inked side (powder will only be in embossed areas of design). Heat with heat gun. Brush off excess cornstarch later with a paintbrush.

6

WRAP A SWEET THANK-YOU

May is full of important days of remembrance: National Teacher Day, the "Stamp Out Hunger" food drive by letter carriers, Mother's Day, Armed Forces Day and more. Follow Noel Culbertson's lead and use your scrapbooking supplies to create a decorative wrap for a thank-you candy bar! Start with three pieces of paper: 7″ x 11″, 3″ x 11″ and 2¹⁄₂″ x 11″.

Candy Bar Wraps *by Noel Culbertson.* **Supplies** *Software:* Adobe Photoshop CS3, Adobe Systems; *Cardstock:* Bazzill Basics Paper (blue) and Stampin' Up! (cream and green); *Patterned paper:* BasicGrey (green) and Stampin' Up! (brown, cream and green); *Patterned paper and flower sticker:* Making Memories; *Paper lace:* Creative Imaginations; *Canvas stamp, brads and ink:* Stampin' Up!; *Ribbon and Flourish stamp:* impressrubberstamps.com; *Ink:* VersaMark, Tsukineko; *Embossing powder:* Stampin' Up!; *Digital flourish:* Hipster Plumes Mega Pack 2 by Anna Aspnes, *www.designerdigitals.com;* *Font:* Garamond, Microsoft; *Glitter glue:* Stickles, Ranger Industries; *Other:* Rhinestone and Hershey's candy bars. **ck**

7 *snazzy* solutions

1 ADD "TREAD" TO YOUR TITLE

Want a sports vehicle page that's as rugged as your big or little guy? Follow Brandi Pitts' lead and create a "tire tread" look on your title. First, paint chipboard letters black. Coat each letter with clear embossing ink, sprinkle on clear Ultra Thick Embossing Enamel (UTEE) powder, and heat it. While the enamel is still hot, run the wheels of a toy truck over the letter. Complete each letter before moving on to the next.

Note: Black UTEE could have provided a similar effect here, but Brandi prefers clear because it lets any paint color show through. Says Brandi, "As a variation, paint the letters brown, apply clear UTEE, and the results will look like tire tracks in mud."

Try a *new* approach today

Your Escape *by Brandi Pitts.* **Supplies** *Patterned paper:* BasicGrey; *Chipboard letters, screw snaps and photo turn:* Making Memories; *Rub-ons:* Autumn Leaves (letters), BasicGrey (letters) and Dee's Designs (letters and texture); *Black paint:* Plaid Enterprises; *Black ink:* Memories, Stewart Superior Corporation; *Clear embossing ink:* Ranger Industries; *Clear embossing powder:* Ultra Thick Embossing Enamel, Suze Weinberg, Ranger Industries.

This is what you do to blow off steam. This is where you go to unwind. No matter how scary it looks, you somehow relax when you're in your Jeep. Though I worry the entire time you're gone, I know that this is what you love to do and your sense of adventure is one of the things I love about

BY JANA LILLIE

One of my guilty pleasures is buying cut flowers and organizing them in varying heights in tiny glass vases. I enjoy the time spent arranging them as much as I do looking at them when I am done. I collect tiny vases whenever I travel. They make great practical souvenirs and I use them often. I change the colors and style of the vases, depending on the time of year, and line them up along my kitchen window sill. The more exotic the flowers, the better. I enjoy the vibrant mix of colors and texture. My window box flowers make me happy and feed my soul.

window box *Flowers* make me happy & feed my soul

DATED: June 2007
enjoyed forever

Window Box Flowers *by Karen Wilson-Bonnar.* **Supplies** *Scanner:* Epson; *Software:* Adobe Illustrator and Adobe Photoshop, Adobe Systems; *Cardstock:* Bazzill Basics Paper; *Fonts:* Futura and Zapfino, Internet; *Digital elements:* DesignerDigitals.com.

SCAN NATURE'S BEST FOR A BACKDROP

Whether you'd like to showcase a special flower or leaves from a hike, capture them as part of your page design with a scanner and a little photo editing. Here, Karen Wilson-Bonnar scanned a Godetia flower and stem, then reduced the images' opacity to 80 percent in Adobe Photoshop so she could use them as pretty backdrops for her page design.

Some of Karen's favorite tricks?

■ Combine several scans for beautiful, unique backgrounds.

■ Experiment with different blending modes.

■ For variation, use different material or fabric (such as black velvet) behind the flowers when scanning.

PUNCH A CUSTOM TAB

When Robin Manly needs a custom file tab for a project, she grabs her file tab punch and scrap paper, then makes her own for free! To copy her idea, carefully align the image you want on the bottom half of the tab shape. Don't worry about unwanted text or images on the back of the tab—they won't show. For instant journaling space, punch a tab shape from the lines in a subscription card and write your own message. *Note:* If you don't have access to a file tab punch, trace around an existing tab from your stash.

Custom File Tabs *by Robin Manly.* **Supplies** *3" tab punch:* McGill; *Other:* Paper scraps.

GET A "HANDLE" ON CLOSING GIFT BAGS

Never knowing quite what to do with the handles on gift bags, Brittany Beattie has found the perfect solution in the Tag Curler by Making Memories. She simply uses the tool to clip a tag at the top of the handles—it holds them in place while adding a charming greeting to the bag.

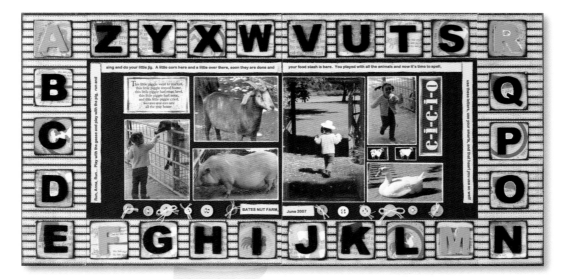

Bates Nut Farm *by Tracey Locher.* **Supplies** *Cardstock:* Bazzill Basics Paper; *Patterned paper, chipboard letters, stickers, coupons and buttons:* Rusty Pickle; *Paint:* Making Memories; *Ink:* Delta Creative; *Dimensional adhesive:* Mod Podge, Plaid Enterprises; *Other:* Velcro and thread.

MAKE MOVABLE LETTERS WITH VELCRO

To help her three-year-old daughter remember their farm outing, Tracey Locher created a fun interactive layout. Each chipboard letter on the border is attached with Velcro for easy removal and handling. Best of all, Anna is learning her ABCs while admiring the layout!

RETHINK AN EVERYDAY OBJECT

Emily Falconbridge's extra shelf liner didn't stay extra for long—she incorporated the material (painted blue) as a funky background for her scrapbook page. Concerned about archival safety? Use the liner (not acid free) on a card or home-decor project instead!

OOH— SIMULATE YOUR CAMERA SETTINGS

The SimCam camera simulator at *www.Photonhead.com* lets you plug in *f*-stop and shutter settings and see how a finished photo will look (digital or film camera). Get instant feedback—the SimCam is one cool tool!

Just the Way We Like It *by Emily Falconbridge.* **Supplies** *Cardstock:* Bazzill Basics Paper; *Letter stickers:* Heidi Grace Designs; *Rub-ons:* BasicGrey; *Paint and gesso:* Matisse Derivan; *Other:* Fabric, rubber shelf lining and thread. **ck**

7 *surefire* solutions

1

EMBOSS FABRIC? YOU BET!

Heidi Sonboul loves to heat emboss and tried it with fabric. It worked! (See the tree below.) To create this look, stamp an image on fabric with watermark ink. Add embossing powder (to remove stray powder from unwanted places before embossing, hold the sides of the fabric and "snap" it by pulling outward). Apply heat evenly with a heat gun. Heidi used this technique successfully on a T-shirt as well!

Save money, save *time*

This Makes Him Happy *by Heidi Sonboul.* **Supplies** *Cardstock:* Bazzill Basics Paper; *Patterned paper:* Anna Griffin; *Leaf stamp:* Autumn Leaves; *Heat gun:* Marvy Uchida; *Bird:* Boy Scouts of America; *Embossing powder:* Stampendous!; *Ink:* VersaMark, Tsukineko; *Other:* Fabric and thread.

BY JANA LILLIE

CREATE FAST "QUILLED" FLOWERS

To make a flower like those on this page by Alicia Thelin:

❶ Punch a circle from cardstock with a 1" circle punch. Apply a generous layer of dimensional glaze to the top.

❷ Cut a thin strip from the cardstock and wrap it around the graduated handle of a large watercolor brush.

❸ Press the spiral into the dimensional glaze on the punched circle and let dry. Adhere the circle to the end of a long, thin strip of green cardstock used for a "stem." Repeat steps 1–3 for two additional flowers.

❹ Punch three ovals from green cardstock. Cut one end of each oval into a point, then score down the middle of each piece to form a leaf. Punch or cut three smaller leaves as well and score down the middle.

❺ Punch two cardstock circles with a ½" circle punch. Adhere leaves and circles as desired for a fun flower look!

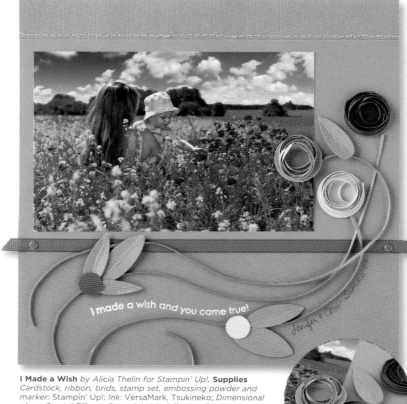

I Made a Wish *by Alicia Thelin for Stampin' Up!.* **Supplies** *Cardstock, ribbon, brids, stamp set, embossing powder and marker:* Stampin' Up!; *Ink:* VersaMark, Tsukineko; *Dimensional glaze:* Crystal Effects, Stampin' Up!; *Adhesive:* Stampin' Dimensionals, Stampin' Up!; *Other:* Oval punch, circle punches (⅛", ½" and 1") and thread. **This is an 8" x 8" page.**

MAKE SCROLL TAGS IN MINUTES

Marla Kress didn't have the gift tags she needed on hand—so she made her own with patterned-paper scraps, chipboard scrolls, a line stamp and baker's twine. "Cutting the paper to fit the shape of the scroll gives each tag a whimsical twist," says Marla. "I used a Galaxy Marker to color the chipboard (originally bright yellow) to fit my color scheme."

Scroll Tags *by Marla Kress.* **Supplies** *Patterned paper:* BasicGrey; *Chipboard scroll:* Bo-Bunny Press; *Line stamp:* It Kit Studio; *Paint:* Making Memories; *Ink:* Ranger Industries; *Pen:* Galaxy Markers, American Crafts; *Other:* Baker's twine.

KEEP HIDDEN TRACK OF DIGITAL SOURCES

Ever forget the names of fonts? How about the sources for digital elements used on a page? Fret no more! Upon finishing a page in Adobe Photoshop, Amy Goldstein creates a new "layer" in Photoshop and types in the names and sources she needs to remember. She then tells the software to "hide" the layer. The information is easy to retrieve but doesn't show when the layout is printed.

GIVE NEW LIFE TO OLD MATS

Use a digital cutter like the Wishblade, Silhouette, or Cricut? Save your old cutting mats. While they may not be sticky enough to use on the machine any longer, Tracey Odachowski finds them perfect for holding small pieces of paper in place while painting, applying glitter, or embossing.

ADD CUTE CHARACTER ACCENTS

Do you love Care Bears, Disney characters, or other cute illustrations? Create fast, custom page accents with downloadable printables or cartoon images cut or scanned from a coloring book! To create the darling bears for her page, Tiffany Tillman downloaded black-and-white Care Bear printables and colored them electronically after opening the file in Adobe Photoshop Elements.

Care Bear by Tiffany Tillman. **Supplies** Photo-editing software: Adobe Photoshop Elements 5, Adobe Systems; Cardstock: Prism Papers; Chipboard letters: Redmond Stencil Creme, Scenic Route; Font: Georgia, Internet; Printables: www.agkidzone.com.

Tag and Flowers by Detta Owens. **Supplies** Patterned paper: Piggy Tales; Tag: Office Depot; Punches: EK Success (flower on tag), McGill (loose flower) and Stampin' Up! (scallop); Brad and ribbon: Making Memories; Stamp: Close To My Heart; Blue ink: ColorBox, Clearsnap; Alcohol inks and blending solution: Tim Holtz, Ranger Industries; Glitter glue: Stickles, Ranger Industries; Adhesive: Glue Dots, Glue Dots International; Scotch ATG, 3M; Other: Coffee-can lids and craft gem.

PUNCH SHAPES FROM LIDS!

Detta Owens loves the look of "ghost flowers" and discovered that she can create something similar with a coffee-can lid! She simply trims off the outside rim and punches shapes from the inner portion. While the shapes are not archivally safe for scrapbook pages, they make quick, fun accents to dress up cards, gift tags, and other projects! **ck**

6 *sizzling* solutions

EMBROIDER A CUSTOM DESIGN

When Mou Saha's daughter received a love note, Mou couldn't wait to scrapbook it, complete with a boy character she drew herself. After drawing the figure lightly in pencil, Mou stitched the outline with embroidery floss.

Create cute projects *fast*

One Little Love Note *by Mou Saha.* **Supplies** *Chipboard word:* Die Cuts With a View; *Letter stamps:* K&Company and Stampendous!; *Ink:* Tsukineko; *Embroidery floss:* DMC; *Pen:* Marvy Uchida; *Other:* Cardstock.

BY JANA LILLIE

CREATE A MOSAIC WITH SCRAPS

C.D. Muckosky used to discard the scraps from her Bind-it-All machine—now she turns them into cool mosaic pieces for accents. After overlapping the pieces (you can also use paper or fabric scraps), she secures the mosaic with tacky glue (dries clear).

Superstar by C.D. Muckosky. **Supplies** *Watercolor paper:* Strathmore; *Watercolor paints:* Prang; *Binding machine:* Bind-it-All, Zutter Innovative Products; *Corner rounder:* Fiskars; *Pencil crayons:* PrismaColor, Newell Rubbermaid; *Metallic embroidery floss:* DMC; *Pens:* Pigma Micron (black), Sakura; Uni-ball Signo (white), Newell Rubbermaid; *Adhesive:* Aleene's Tacky Glue, Duncan Enterprises; Foam Squares, Fiskars; Duck Tape, Beacon Adhesives; *Other:* Stretch cord, glitter glue and tape (electrical and masking).

BOOST A BACKPACK'S PIZZAZZ

To add a personal, playful touch to her daughter's backpack, Deena Wuest created a digital tag on her computer. She printed the tag, folded it lengthwise, and "laminated" the tag with clear packing tape. Next, she trimmed the tape to ¼" from the tag sides, punched a hole in the tag, and tied it onto Savanna's backpack with scrapbook ribbon.

CREATE YOUR OWN RUBBER STAMPS

Here's a cool discovery from Danielle Ryerson: with the cuttable, 6" x 9" rubber stamp material at ScrapbookDiecutter.com, you can create your own custom stamps. The material, available by the sheet or in a kit, can be cut on the Cricut (requires an extra blade), Silhouette, Wishblade, and more!

Backpack Tag by Deena Wuest. **Supplies** *Software:* Adobe Photoshop Elements 4.0; *Digital paper:* Seaside by Katie Pertiet; *Digital letters:* Jack-n-Me Alpha by Katie Pertiet; *Digital accents:* School Days Felt Board Friends by Pattie Knox; *Font:* AvantGarde, Internet; *Other:* Ribbon. All digital elements downloaded from *www.designerdigitals.com*.

frame 124

from there......................................to here.

124 frames

From Here to There *by Aly Dosdall.* **Supplies** *Software:* Adobe Photoshop 7.0; *Digital background and patterned paper:* Mailroom No. 1 Paper Pack and Web Challenge Freebie (2/10/08) by Katie Pertiet; *Digital flower eyelets:* Brad Bonanza by Pattie Knox; *Digital border:* Web Challenge Freebie by Mindy Teresawa; *Fonts:* Fling LET, *www.fonts101.com;* Futura Light, Microsoft. All digital elements downloaded from *www.designer-digitals.com.*

SUBJECT WON'T SIT STILL

Aly Dosdall dreams of owning a digital SLR camera someday, but until then, she's found an easy way to capture her active kids with her point-and-shoot camera: use the "continuous" setting. If your camera offers this feature (check your manual), you can hold down the shutter-release button and take rapid, continuous shots.

For the fun layout here, Aly took 124 shots in continuous mode and ended up with several she wanted to keep.

MAKE A 3" X 3" ALBUM IN MINUTES

Who knew that you could create a 3" x 3" album (with pockets for tags) from a single sheet of cardstock and some patterned-paper scraps? Renee Dorian loves to whip up simple and embellished versions for baby presents, wedding gifts, party favors and more.

Mini Album *by Renee Dorian.* **Supplies** *Patterned paper:* one heart . . . one mind (cover) and Arctic Frog (inside); *Tags:* 7gypsies; *Ribbon:* Target; *Stamp:* Catslife Press; *Ink:* StazOn, Tsukineko; *Adhesive:* Duck, Henkel Consumer Adhesives; Elmer's (glue stick).

NOTE TO SELF

TOP TEN LIST
1.

7 *tempting* tricks

HEAT EMBOSS GHOST LETTERS

Forget the magic potion—all Emilie Ahern needed to create the enchanting title below was ghost letters, embossing ink, embossing powder and a heat tool. "Do this with clear embossing powder," says Emilie, "and it bubbles like water." For step-by-step photos, turn the page. And don't miss the fun leaf looks created in minutes with a Cricut machine and shape cartridge!

cast a spell with **cool** *looks*

Autumn *by Emilie Ahern.* **Supplies** *Cardstock:* WorldWin; *Patterned paper:* October Afternoon and Scenic Route; *Ghost letters:* Heidi Swapp for Advantus; *Embossing ink:* Rubber Stampede; *Embossing powder:* Stampendous!; *Electronic cutter:* Cricut, Provo Craft; *Leaf cartridge:* Accent Essentials (sampler for Cricut Expression but also sold online), Provo Craft; *Corner-rounder punch:* EK Success; *Brads:* Making Memories.

BY JANA LILLIE

HOW TO HEAT EMBOSS GHOST LETTERS

Love Emilie's cool look on the previous page? Here's how to create it yourself:

① Place letter face-down on an embossing pad, using the lid to apply even pressure.

② Use tweezers (or fingernails) to transport and flip the letter onto another surface, so it's face-up. Sprinkle on embossing powder.

③ Shake off any excess powder, then heat with a heat tool.

④ Enjoy the results!

ADD GLITZ WITH GLITTER

Who knew it was so easy to glam up ghost letters? Nia Reddy dressed hers up with a dusting of burgundy glitter. Not only does it add sparkly shimmer, but the glitter covers the adhesive as well.

Wash *by Nia Reddy.* **Supplies** *Cardstock:* Die Cuts With a View; *Patterned paper:* K&Company (green) and unknown; *Glitter:* Martha Stewart Crafts; *Brads:* SEI; *Adhesive dots:* Glue Dots International.

Download this ticket design!

Admission Ticket *by Maggie Holmes.* Photograph by Ryan Johnson. **Supplies** *Software:* Adobe Illustrator CS2; *Fonts:* Thyssen J, Type Embellishments One and Uptown, Internet.

CARVE A DESIGN TO USE LATER

That's right—carve a greeting and friendly (or fiendish) face, then add light inside the jack-o'-lantern and shoot a striking photograph at night like the example above by Ryan Johnson. Use the results for an eye-catching page title, accent or project such as Maggie Holmes' ticket here.

RUB-ONS WON'T STICK? TRY THIS!

When Irma Peredne found herself with a bad batch of rub-ons, she grabbed a foam brush and applied a thin glaze of transparent Liquitex Gloss Gel over her painted paper background. The gel dried clear and a bit tacky in seconds, which was just enough to get the stubborn rub-ons to transfer. Quick fix!

Rock On *by Andrea Chamberlain.* **Supplies** *Software:* Adobe Photoshop CS2; *Fonts:* Palatino, Retro Rock Poster and Undecapped Vinyl, Internet.

ROCK ON WITH A TWO-TONE TITLE

To create a title as funky as her daughter, Andrea Chamberlain typed text in Adobe Photoshop, applied a thin black stroke (5 pixels) inside each letter, then changed all the blending modes to "lighten." No text rasterizing required!

"TAPE" FOR QUICK GRUNGE

To create a weathered look in minutes, Lovely Cutler covered chipboard letters and a 4" x 5" piece of cardboard with masking tape, then cut the excess flush with the edges of the letters or cardboard. (She left some "ridges" of the torn cardboard uncovered.) Next, she painted the surface with acrylic paint. Once the paint was almost dry, Lovely lifted off portions of the paint with another piece of masking tape. Wickedly fast and fun!

Boo! *by Lovely Cutler.* **Supplies** *Masking tape:* Scotch, 3M (works best; the older, the better); *Chipboard letters:* Fancy Pants Designs; *Velvet silhouette stickers:* Making Memories; *Other:* Cardboard, paint, jute and staples.

CREATE THESE "DREAMY" DAISIES

Ooh, love these daisies! To create them, Eileen Collins stamped mulberry paper with a daisy stamp (note its doodled, multi-line look) and moistened the perimeter of the shape with a wet cotton swab. She then carefully tore around the edges. For the flower centers, Eileen repeated the same steps with a smaller daisy stamp (from the same set as the larger daisy) and added orange punched circles on top.

Daisy Thank-You Card *by Eileen Collins for Technique Tuesday.* **Supplies** *Cardstock:* Bazzill Basics Paper; *Flourish tile:* Tile Toppers, Technique Tuesday; *Stamps:* Delightful Daisies, Technique Tuesday; *Ink:* VersaMark, Tsukineko; *Other:* Mulberry paper. *Note:* To change the color of the white flourish tile, Eileen rubbed a light-green chalk inkpad over the surface.

tips & tricks

BY MEGAN HOEPPNER

LAYER IT ON THICK

We're not sure if Natasja Verbeek was inspired by a freshly raked pile of leaves when creating this layout, but her stacked page design sure reminds us of one. Notice how she layered several different paper types to create a colorful and energetic pile that looks anything but messy. All you'll need are several different types of paper. Start with a natural patterned paper base, followed by a sheet of book paper (either torn from an old book or photocopied from one). Next, add a bit of distressed cardstock, and top your pile off with a piece of rugged cardboard. The various finishes will leave you with a layered look others will want to dive right into.

ten creative tips to try

Outdoor Diva *by Natasja Verbeek.* **Supplies:** *Cardstock:* Bazzill Basics Paper; *Patterned paper:* Cosmo Cricket and Skipping Stones Designs; *Ink:* Ranger Industries; *Stickers:* American Crafts and Cosmo Cricket; *Chipboard:* Advantus; *Other:* Pen and adhesive.

CHECK PLEASE

Requesting the check just got a lot more fun thanks to this journaling tip provided by Ginger John of Glitz Design. Record your memories on a blank bill for a fresh, found-items approach. It will give your layout lots of character. Various receipt forms can be found at your local office-supply store. This is definitely an idea to check out!

Gift by Ginger John for Glitz Design. **Supplies:** *Patterned paper:* Glitz Design, Graphic45, and Pink Paislee; *Stickers:* Glitz Design and Jenni Bowlin Studio; *Rub-ons and die cut:* Glitz Design; *Button and pearl accents:* Jenni Bowlin Studio; *Pen:* Bic; *Adhesive:* Ranger Industries and Tombow; *Other:* Acrylic paint, cardboard, guest check, lace flower, ledger sheet, mirror, rhinestones, staples, vintage card, and sheet music.

MORE FORM FINDS

In your quest for unique journaling spots, don't stop at receipts. Game scorecards, calendar slips, and even purchase orders will set your layouts apart.

TRAY CHIC

The next time you sit down to create, don't forget an ice tray and/or silicone cupcake liners. No, these aren't for ice-cold beverages or tasty snacks. Instead, they're to keep the smallest of accents together and organized. This cool plan, provided by reader April Street, is simple: fill your tray with the small accents you're planning to use on your next project, and free up space on your desk for creating as well as keeping track of even the bittiest beauties.

LEAF YOUR MARK

Creating a truly unique look on your layouts just got a lot more colorful thanks to this technique by Liz Hicks. She made leaf accents to add color and dimension to her work of art. You can achieve the same standout look by following the tips below:

Be YOU-nique *by Liz Hicks.* **Supplies:** *Cardstock:* Couture Cardstock; *Paint, spray ink, and stamps:* Tattered Angels; *Ink:* Tsukineko; *Thread:* Gutterman; *Font:* Times New Roman; *Adhesive:* Beacon Adhesives and Scrapbook Adhesives by 3L.

❶ Hand cut leaves and stamp with water-safe ink (such as StazOn), which won't bleed when misted.

❷ Paint leaves.

❸ Spray painted leaves with coordinating spray ink.

❹ Coat leaves with clear, liquid adhesive to create glossy look.

LETTER STANDOUT

Making your smaller letters stand out on a larger layout is easy with a little stitching. Simply adhere your bitty title, whether it's created from small letter stickers or typed and trimmed, as Liz did. Then stitch both above and below your statement using a contrasting color of thread for a little look that's big on impact.

Happy Just Being by Kim Watson. **Supplies:** Cardstock: American Crafts; Patterned paper: American Crafts and BoBunny Press; Rub-ons: Fancy Pants Designs and Hambly Screen Prints; Eyelet: Making Memories; Stickers: American Crafts and Scenic Route; Plastic accents: American Crafts; Stamps: Croxley Stationery and Technique Tuesday; Ink: Close to My Heart; Tools: EK Success, Fiskars Americas, and Making Memories; Pens: American Crafts, EK Success, and Sakura; Font: Typewriter; Adhesive: American Crafts, Scrapbook Adhesives by 3L, Therm O Web, and Tombow; Other: Bubble wrap.

PEN PRETTIES

Put your mark on puffy accents with a few pen doodles. It's a fun and creative way to turn a pre-made product into an accent all your own. And, thanks to Kim Watson, it's easy to do. Here's how:

❶ Draw practice doodles on scratch paper.

❷ Draw doodles on accents (see "Pen Lineup" for which pens to use).

❸ Adhere accents to layout, and doodle leaves and swirls.

PEN LINEUP

Kim tested several pens and, after a little trial and error, came up with the perfect pen assortment to use for this technique.

- **White Galaxy Marker by American Crafts:** This opaque writer will give you bright white, solid lines that won't rub off the plastic.

- **Colored Souffle Pens by Sakura:** These opaque colors will glide on evenly and stay put on plastic.

- **Black Zig Photo Writer by EK Success:** This writing tool will give you a solid line without smudges. It works for doodling on paper as well.

For more on pens, check out our pen product review, found in the September 2010 issue of *Creating Keepsakes*.

CHALK IT UP

You're just a chalk palette away from 100 percent original flocked paper. Mou Saha discovered this when she colored the flocking on her patterned paper to create a vivid look for her layout. Flocked paper is fuzzy and will take the chalk color easily. So all you have to do is use a small applicator, such as a cotton swab, to add your own bright imprint directly on the flocked surfaces of your paper.

Priceless by Mou Saha. **Supplies:** *Patterned and flocked papers, flower, and stickers:* Anna Griffin; *Chalk:* Deluxe Designs; *Pen:* American Crafts; *Adhesive:* 3M.

For more ideas for using chalk, turn to page 245.

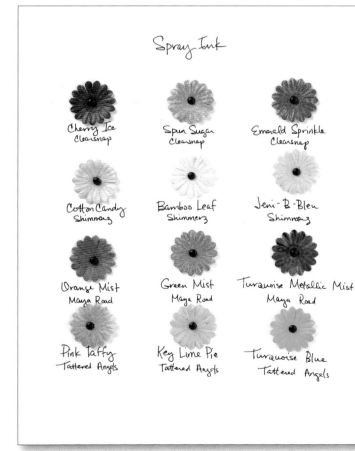

LET THE FLOWERS BE YOUR GUIDE

Are you a fan of spray ink? This popular product is popping up all over the place, as are unique ways to organize it, including this idea from reader Hope Smyth. To keep track of the beautiful colors she owns, she sprays a white paper flower with each color, then adheres them to a piece of cardstock and jots down the name of the color. This effortless idea is not only functional, it's also pretty. And doesn't being pretty make organizing that much more inspiring?

WRITE A LOVE LETTER

Use your journaling skills to connect with your family. Whether you write formal letters or just leave little notes around the house, the written word is a wonderful way to connect with those you care about. A loyal reader on Club CK suggests writing a letter to your grandchildren. She writes a note to her grandchildren on their birthdays, telling them what's going on in their lives at that time and how they've changed over the last year. She then includes a special life lesson, seals the note, and stores it in a secure place. Her plan is to give these heartfelt letters to her grandchildren when they turn 18. What a wonderful surprise that will be!

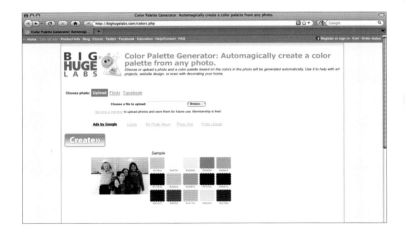

ONLINE COLOR HELP

Ever find yourself stumped when it comes to selecting a color combination to work with on a layout? Thanks to reader Annie Tsai, we have the answer—let your photos be your guide. All you have to do is upload your image(s) to Big Huge Labs *(bighuge labs.com)*, and it will come up with not one, but three complementary color-palette options. Annie swears by this color coach and was nice enough to share the tip with us. Thanks, Annie!

WANTED: YOUR BEST TIPS

Do you have a great tip up your creative sleeve? We want to hear from you! Your idea could be published in a future issue of the magazine. Simply e-mail your tip or technique (easy to advanced) to *editorial@creatingkeepsakes.com* and include "Tips & Tricks" in the subject line. **ck**

9 *tricks* you've gotta try

1 ARRANGE WORDS CREATIVELY IN SECONDS

Aly Dosdall's "word cloud" looks difficult to create—but it's easy and fast. To create your own clever arrangement, go online to Wordle.net, click on "Create your own" and type in any words with a space between them. Click on "Go" and the site will generate a random configuration. Change colors, fonts, styles and more!

scrap *faster* **and better**

Snow *by Aly Dosdall.* **Supplies** *Software:* Adobe Photoshop CS2; *Paper and journaling tag:* BasicGrey; *Circle and snowflake punches:* EK Success; *Brads:* The Paper Company; *Dimensional foam squares:* 3M; *Font:* BigMisterC.

BY JANA LILLIE

CHALK UP A COOL TITLE EFFECT

Whoa—is this chalkboard effect cool or what?! Sarah Hodgkinson achieved the look in three easy steps:

❶ Adhere chipboard letters face-up with adhesive dots to a cutting mat, using its measuring grid as a guide for centering and alignment.

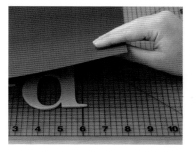

❷ Adhere white-core cardstock face-up to the mat with adhesive dots to keep the cardstock from shifting.

❸ Sand gently over the letter area until the desired amount of white is achieved. Sand the edges of the paper as well after lifting it carefully off the mat.

Field Trip by Sarah Hodgkinson. **Supplies** *Specialty cardstock:* All in the Family and Black Magic, Core-dinations; *Title strip ("trip"):* Opposites Attract, Cricut; *Chipboard letters:* BasicGrey; *Software:* Print-Master Gold, Broderbund; *Cutting mat:* Creative Memories; *Adhesive dots:* Glue Dots International; *Other:* Sandpaper.

STACK FOR A DIMENSIONAL LOOK

To add dimension to her titles, Mary Rogers prints out the same word five times on cardstock with her Cricut machine. She then stacks the die-cut versions, applying adhesive between the layers. "People are amazed at the difference this makes," says Mary. "The titles really pop visually, and they're so easy to create using your basic supplies."

Brr by Mary Rogers. **Supplies** *Cardstock:* Bazzill Basics Paper; *Patterned paper:* BasicGrey; *Die-cut letters:* George and Basic Shapes cartridges, Cricut, Provo Craft; *Snowflakes:* Heidi Swapp for Advantus; *Brads:* Making Memories; *Ink:* Tim Holtz Distress Ink, Ranger Industries; *Adhesive:* EK Success and Xyron; *Other:* Glitter.

CREATE A PANORAMIC VIEW...FOR FREE

Ever wish you could easily capture a panoramic view of a room or another location? You can! Brenda Arnall created her "room with a view" in a free Microsoft download called Windows Live Photo Gallery (visit it at *http://explore.live.com/windows-live-photo-gallery*).

Says Brenda, "The gallery turns a series of photos into a panoramic picture. You don't need to be ultra-precise when lining up the photos but do need a little overlap. The download automatically stitches everything together into a single photo." Sweet—and the online instructions are easy to follow!

The View from My Chair *by Brenda Arnall.* **Supplies** *Cardstock:* Bazzill Basics Paper; *Patterned paper:* Making Memories and Scenic Route; *Chipboard letters:* October Afternoon; *Rub-ons:* 7gypsies; *Letter stickers, tag and metal accent:* Making Memories; *Stamp and ink:* Technique Tuesday; *Paint:* Golden Artist Colors; *Paper trim:* Doodlebug Design; *Brads:* Making Memories; *Pen:* Staedtler; *Fonts:* CK Swing and Zurich Ex BT.

REMOVE RUB-ONS IN A FLASH

Rub-ons are remarkably versatile—and sticky. What's a scrapper to do when she goofs on one? Remove it painlessly with an adhesive eraser (under $5). This works for Fresh Face Yvonne Winters, and it can work for you, too!

Thank You Tag *by Yvonne Winters.* **Supplies** *Paper and ribbon:* Close To My Heart; *Die-cut letters:* Cricut; *Rub-on:* Bo-Bunny Press; *Adhesive eraser:* Xyron.

CARRY SPARE BATTERIES IN THE COLD

You can capture awesome photos outdoors this winter . . . if your camera batteries don't succumb to the cold. (It zaps their power.) If you're headed to a ski slope, a sledding hill or another winter scene, carry an extra set of batteries in a pocket near your body so you'll have a warm set on hand that holds power. When you load the warm batteries into your camera, place the original set near your body so they'll be ready again once they warm up. Better safe than sorry!

GLAM UP A HOLDER FOR IPOD OR CELL PHONE

Sure, you can carry your iPod or cell phone in a standard holder, but why not make yours special? Whip up a fun, funky holder with a 5" x 11" piece of felt or fabric and a few of your favorite supplies. That's what Sue Thomas did here!

note: To adjust for smaller iPods or cell phones, simply measure the height and width of your iPod or cell phone and add 1½" to the height measurement and 2" to the width measurement to get the starting size of your front and back piece of felt or fabric.

STREAMLINE YOUR BUTTON PROCESS

Liz Michaud loves to dress up her layouts with buttons, but creating a button border or adding stitching to several buttons can be time-consuming. As a shortcut, glue on all your buttons, then take a needle and quickly punch through all the button holes through the paper. (You'll be able to see from the back.) Next, with a needle and a long piece of thread, sew through all the buttons. This saves time, and the buttons lie flatter without the bulk of extra knots.

MAKE "INCHIES" IN SPARE MINUTES

Busy year ahead? Get a jump-start by making "inchies" like Shari Carroll's whenever you have a few spare minutes. Decorate the 1" paper squares with stamps, eyelets, brads, bows, whatever—you can make your mini masterpieces as simple or as elaborate as you like! Use the inchies in a pinch to adorn scrapbook pages, cards or any project.

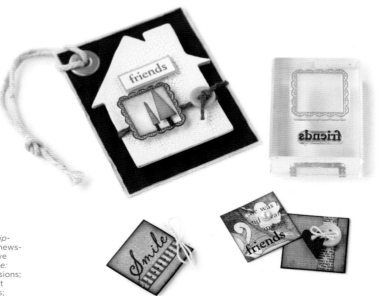

Card and Accents by Shari Carroll. **Supplies** *Cardstock and chipboard circle:* Bazzill Basics Paper; *Patterned paper:* 7gypsies (newsprint), BasicGrey (stripe, floral and butterfly) and My Mind's Eye (green); *Stamps, pearls and flower:* Hero Arts; *Chipboard house:* Maya Road; *Punches:* EK Success; *Silk ribbon:* Creative Impressions; *Ink:* Clearsnap (chalk), Ranger Industries (distress) and Stewart Superior Corporation (shadow); *Eyelet:* We R Memory Keepers; *Other:* Color pencil, book text, button and string.

7 *creative* & clever twists

1 PUNCH A MESH LOOK IN MINUTES

To create an airy backdrop for her photos, Irma Peredne punched holes in paper with an anywhere punch. She kept the spacing even by punching over the paper's preexisting dot pattern. (You can also use a separate sheet of dot patterned paper as a guide.) To save time, Irma punched only the portion of paper that would show. To determine this area, she placed her page elements on the paper and lightly traced around them to see the area they would cover. Total punching time? Under 10 minutes! **>>**

add *pretty* touches sure to inspire

Boys to Men *by Irma Peredne.* **Supplies** *Cardstock:* Bazzill Basics Paper; *Patterned paper:* BasicGrey (background), Kelly Panacci for Sandylion (plaid) and SEI (blue punched); *Journaling spot:* Heidi Swapp for Advantus; *Metal tag and letter stickers:* Making Memories; *Number sticker:* Creative Imaginations; *Rub-ons:* BasicGrey; *Ink:* ColorBox, Clearsnap; *Circle template:* Coluzzle, Provo Craft; *Font:* Arial.

BY JANA LILLIE

TRY THIS FOR A MORE NATURAL SMILE

"Cheesy" or "fake" smiles a problem during photo sessions? Try Allison Orthner's expert advice. Instead of encouraging people to say "cheese," ask them to say "hi" over and over in as many ways as possible. Snap pictures at the end of the word "hi." People start having so much fun that their genuine smiles come across!

BEFORE

AFTER

PHOTOS BY ALLISON ORTHNER

DELIGHT WITH THESE DARLING CLIPS

How cute are these?! Annaka Crockett used her scrapbooking supplies to dress up binder clips. They're definitely conversation pieces, whether used as standalone designs or fun photo holders.

To decorate a clip, cut patterned paper into a strip as wide as the clip. Measure the plastic portion of the clip from the top of one side to the top of the other, base included. Add ½"—you can always trim more if needed. Attach the paper around the clip with numerous adhesive dots, then tuck it under the plastic folds of the clip. Embellish as desired.

Decorated Clips *by Annaka Crockett.* **Supplies** *Cardstock:* Bazzill Basics Paper; *Patterned paper:* 3 Bugs in a Rug (grid), Chatterbox (pink), Scenic Route (stripe) and unknown; *Acetate butterfly and star:* Heidi Swapp for Advantus; *Teal flowers and rub-ons:* 7gypsies; *Pink flower:* Keepsake Trends; *Circle punch:* McGill; *Paint:* Plaid Enterprises; *Art glitter:* Barbara Trombley; *Glaze:* Diamond Glaze; *Embroidery floss:* DMC; *Font for letter "M":* Monotype Corsiva; *Adhesive dot:* Glue Dots International; *Other:* Ribbon, hand-cut tag, binder clips and black monogram letter.

CREATE EASY JEWELED CENTERS

While playing with Stickles dimensional adhesive, Janet Kannenberg discovered an easy way to create a faux-jewel center for silk flowers. Simply attach an eyelet to the center of a flower and carefully squeeze a bit of dimensional adhesive into the eyelet. (Janet prefers the "puffier" varieties of Stickles by Ranger Industries.) Let the adhesive dry thoroughly, then add a second coat for more dimension.

PLAY WITH PAINT ON PAINT

Heidi Sonboul was tired of "doing the same ol' thing," so she got creative with puffy and acrylic paints on her "Bubbles" page. While she initially hesitated over the mess, she loved the results so much that she has used this technique a few times since! "Just think of the possibilities," says Heidi. "You can make 3-D titles, frames, and so much more. Even after months, the puffy paint has held up beautifully in my page protectors."

Blissful Bubbles by Heidi Sonboul. **Supplies** Cardstock: Bazzill Basics Paper; Patterned paper and pen: American Crafts; Circle template: Fiskars; Paint: Making Memories (acrylic) and Duncan Enterprises (puffy); Stamps: Inkadinkado; Tag: K&Company; Letter die cuts: Street Sign Solutions Cartridge, Cricut, Provo Craft.

to create this look:

❶ Trace or draw a shape or design (use a template if desired).

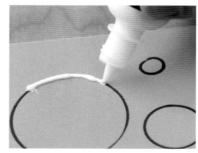

❷ Tap the tip of the puffy paint container on a second piece of paper to get out any air bubbles. Apply puffy paint along the drawing's outline and let it dry completely.

❸ Apply acrylic paint over the puffy paint and background.

note: Match the paint colors to avoid the need for multiple layers—they can make the paper wavy.

PROTECT YOUR IMAGES AND TEXT

Ouch! My home computer's hard drive crashed, and after high stress and a bill of $1,800 to retrieve irreplaceable photos and documents, here's what I would encourage:

❶ Choose a backup system you'll use. My previous system was unwieldy and tedious. Find something easy and use it.

❷ Keep a paper printout of how your current computer files are organized. I had hundreds of files, old and new, saved in dozens of folders, as did my sons and husband. When the recovery guy asked which files were most important (he'd be pulling random files—no nicely organized folders), I couldn't recall enough specifics. I now keep a printout of how things are organized in folders on my computer.

OOH—FILL A SHAPE WITH BUTTONS

To emphasize how much she loves New York City, Julie Fei-Fan Balzer penciled in a heart shape on her scrapbook page. After filling the shape creatively with buttons, she erased the pencil lines. Use this clever design idea with a variety of shapes!

I Love NYC by Julie Fei-Fan Balzer. **Supplies** Cardstock: Bazzill Basics Paper; Buttons: Autumn Leaves (acrylic) and Maya Road (felt); Rub-ons: Autumn Leaves; Embroidery floss: DMC; Pen: Zig Writer, EK Success; Other: Pencil.

8 *stylish* solutions

TRY THIS JOURNALING TRICK

Tracey Odachowski chose lined patterned paper for a background but wondered how to journal effectively on top of the pattern. To keep things readable, she lightly sanded a portion of the patterned paper with sandpaper. She then redrew a few of the lines before journaling on them.

sand, store and *create* with ease

Daydreaming *by Tracey Odachowski.* **Supplies** *Cardstock:* Bazzill Basics Paper; *Patterned paper, die cuts and stamps:* October Afternoon; *Pens and ink:* Stampin' Up!; *Jewels:* Heidi Swapp for Advantus; *Adhesive:* Therm O Web; *Digital cutter:* Xyron; *Font:* Fling; *Other:* Sandpaper.

BY JANA LILLIE

SPEED SCRAP YOUR "ORPHAN PHOTOS"

Self-proclaimed camera nut Stefanie Eskander has nearly 20,000 digital photos organized by date and event on two computers. Even though she scraps digitally and often, many photos she hoped to scrapbook (her "orphan photos") have never made it onto a layout.

Her solution? Stefanie is creating an orphan-photos album for each year, with multiple cropped photos on each monthly spread and journaled highlights at bottom right. "I love having a pictorial history for my family," says Stefanie, "and this makes it so easy to see at a glance what we did." For details on Stefanie's grid format, visit *creatingkeepsakes.com* and click on "Magazines."

March *by Stefanie Eskander.* **Supplies** *Software:* Adobe Photoshop CS3; *Fonts:* MemphisTBol, MemphisTMed and MemphisTExtLig.

CREATE CUSTOM POST-IT COVERS

Whether you use Post-it Notes at home or in the office, whip up custom covers like these by Jaime Ward. (Visit *creatingkeepsakes. com* and click on "Magazines > Past Issues > March 2009" for step-by-step instructions. You'll also get a peek at her paper-clip holder and pen holder.) Not only are the items a fun use of favorite or leftover scrapbook supplies, but you'll wow everyone with your sense of style as well!

Post-it Covers *by Jaime Ward.* **Supplies** *Cardstock:* Provo Craft and Stampin' Up!; *Digital supplies:* Digi Keepsakes by Monica; *Magnetic snaps:* BasicGrey; *Post-it Notes:* 3M; *Tacky tape:* Provo Craft. *Note:* Idea inspired by Grace Tolman; instructions adapted from her blog at TolmanChronicles.Blogspot.com.

TURN PLASTIC INTO PAINT TRAYS

Noel Culbertson stretches her scrap dollars by removing the plastic backings from product packaging and using them as paint trays. (She especially loves the plastic backings from Heidi Swapp's acrylic shapes.) The backings are small, can be rinsed and reused several times, and they're free. How's that for helping your budget and recycling?!

SHOW YOUR ARTISTIC SIDE

April Massad loves to experiment, and she's come up with two eye-catching (and easy) looks with alcohol ink. Relax—while the results are stunning, the steps are simple.

Home by April Massad. **Supplies** *Patterned paper:* Scenic Route; *Chipboard and stamps:* Technique Tuesday; *Buttons:* Autumn Leaves; *Felt applicator tool, felt, alcohol ink, blending solution, brown ink and ultra-thick embossing enamel:* Ranger Industries; *Border punch for flaps:* Fiskars; *Eyelets:* Making Memories; *Ink:* StazOn (black) and VersaMark (embossing), Tsukineko; *Embroidery floss:* DMC; *Font:* CK Newsprint.

button technique

After flipping a clear button onto its smooth side:

❶ Using a Tim Holtz Alcohol Ink Applicator, stick the alcohol ink nib into the felt and squeeze gently. Repeat until the felt contains several dots of ink.

❷ Press the tool onto the button to ink it. Lightly blow on the button to start the ink drying, then ink quickly again with the tool. Repeat as desired for darker, more pronounced colors.

crackle technique

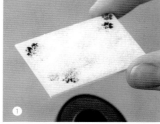

❶ Ink your chipboard the desired color, stamp your design and let it dry. Cover chipboard with embossing ink and pour on Ultra Thick Embossing Enamel (UTEE). Heat the chipboard's underside with a heat tool to minimize crystals blowing off during the embossing. Heat until the crystals melt and merge.

❷ With a felt applicator tool, ink the felt by sticking the alcohol ink nib into the felt and squeezing gently. Repeat until the felt contains several dots of ink. Ink the chipboard with the felt applicator by pressing it into the UTEE until you

cover the surface. To remove some alcohol ink from your stamped image, drop a few drops of blending solution on it. Dab the solution as needed with the felt applicator tool. Repeat as desired and let the layer dry.

❸ Ink the chipboard again with embossing ink. Add another layer of UTEE, repeating step 1. You'll see the ink "crackle" as you heat the second layer of UTEE. Let it cool, and you're done!

CHOOSE A POWDER SHADE IN SECONDS

When April Massad needs the perfect shade of embossing powder, she turns to her trusty ring of samples. "I took the centers of chipboard letters like 'O' or 'B' and embossed them with the shades of embossing powders I use most," says April. "I then punched a hole in each end, put the pieces on an inexpensive metal ring and tied ribbon on it. I can find what I need in seconds."

Embossing Samples *by April Massad.* **Supplies** *Chipboard pieces:* BasicGrey; *Embossing powders:* Ranger Industries; *Metal jump ring:* The Jewelry Shoppe; *Other:* Ribbon.

MAKE $ WITH YOUR PHOTOS

Do you specialize in taking sports photos of individuals or teams? How about school or wedding pictures? If people regularly offer to buy copies, check out the Pro Gallery options at *shutterfly.com.* (Click on "Professional Photographers" at the bottom of the screen.)

For an annual $99 fee, you receive 5GB of hosting space in an online storefront. Post your photos (in one or multiple galleries), specify print sizes and prices, and let Shutterfly handle the processing, delivery, accounting and more for a small percentage. Profits are deposited directly in your bank account.

PHOTO BY LINDA RODRIGUEZ

WRITE PERFECTLY EVERY TIME

Need help spacing your handwriting on sheer journaling cards like this design by Maya Road? Here's a handy solution from Suzy Plantamura:

① In Microsoft Word, create a text box that's the same size as the journaling card. Find a simple-to-read font that lets you space your journaling in the same number of lines as those on the card. Type your journaling to fit.

② Print the text box, then lay sheer card on top of the journaling (you may need to make some adjustments). Handwrite your journaling on top of the printed journaling with a permanent marker like Suzy's Sharpie.)

③ Remove the printed copy behind the sheer journaling card. Enjoy—you've got perfectly spaced handwriting in minutes without any spelling mistakes! **ck**

tips & tricks

BY MEGAN HOEPPNER

PAINTING THE CLOUDS BLUE

When it comes to handmade whimsy, Stacy Cohen has got the style mastered. She used acrylic paint—a few drops of teal with a dash of white—to create a soft cloud in the corner of her page. To add more definition to her design, she stitched a border with embroidery floss. This is a lovely way to fill in an open corner on a page and have a little artistic fun while you're at it.

create
clouds, roses, and more

Sing Your Best Life *by Stacy Cohen.* **Supplies** *Cardstock:* Bazzill Basics Paper; *Patterned paper and trim:* Webster's Pages; *Paint:* Making Memories (white and teal) and Shimmerz (brown glitter); *Stamp:* Creative Imaginations; *Ink:* Clearsnap; *Glitter glue:* Ranger Industries; *Embroidery floss:* DMC; *Pearls :* KaiserCraft; *Circle cutter tool:* Provo Craft ; *Pen:* American Crafts; *Butterfly (used as template):* Heidi Swapp for Advantus; *Font:* Georgia; *Adhesive:* Beacon's and Tombow; *Other:* Bead wire (for butterfly), gems and thread.

INKING THE ROSES RED

Stacy's fancy-free design on page 72 didn't stop at the painted cloud. She folded paper roses for extra dainty dimension. Grow your own paper-rose garden in four easy steps:

Ink: Quick Quotes.

❶ Draw a spiral and cut out the shape. Cut in a curved motion for a more decorative edge.

❷ Ink the edges. Note: Stacy only inked her cardstock flowers, leaving the busier patterned paper posies clean.

❸ Start from the outside of the spiral and roll the paper in towards the center.

❹ Adhere the rolled flower to the spiral's center and open the bloom by bending the edges back.

ORGANIZED DÉCOR

Nip those disorganized accents in the bud with a little flower-pot placement. Laura Stoller planted this idea in our heads when she attached small embellishments to foam balls for quick storage and easy access. You, too, can grow an orderly garden with a few basic supplies from the craft and home-improvement stores.

❶ Stick floral picks into foam ball and insert embellishments.

❷ Insert second foam ball into small flower pot and pierce accent flower into place.

❸ Roll scraps of ribbons and trims around pins and insert into the base.

Optional Step:
Paint your flower pot and/or add rub-ons or stamps for a more decorative look.

DESIGN ON A LINE

Capture an entire day's worth of moments on one layout and still keep things in chronological order using label stickers and photo lines. Shelly Jaquet's Easter celebration was full of memorable moments. Rather than create individual pages for each colorful activity, she typed labels for them, stitched them to a strip of patterned paper and then lined up her photos in rows according to each category (neigh-borhood party, coloring eggs and Easter morning). Try this for wedding pages with rows for each lovely step of the special day (the shower, the ceremony and the reception) or for birthday parties (the gifts, the cake and the décor). With this design approach, you can fill your album with row upon row of orderly bliss.

Easter Celebrations *by Shelly Jaquet.* **Supplies** *Cardstock:* Bazzill Basics Paper; *Patterned paper and trim:* Jenni Bowlin and Scenic Route; *Chipboard letters:* Heidi Swapp for Advantus; *Label stickers:* October Afternoon; *Border punch:* Stampin' Up!; *Pen:* American Crafts; *Font:* Rough Typewriter; *Adhesive:* Duck, EK Success and Glue Dots International.

PRINT ON LABELS

Creating printed labels like Shelly used on her layout may seem intimidating, but it's actually as easy as 1, 2, 3. Check it out!

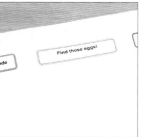

❶ Print the words you want to appear on your labels, selecting a font and size that fits.

❷ Adhere your labels directly over the printed phrase as you want them to appear on your stickers.

❸ Print your words a second time on the labeled sheet, cut the labels out and adhere them to your layout.

6 *inventive* twists

BY JANA LILLIE

1 STEP OUT IN STYLE

Jackie Stringham's daughter Katie is eight and already shares her mom's love of shoes. Jackie captured the fun on a playful page—check out her stylish shoe accent. And check out the paper shoe by Ellen Hutson! She's sharing her pattern and instructions for free at *creatingkeepsakes. com (click on Downloads, May 2009)*—plus you'll see that the shoe here is one of an amazing trio. Created in spring's hottest hues, the shoes are a sure conversation piece and gift idea! Fill them with candy, flowers or a simple note of appreciation!

play with **paper** and color

trying on **my shoes**

I found her today all dressed up in my high heels doing Danny's hair up in little pony tails. She sounded like me, she looked like me and she was acting like me. The little mom in every way. I hope one day her little brothers realize how lucky they are to have such a nurturing big sister.

Trying on My Shoes *by Jackie Stringham.* **Supplies** *Cardstock:* Bazzill Basics Paper (pink and orange) and Provo Craft (white); *Patterned paper:* October Afternoon (pink floral) and Scenic Route (green dot); *Die cuts:* Silhouette, QuicKutz; *Beads:* Provo Craft; *Fonts:* Bernhard MT Condensed (title) and Miaindra GD (journaling); *Adhesive:* Tombow; *Other:* Silk flower.

2 GET FREE HELP COMBINING COLORS

Pam Callaghan wanted a bright mix of complementary background colors for the page shown here—she just wasn't sure where to start. "I found the perfect color palette online at *colorschemer.com/schemes* and matched my colors to that," says Pam. "I love how everything turned out! You can create your own color schemes by using a trial version or buying the color schemer for your own use. The site is one of my best new color tools!"

Your Smile by Pam Callaghan. **Supplies** *Cardstock:* Bazzill Basics Paper and Die Cuts With a View; *Patterned paper:* American Crafts; *Chipboard letters:* Heidi Swapp for Advantus; *Letter stickers:* Doodlebug Design; *Flowers:* Making Memories; *Brads:* Die Cuts With a View; *Digital circle text path:* Jen Lessinger at TwoPeasinaBucket.com.

3 SAY "THANKS" IN A SWEET WAY

May's the perfect time to say "thanks" to a dear friend or family member. Sweeten your message with candy or a personal note in this clever purse holder! To create it, simply cut out a purse shape, assemble it and stamp on designs or apply rub-ons. Tie two butterfly shapes together with crochet thread and adhere. To create the purse handle, punch a hole in each side of the purse with a ¼" circle punch and thread grosgrain ribbon through each hole.

Purse Holder by Paula Hogan for Stampin' Up!. **Supplies** *Cardstock, patterned paper, rub-ons, stamps, ink and ribbon:* Stampin' Up!; *Die-cutting machine and dies:* Sizzix; *Other:* Circle punch and crochet thread.

MAKE YOUR OWN EMBOSSED DIE CUTS

Love the dimension that embossing adds to your designs? Follow Betsy Veldman's lead and create ingenious, embossed die cuts with your Cricut and Cuttlebug machines! Betsy has created numerous folders that she files after labeling each with the Cricut cartridge used and the cut size. "I love that I can make the die cuts any size I want," says Betsy. "To save time, I've also created sets of squares and circles to use as mats on future projects."

Spring Ride *by Betsy Veldman.* **Supplies** *Patterned paper:* BasicGrey (solids), Sassafras (striped scalloped border) and SEI (green print); *Die-cut cartridges:* Storybook (frames) and Sans Serif Solutions (letters), Cricut, Provo Craft; *Stickers and buttons:* BasicGrey; *Font:* Arial.

Here's how to create results like Betsy's:

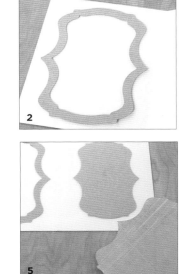

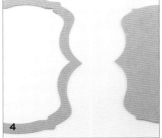

❶ Select an image from a Cricut design cartridge that has a solid blackout image to match. Cut the desired image from chipboard with the Cricut's multi-cut feature.

❷ Fold a small piece of cardstock in half to create a folder. Adhere the outside portion of the cut design to one side of the folder.

❸ Place the inner portion of the cut design inside the outer portion and apply glue to the top. Close the folder and apply pressure over the glued area to secure in place.

❹ Open the folder to confirm the inside portion of the design is stuck to the other side of the folder as shown.

❺ Place matching blackout image over the chipboard die cut that has the outer ring. Place it facedown for a raised image center or faceup for raised edges. *Tip:* Put a tiny dot of repositionable adhesive on the back of your die cut to keep it from moving around.

❻ Run the combination through a Cuttlebug embossing machine for the results shown. Betsy used the following sandwich stack from bottom up: A plate, B plate, die cut inside folder, C plate.

5 ADD A BURST OF COLOR

Aly Dosdall could have spent hours creating a colorful backdrop for her St. Louis pictures. Instead, she downloaded a digital kit in minutes with a pixel look she loves. The design even includes squares for 14 photos or accents!

Colors of St. Louis *by Aly Dosdall.* **Supplies** *Software:* Adobe Photoshop CS2; *Digital template:* Express Chick Out Lane: Hip 2B Squared Edition by 3 Pixel Chicks; *Letters:* Crackly Alpha Brushes-n-Stamps by Katie Pertiet; *Mini letters:* Tranquillite Elements by Angel Hartline; *Font:* Times New Roman.

6 WOW WITH ALCOHOL-INK LEAVES AND DESIGNS

Ooh—as shown at right, Irene Tan of Malaysia creates cool leaf effects we couldn't resist. Her secret? Alcohol ink for a stained-glass look. Here's how to duplicate her results:

Leaf Samples *by Irene Tan.* **Supplies** *Leaf stamps:* Impression Obsession; *Felt applicator tool, felt, alcohol ink and blending solution:* Ranger Industries; *Black paint:* Making Memories; *Dimensional paint:* Liquid Pearls, Ranger Industries; *White pens:* Uni-ball Signo, Newell Rubbermaid; Zig Painty, EK Success; *Other:* Transparency.

❶ Apply alcohol inks randomly to a felt applicator tool and apply to a transparency. Use blending solution as needed. Next, dab to get the desired look and let dry. Stamp designs (like Irene's leaves) on the inked transparency using a solvent-based ink.

❷ Accentuate each stamped leaf with dots (before or after trimming the leaf and stem images) and let dry. Irene likes to add her dots prior to trimming for added control.

9 *ways* to save time and $

1

PRETTY UP YOUR CHIPBOARD

To save money and add sizzle, April Massad covers plain chipboard flowers with paper scraps. (Just trace, cut, adhere, and then sand the edges.) She also buys plain chipboard letters and embosses them the color she wants—it's much quicker than painting! For additional tricks used on the layout below, turn the page. >>

try these **quick** *solutions*

Summer Time *by April Massad.* **Supplies** *Cardstock:* Bazzill Basics Paper; *Patterned paper:* We R Memory Keepers; *Transparency:* Hambly Screen Prints; *Labels:* Creative Imaginations; *Chipboard:* BasicGrey (letters) and Fancy Pants Designs (flowers); *Buttons:* Autumn Leaves; *Beads and wire:* Crafts Etc.; *Embossing powder:* Ranger Industries; *Ink:* Stampabilities; *Pen:* Zig Writer, EK Success; *Craft knife:* EK Success; *Sandpaper and files:* BasicGrey; *Adhesive:* E-Z Runner, Scrapbook Adhesives by 3L; Adhesive Foam Squares, The Paper Studio.

BY JANA LILLIE

<< continued from previous page

MORE CREATIVE TRICKS BY APRIL MASSAD

April Massad's ingenuity didn't end with the custom chipboard looks shown on the previous page. We also love how she:

- **Used labels for her journaling strips.** "I staggered the self-adhesive label strips, trimmed the longer pieces off the side of my page, and then journaled on the remaining pieces," says April. "It was much quicker than measuring out cardstock strips, and I love the color the labels add to my layout."

- **Jazzed up her button flower centers.** Instead of using ribbon or thread, April put beads on a wire and strung the wire through the buttonholes—it's "much easier!" she says.

For more details on how April covered the chipboard flowers with patterned paper, see the June 2009 Tips & Tricks online extension at *creatingkeepsakes.com.*

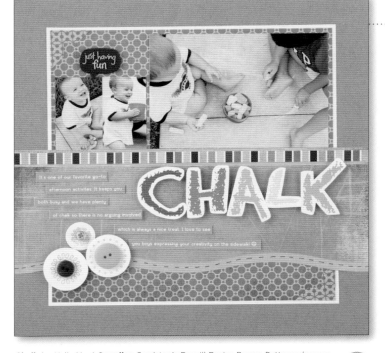

Chalk *by Kelly Noel.* **Supplies** *Cardstock:* Bazzill Basics Paper; *Patterned paper and buttons:* BasicGrey; *Stamps:* Hero Arts; *Ink:* Autumn Leaves; *Charm:* October Afternoon; *Punch and pen:* EK Success; *Fonts:* Eraser Dust and Surrounding; *Adhesive:* Tombow.

MIMIC A CHALK LOOK

The moment Kelly Noel saw the Eraser Dust font at Dafont.com, she knew it would be perfect for a page about her sons playing with chalk on the driveway. "I typed the word 'CHALK' in the font, changed the color of each letter, printed the word on white cardstock and cut the letters out," says Kelly. "I elevated each letter with dimensional adhesive, and I was done—I got the look I wanted without the mess of real chalk."

HELP YOUR PHOTO SUBJECT RELAX

We've all experienced it—the photo subject who feels awkward in front of the camera. For a quick fix, add a child to the mix. "It takes the pressure off being photographed," says Joanna Bolick. "For this photo, I encouraged my son Cole to give his grandfather a big hug from behind. I asked my dad to get down to Cole's level so they would be face-to-face in the photo." Try this trick on pictures with Dad or Grandpa on Father's Day!

GET A GREAT GROUP PHOTO

During summer months, family members are often asked to pose for group pictures. (Think family reunions, graduations and weddings.) Some family members will be excited, others will not. Here's terrific advice courtesy of Terri Davenport: set the tripod up and have a young member of the family be the one to push the camera-release button. Relatives are typically more willing to pose for a child, and their facial expressions will generally be more relaxed and natural.

TRY THIS NEW TAKE ON A GUEST BOOK

Gail Robinson delighted us with a fun take on a guest book she created for her niece's wedding. To "do something a little different," she let her niece choose a favorite song ("I Love" by Tom T. Hall), and she incorporated the words as part of her design. Gail printed the lyrics on envelopes, which she hole-punched and placed between the pages of the guest-book album. Guests in the wedding line viewed the album and filled out scallop circle cards lying on the table instead of signing a book. After the reception, the scallop cards were placed inside the envelopes, and the album was finished.

Wedding Guest Book *by Gail Robinson. Photos by Julie Hess.*
Supplies *Album and ribbon:* Making Memories; *Cardstock:* Bazzill Basics Paper; *Envelopes and cards:* Archiver's; *Flowers:* Heidi Swapp for Advantus; *Photo corners:* Scrapbook Adhesives by 3L; *Letter stickers:* American Crafts; *Paint:* Delta Creative; *Buttons:* Lasting Impressions for Paper; *Pearls:* Kaisercraft; *Other:* Brads.

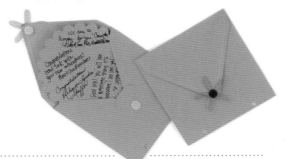

SPLIT A DOT OR SQUARE

Here's a popular, handy trick: the next time you need to elevate a page accent, cut your foam square or adhesive dot in half. Not only will you still get the lift you need, but your stash of dots and squares will last longer as well.

CREATE A "FRY BOX" PARTY FAVOR

Sure—at your next party you can always fill bags with prizes for party guests, but why not hand out cute "fry box" favors instead? Jamie Ward has created fun variations for her children's parties, and she is happy to share her free download at *creatingkeepsakes.com (click on Downloads, June 2009)*. See what *you* can create with your extra supplies!

Girly Fry Box *by Jaime Ward.* **Supplies** *Cardstock:* Provo Craft; *Patterned paper:* Glitz Design; *Stamp, ink, embossing powder and scallop punch:* Stampin' Up!; *Ribbon:* C.M. Offray & Son; *Adhesive:* Duck Products, Henkel Corporation.

Here's how to create a "fry box" favor:

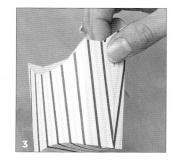

❶ Download the "Fry Box Scoring Guides" PDF from CreatingKeepsakes.com. Put the desired scrapbook paper in your printer (positioned so it will print on the wrong side) and print the file.

❷ Trim along the outer solid lines of each box (the pattern includes two). Use a bone folder or embossing stylus to trace along the dotted lines, applying heavy pressure to score the paper. *Tip:* Use a ruler to help when tracing along straight lines.

❸ Fold along the lines (positioning the front flap on top of the back flap) and use adhesive to glue the sides shut. When the box is folded, the bottom will curve up like a fry box does. Fill the completed box with goodies, and you're done!

Visit *creatingkeepsakes.com* for steps and files to create this same look digitally!

PICK 'EM UP WITH PANTYHOSE

Ever dropped an open container of beads, eyelets or other tiny accents on the carpet? Try this trick by Michelle Novella! Slip the foot portion of a pair of knee-high pantyhose over the end of your vacuum attachment. Stretch the material tight and secure it with a thick rubber band. Turn on your vacuum and let the suction pick up the tiny pieces for you! When ready to release the items into a container, simply turn off the vacuum.

use common *household items*

1 PUT ON A SPRITZ

Creating handmade flower accents just got a lot more sparkly thanks to this tip from Steph Caskey-Devlin. She turned ordinary white tissue paper into a blooming page accent by cutting it into circles, fastening them together with a button, and spraying on some Glimmer Mist by Tattered Angels. Read on to learn how. >>

Try these *affordable* ideas

BY MEGAN HOEPPNER

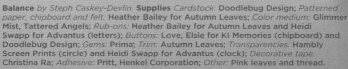

Balance *by Steph Caskey-Devlin.* **Supplies** *Cardstock:* Doodlebug Design; *Patterned paper, chipboard and felt:* Heather Bailey for Autumn Leaves; *Color medium:* Glimmer Mist, Tattered Angels; *Rub-ons:* Heather Bailey for Autumn Leaves and Heidi Swapp for Advantus (letters); *Buttons:* Love, Elsie for KI Memories (chipboard) and Doodlebug Design; *Gems:* Prima; *Trim:* Autumn Leaves; *Transparencies:* Hambly Screen Prints (circle) and Heidi Swapp for Advantus (clock); *Decorative tape:* Christina Ra; *Adhesive:* Pritt, Henkel Corporation; *Other:* Pink leaves and thread.

<< continued from previous page

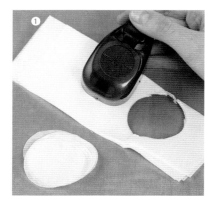

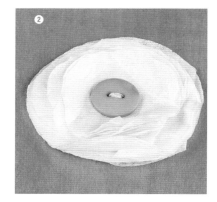

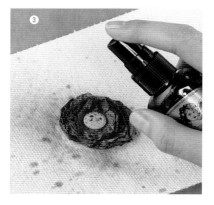

STEP 1: Cut (or punch) several tissue-paper circles (Steph used 2″ and 2½″ circle punches). To speed up the process, first fold your tissue paper several times before cutting circles.

STEP 2: Crumple and then flatten your circles for added texture. Secure them together with a button and thread.

STEP 3: Apply Glimmer Mist (or other spray ink), lifting the petals to get the color in the crevices of each layer; let dry. *Note:* You can speed up the drying process with a heat tool, but do so with caution by keeping the tool at a safe distance (a few inches) from the paper.

TAKE NOTE WITH HANDMADE JOURNALING SPOTS

There was a time when seeing a pile of note cards in my top desk drawer sent shivers down my spine, as they immediately transported me back to the days of college speech classes. That is, until I was forced to conquer my fear late one night while in desperate need of a lined journaling spot (I can't write straight to save my life). With little more than my imagination, some cardstock and a few shape punches, I turned this staple office supply into a fun and completely unique place to hold my journaled thoughts.

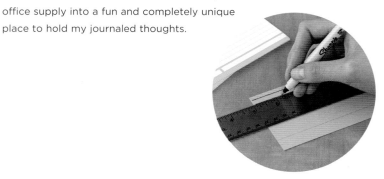

NOTEWORTHY TIDBIT

Note cards are available in cool colors, like the green Post-it Note cards shown here, but you can also transform those standard blue lines into different colors with a fine-point marker and a ruler.

CUT SHAPELY PHOTOS

Add interest to a layout with photos in multiple shapes and sizes. As Jamie Harper shows us, you don't have to invest in multiple shape punches or go digi to master this look. Instead, grab clear objects in a variety of shapes and sizes and use them as tracing templates—using a clear object allows you to see exactly where you want your cut.

(You can also use hollow-centered items, such as the center of a roll of tape or a tag rim.) Position the shape over the image for perfect placement, trace around the shape and then cut. Remember to use pens that won't smudge on a smooth photo, like Slick Writers from American Crafts, to avoid messy mishaps.

 **My Family** *by Jamie Harper.* **Supplies** *Cardstock:* Bazzill Basics Paper; *Patterned paper:* Art Warehouse and Dream Street Papers (solid blue dots); *Stickers:* Adornit - Carolee's Creations (flowers) and Making Memories (letters); *Adhesive:* Scotch ATG, 3M; *Font:* Typical Writer.

TEMPLATES AROUND THE HOUSE

See acrylic stamping blocks in a new way. With the numerous shapes and sizes they come in (some are even scalloped), you can trace all sorts of fun photo shapes with this stamping tool. Don't be afraid to try this idea with larger shapes. Clear plates, cups and jar lids make great and affordable templates.

USE THOSE SCRAPS

Now more than ever it feels like a waste-not, want-not world, which means making the most of leftover patterned paper scraps. Instead of throwing them out, turn them into accents to use on future projects by punching shapes from what's left of your sheet(s). Store the punched shapes in a plastic bag or jar for quick and easy access when it comes time to create again. Before long, you'll have lots of decorative bits to pull from and far fewer trashed scraps.

CONSIDER ON-THE-GO RIBBON STORAGE

Most scrapbookers will agree that ribbon is a crafting must. Unfortunately, it's not always easy to take along when scrapping on the go. A tote full of ribbon spools? I think not. A bulky, jumbled bag of scraps? Forget about it! Lucinda Messman has an idea that's as orderly as it is easy. Wrap ribbon strands around craft sticks, secure them in place with small straight pins or paper clips and pack the sticks in a quart-size sandwich bag. That's a wrap!

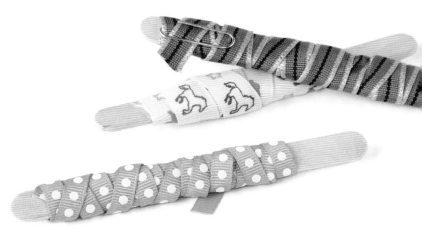

SIMPLE SOLUTION: LETTER STICKERS

This clever idea comes from Marnie Flores. To give her title an extra bit of spunk while also stretching her sticker sheet further, she used the outline of a letter to create her "t." Often times, stickers bleed beyond the border, leaving a thin layer of color. Follow Marnie's lead and cut these outlines out and use them as original letters on your page. On the letters with centers (such as "A," "B," "D," "e" and "g"), save and use the middles. If you create a page with a white background like Marnie's, you can simply peel and stick these centers. If you go with another background option like patterned paper or photos, you can use a craft knife to cut around the edge. **ck**

Outwit by Marnie Flores. **Supplies** *Cardstock:* Prism Papers; *Patterned paper:* We R Memory Keepers; *Letter stickers:* **SEI;** *Ribbon:* C.M. Offray & Son; *Pen:* Tombow; *Adhesive:* Creative Memories and Kokuyo.

take a
creative journey

1

OUTLINE YOUR TITLE

Jen Jockisch has an idea that really rocks. She outlined the letter stickers in her title with a fine-point marker! This technique helps her title stand out as a star performer on her page, which is especially useful with a page that has numerous elements. Plus, it's an easy and inexpensive way to add a little emphasis to the lighter letter stickers in your collection. Way to rock it, Jen.

8 unique *ideas* **to try**

Rock Star by Jen Jockisch. **Supplies** *Brads, cardstock, letter stickers, ribbon and rub-ons:* **American Crafts;** *Flower and patterned paper:* **Sassafras;** *Buttons:* **American Crafts and Sassafras;** *Punches:* **EK Success;** *Adhesive:* **The Paper Studio and Scotch, 3M;** *Other:* **Gems.**

BY MEGAN HOEPPNER

CREATE A SHAPED ALBUM

The always-inspiring Suzy Plantamura made the cover to a beach-themed mini album from actual seashells to complement her project's theme. She paired two shells together and used a drill to hollow out holes in the album "spine." Then using the shells as a template, she traced and cut inside pages from chipboard, decorated them, punched holes and attached everything together with jump rings. For added shell appeal, she attached smaller shells to the outside of her album, both on the cover and hanging from the jump rings.

ORDER SHELLS ONLINE

Suzy picked up her shells at a local shop (she lives in a beach town, lucky girl!), but that doesn't mean you can't get this look if you're landlocked. The following online shops sell shells of many shapes and sizes that are sure to get your creativity swimming:

- *SeashellCo.com*
- *SeashellWorld.com*
- *NaplesSeashellCompany.com*

CREATE A SHELL LOOK AT HOME

Shell we continue? Yes! If you don't have a real shell, you can create Suzy's paper alternative that's as cute as the real deal but only half as heavy and fragile. Here's how:

❶ Cut two shell shapes from chipboard.

❷ Measure four pieces of patterned paper to the height of the shell and twice the width. Crimp each piece with a paper crimper.

❸ Adhere the patterned paper pieces to the shell. When adhering the top and bottom covers, slightly gather the paper to create raised ridges. *Note:* A strong adhesive like Aleene's Tacky Glue works well.

❹ Lightly brush on streaks of paint in white and orange, accenting the crimped area.

❺ Punch two holes in each cover and attach them together with jump rings.

ORGANIZE WITH BITTY BOXES

Inspired by a blog comment from Peggy W., I created this organizational system to hold my smaller scrapping accessories like eyelets, brads, bling, buttons, small tags and flowers. Each accessory is organized by color in small boxes that fit nicely into a single storage drawer. To identify the supplies within each box, I attached accessories to the lids. My personal favorite: the eyelet boxes. By putting grommets in the lids, I can stick my finger in the holes to quickly remove the boxes from the drawer they're housed in. Plus, I can dispense eyelets directly from the holes instead of opening the boxes. These 2″ cubed boxes are available at xpedx stores (*XpedxStores.com*).

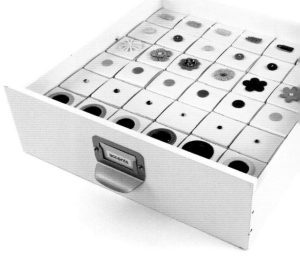

That's My Boy *by Marianne Hope.*
Supplies *Cardstock:* **Scenic Route;**
Patterned paper: **7gypsies;** *Oil pastels:*
Faber-Castell; *Stamps:* **Autumn Leaves
and unknown ("boy");** *Stickers:* **Flair
Designs;** *Adhesive:* **Aleene's Tacky
Glue, Duncan Enterprises; Glue Dots
International;** *Other:* **Masking tape and
handmade crochet flower.**

5 UNMASK THE BENEFITS OF TAPE

When I think of masking tape, I think of quick home repairs and hanging yard-sale
signs. Lucky for us, Marianne Hope sees beyond these basic uses to unlock masking
tape's real creative potential. Sticking to this common household item and oil pastels, she created a stylish frame for her layout in three easy steps:

❶ Color four strips of tape with a base color using oil pastels.

❷ Add a second, darker color and blend with a paper towel.

❸ Cut your frame and add a darker shade of oil pastel to the edges; blend with a
paper towel.

HANDMADE POSTCARDS AND LUGGAGE TAGS

Travel in style with handmade luggage tags. Wendy Sue Anderson has two creative options for scrapbooking a tag from home:

❶ Place a block with your personal information inside two pieces of punched transparencies, and then stitch around the edges to secure the tag.

❷ Dress up a preexisting tag with patterned paper, ribbon and rub-ons.

Once you reach your destination, don't forget to write to your loved ones back home. Wendy's postcard ideas will put any gift-shop option to shame.

❶ Create a photo postcard by adding rub-ons to a picture of you and your family at your travel location.

❷ Stamp a scene straight out of a fairytale and use it as a postcard that can be sent for any occasion.

Postcards and Luggage Tags by Wendy Sue Anderson. **Supplies** *Cardstock:* Bazzill Basics Paper; *Patterned paper and ribbon:* **American Crafts;** *Eyelet and printed acetate:* **Making Memories;** *Photo paper:* **Canon;** *Rub-ons:* **American Crafts, Colorbök and Making Memories;** *Stamps:* **gel-à-tins;** *Ink:* **Clearsnap;** *Flower:* **Doodlebug Design;** *Circle punch:* **Marvy Uchida;** *Fonts:* **Delicious Heavy and Smiley Monster;** *Other:* **Luggage tag, ribbon, staples, thread and vellum.**

PRINT POSTCARDS

Sending handmade photo greetings is easier than ever thanks to postcard photo paper from Canon. The front side of the paper is traditional photo paper, while the back side has all the markings needed for a real postcard. Your personalized designs will have others wishing they were there, even if "there" is your own backyard.

SIMPLE SOLUTION: SAVE TIME AND PRINT IN STYLE

Meet the Selphy ES3 from Canon. It's a portable printer that's full of time-saving options. Not only does it read a variety of memory cards, but it will also print photos wirelessly from Bluetooth-enabled cell phones. Wow!

This gadget does far more than print. It's loaded with editing options, including these: soft focus, pinhole camera, image cropping, lighter skin/darker skin (instant tan—sweet!), faded edges and many more! The fun doesn't stop at editing. There are oodles of border and clip-art options to play with, including the always-enjoyable talk bubble. Another unique feature you'll find with this printer is the way its paper and ink are combined in a single cartridge called an "Easy Photo Pack." These integrated cartridges are available in several paper and ink types for your many scrapbooking needs (including the postcard paper shown above). This printer retails for $199.99. **ck**

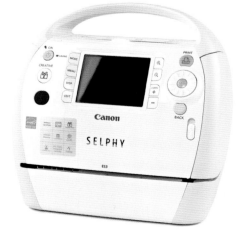

tips & tricks

BY MEGAN HOEPPNER

WRAP TO ADD INTEREST

Here's a sweet idea for adding texture to your next layout—wrap floss around your paper. Laura Vegas only wrapped embroidery floss around the pieces of paper with subtle patterns to keep the design from getting too busy. Creating this look is easy. All you have to do is lightly distress the edges of your paper (to help secure thread), tie some coordinating floss around each, and adhere the paper to your layout with dimensional adhesive. *That's a wrap!*

color coaching and a creative *teacher gift*

Sweet *by Laura Vegas.* **Supplies:** *Cardstock:* American Crafts; *Patterned paper:* Crate Paper; *Embroidery floss:* DMC; *Borders:* Bazzill Basics Paper and Doodlebug Design; *Brads and stickers:* Making Memories; *Font:* Old Remington; *Adhesive:* Glue Dots International and Scrapbook Adhesives by 3L; *Other:* Pom-pom trim and staples.

SHOW YOUR SCHOOL COLORS

When it comes to choosing school colors, we can't help but wonder if there's a committee somewhere that seeks out and assigns the most unflattering pairings. Okay, so maybe not all school color combos are bad, but when it comes to scrapbooking, some colors can certainly pose a challenge. Either they're too loud together (royal purple and gold), they're simply outdated (hunter green and yellow), or they're on the bland side (maroon and gray). Don't let your crazy school colors keep you from showing your school spirit on layouts. As this page by Jen Jockisch illustrates, there are simple design tricks you can use that will turn even the most challenging combos into an A+ design.

20 Years *by Jen Jockisch.* **Supplies:** *Cardstock:* Bazzill Basics Paper; *Patterned paper:* American Crafts, Bella Blvd, Jenni Bowlin Studio, and Studio Calico; *Chipboard:* Heidi Grace Designs; *Brads:* Crate Paper; *Punches:* Fiskars Americas; *Pens:* American Crafts; *Adhesive:* 3M; *Other:* Buttons, floss, staples, and tag.

COLOR CLUE #1: PLAY WITH SPECTRUM

Do your school colors compete? Leave the school rivalries to the basketball court and adjust the intensity of one or both of your shades for a more harmonious outcome, just as Jen did with her bold blue and orange duo.

COLOR CLUE #2: ADD A NEUTRAL

Whether your colors are too loud or too drab, sometimes all it takes is a third-party neutral to find that happy medium. For Jen, that neutral came in the form of her kraft background, which helps subdue her palette.

COLOR CLUE #3: ACCENTUATE THE POSITIVE

If you love one of your school colors but despise its partner, work primarily with your favored shade and only accent with its not-so-attractive cohort. You'll still meet your school's color code, just with quantities that work for you and your tastes.

DORM-ROOM DESIGN

Speaking of school colors, this is the perfect time of year to add vibrant organization solutions to your craft space. Stores often introduce dorm-room décor in cheerful hues and patterns, which look great in craft rooms. With fun lamps, stylish bins, sassy desk supplies, and more, these seasonal lines are just what you need to make the organization grade!

ADD A LITTLE FAIR-RIBBON FLAIR

Create an award-winning look on your next layout with these blue-ribbon accent designs created by Laura Vegas. We've set up this key to help you easily identify each creative part needed to create your own ribbon.

KEY

base   center   tails

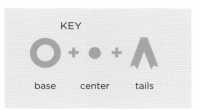

For a list of supplies Laura used to create her fair ribbon accents, visit us online at *creatingkeepsakes.com (click on Magazines, Scrapbooking Tips & Tricks, September 2010).*

die-cut paper   badge   patterned paper

Cut your paper from circular nesting dies and layer the circles to create a quick ribbon base.

punched circles   felt star   ribbon

Make your ribbon base shine with a little glitter and scalloped circles punched from several different mediums (canvas, cardstock, book paper, etc.).

journaling spot   brads   border stickers

Build your ribbon tails with border stickers, which are naturally long and lean. Also, note the brad cluster Laura added using the iTop tool from Imaginisce *(imaginisce. com).* For instructions on how to use this tool to make your own brads, check out our online technique extra at *creatingkeepsakes.com.*

flower accents   button   trim

Why stick to a single button for your center when you can layer several for an eye-catching finish?

looped ribbon   tissue & tag   cardstock

Loop several different trims for a wonderfully whimsical ribbon base.

Giggle Fit *by Kimberly Neddo.*
Supplies: *Cardstock:* Bazzill Basics Paper; *Patterned paper, and borders:* Sassafras; *Stickers:* Jenni Bowlin Studio and Making Memories; *Pins:* Making Memories; *Button:* Buttons Galore; *Decorative-edge scissors:* Fiskars Americas; *Mask:* Advantus; *Spray ink:* Tattered Angels; *Pen:* Newell Rubbermaid; *Adhesive:* Kokuyo; *Other:* Trim.

PAPER YO-YOS

Autumn may be around the corner, but that doesn't mean you can't hold on to that floral feeling. With this technique by Kimberly Neddo, you can create yo-yo flowers on your layout with ease, no matter the season. Planting your paper garden is simple. Here's how:

❶ Punch or cut a 2½" circle from cardboard, and cut 4" square from patterned paper.

❷ Wet patterned paper completely to soften, and then pat off excess water.

❸ Gather and pinch paper together in center, and secure with either thread or small rubber band.

❹ Carefully wrap paper around cardboard circle, rubber band end facing down; set aside to dry.

10 creative tips

PICTURE-PERFECT JOURNALING

Have you ever created a sweet poster using candy bars in place of words? Well, Rita Shimniok's idea is just as sweet but won't cause a toothache. She used chipboard accents from Cosmo Cricket to doll up her journaling by replacing some words with the premade accents. With the number of scrapbook accents on the market, your picture-perfect journaling is only a scrapbook aisle away!

Rita's journaling reads:

"Before [phones] went cordless, when we still wore [high heels], we played [music] and sang [Heart] at the top of our lungs. Now we hardly see each other, but when we do, we [giggle] and laugh just like old times."

Longtime Friends by Rita Shimniok. **Supplies** *Cardstock:* Canson and The Paper Company; *Patterned paper, chipboard accents, ribbon and stickers:* Cosmo Cricket; *Rub-ons:* Making Memories; *Stamps:* Autumn Leaves (flourish) and Sandylion (clock); *Ink:* Tsukineko; *Brad:* Bo-Bunny Press; *Gems:* Doodlebug Design and Making Memories; *Flowers:* Making Memories and Prima; *Paint:* FolkArt, Plaid Enterprises; *Pens:* Ranger Industries (white) and Sakura (glaze); *Font:* CK Scratch Box; *Adhesive:* Glue Dots International and Scotch, 3M; *Other:* Buttons.

LET YOUR RIBBON BLOOM

To create ribbon flowers like the ones on Rita Shimniok's layout, staple the centers of several small strips of ribbon and adhere the stapled ribbon bits together, using an embellishment (brads, buttons, stickers, etc.) to hide your adhesive and give your blossom a happy center.

BY MEGAN HOEPPNER

TAG YOUR TITLE

Make your journaling and titles stand out with one hit of the "easy button" and a quick shopping trip to your local office-supply store. You may even find the tags you want in your own stash! Take Brenda's cue and use tags as a disguised "mat" or block to house your title and journaling. Brenda inked the edges of the tags so they pop just enough without taking the attention away from her story. Easy!

Carving Pumpkins by Brenda Neuberger. **Supplies** *Cardstock, patterned paper, tags, buttons, letter stickers, rub-ons and trim:* Rusty Pickle; *Font:* Arial; *Adhesive:* Beacon Adhesives and GlueArts; *Other:* Staples.

PHOTO-CORNER CREATIVITY

Sure, border punches are great for turning a piece of paper into a decorative strip, but did you know that you can also use them to make super-cute photo-corner accents? With this tip, provided by EK Success, you can have completely unique photo corners in just a couple of folds.

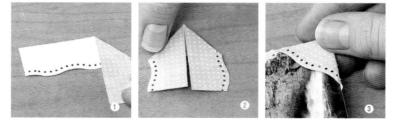

HOW-TO: CREATE PHOTO CORNERS FROM BORDER STRIPS

❶ Punch a border strip using your favorite border punch.
❷ Fold the edges over to create a triangle at the middle.
❸ Flip the triangle over, adhere it to your page and insert your image.

VISIT THE STAMP FACTORY

The Push and Print Stamp Factory from Fiskars Americas is a self-inking tool that makes stamping a breeze. Simply load an ink pad (ink-side down), attach your stamps to the stamp plate and give the tool a push. Since the machine re-inks the stamp between each impression, you can create for hours!

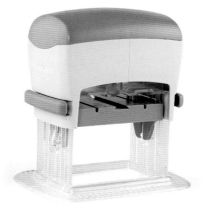

CUSTOMIZE YOUR RIBBON

The Stamp Factory has a number of accessories available, including the Ribbon Stamp Plate and Frame Attachment that make stamping ribbon a breeze. You can stamp photo captions, create completely personalized gift bows and more—the tool's guide helps you make sure the stamp is aligned in the perfect place every time!

STAMP MAT MAGIC

How many times have you thoroughly covered a stamp in ink, held that stamp snuggly with both hands and then stamped it straight down on your paper . . . only to find that part of the image didn't transfer? No, this isn't a sign of sub-par stamping. In fact, it sounds like you're doing everything right. This is just something that happens to the best of us from time to time, even with perfect technique and high-quality stamps . . . until now.

Stamp with a foam mat (also known as "craft foam" or "fun foam") resting between your paper and your table. The slightly squishy surface of the foam makes for a more evenly stamped impression every time. Check out my without-foam vs. with-foam test at right! The proof is in the stamping.

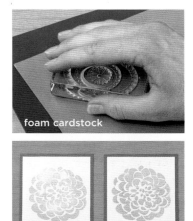

foam cardstock

without foam   with foam

BUILD YOUR OWN BRADS

One-of-a-kind brads are only a punch away with the Easy BradMaker Starter Kit from Chatterbox. Simply punch your paper of choice (patterned paper, cardstock or even photos), cover the punched piece with a clear top and adhere the element to a brad base. In a few minutes, you can have customized brads that go with any project.

SAY IT WITH BRADS

As if turning photos into brads and creating attachments to match every layout weren't enough, you can also use The Easy BradMaker Kit (shown above) to create a classy title. Just add letter stickers, stamps or rub-ons to your punched circles before adhering the clear brad tops. With this idea, your titles are sure to rock!

SIMPLE SOLUTION: MAKE IT MONOCHROMATIC

As much as I adore patterned paper, I was instantly drawn to this page by Wendy Sue Anderson, which has cardstock stealing the show. She created a subtle, monochromatic background by punching shapes from her cardstock and layering them over her cardstock background pieces (see the blue and brown dots and the green stars). This simple trick is a great way to add personality to a page and use up those leftover paper scraps!

So Handsome *by Wendy Sue Anderson.* **Supplies** *Cardstock:* American Crafts (brown and white), Chatterbox (blue) and Die Cuts With a View (green); *Patterned paper:* Making Memories; *Brads:* SEI; *Ribbon:* American Crafts; *Punches:* Fiskars Americas (star and large circle) and Marvy Uchida (small circle); *Pen:* American Crafts; *Adhesive:* Tombow and Xyron. **ck**

customizable stamps, photo videos & more!

BUILD A BACKGROUND

Put extra bits of paper to good use by turning them into an interesting background for your page. Heidi Sonboul cut shapes with her Cricut die-cutting machine to create this seasonally stunning design—an approach that made this project quick and easy.

You don't have to own a die-cutting machine to pull off this look. With a little time and a few basic punches, you can achieve a similar look on your layout, as shown below.

make your own
foam
stamps

Colorful Leaves by Heidi Sonboul. **Supplies** *Cardstock:* BasicGrey and Bazzill Basics Paper; *Patterned paper and chipboard:* Cosmo Cricket; *Rub-ons:* Cosmo Cricket and Creative Imaginations; *Tags:* K&Company; *Stickers:* October Afternoon; *Brads:* BasicGrey; *Tools:* Fiskars Americas and Provo Craft; *Adhesive:* Scotch, 3M; *Other:* Thread.

BY MEGAN HOEPPNER

HOW-TO: MAKE A QUILTED BACKGROUND

❶ Punch 60 squares from coordinating patterned papers.

❷ Use a corner-rounder punch to curve two opposing corners from each square, and then assemble your squares on your cardstock as shown.

HOW-TO: MAKE A PHOTO SLIDESHOW

① Open Picasa and import the photos you want to use by clicking on the "import" button in the upper-left corner of the screen. Drag the images from your library into the "selection" box found on the lower-left corner of the screen.

② Click the "Create" menu and select "Movie. . . ." The images you've selected should appear under the "Clips" tab. Click on the plus sign, and they will be added to your slideshow. At this stage, you can add captions and also add music by uploading audio under the "movie" tab.

③ Once your slideshow is the way you want it, click "create movie" and your slideshow will be saved as a .wmv file (Windows Media Audio/Video file), which can be copied onto a CD-R or a CD-RW.

GIVE THE GIFT OF PICTURES

Impress your loved ones this holiday season with a gift that's both easy to create and incredibly affordable: a photo slideshow on CD. Unlike traditional photo cards, which hold a few photos at best, this approach allows you to send a year's worth of images. Plus, in just a few simple steps you can set the pictures to music and even add captions for a unique and heartfelt greeting that friends and family will treasure. Follow the steps at right to create one using Picasa, a free web software (*Picasa.com*).

Merry and Bright CD card *by Megan Hoeppner.* **Supplies** *Cardstock, number stickers and ribbon:* American Crafts; *Stickers:* Making Memories (letters) and My Mind's Eye (holiday); *Adhesive:* Glue Arts; *Other:* Ribbon (green) and thread.

BONUS IDEA

Are you hosting a party this holiday season? Create a photo slideshow and have it playing on your TV for guests to enjoy. Here are two options that make creating photo DVDs easy:

My Digital Studio is a software program from Stampin' Up! that offers you many creative possibilities. Not only can you make your own photo DVD with it, but you can also create cards, scrapbook pages, photo books and more. Plus, it comes loaded with Stampin' Up! artwork and colors, all for only $79.95 (U.S.). *StampinUp.com*

Turn your digital photos and video clips into a DVD to share with family and friends using SmileShow by YesVideo. You create your movies online, and pricing starts at only $4.99, making this an easy and affordable option. *SmileshowDVD.com*

BRADS IN A SQUEEZE

Previously, I brought you a brad-maker tool from Chatterbox that makes elegant brads in a few simple steps. In the spirit of personalized brads, I wanted to share another option with you. The i-top Brad Maker tool from Imaginisce is a user-friendly gizmo that will have you turning numerous mediums into your own brad-iful creations in just a couple of squeezes. I've made a few here to jump-start your creativity.

CANDY WRAPPER

FABRIC

JOURNALING SPOT

RIBBON

PAPER

PHOTO

HOW-TO: CREATE PERSONALIZED BRADS WITH THE I-TOP TOOL

❶ Prepare your brad top. Imaginisce has designed punches to work with this tool so that preparing your brad top is effortless. Simply punch your desired size from a paper, photo or other flat item.

❷ Insert your punched brad top into the rubber head (select the head according to the size of brad you're making—small, medium or large). Layer the metal shell over the paper, smooth side down, and squeeze the handle.

❸ Fold the paper edges around the shell. Position the brad base in the tool's metal head (selecting the size that matches the size of the brad shell). Squeeze the handle to attach the two pieces. Remove your finished brad.

MAKE YOUR OWN STAMPS

This idea, provided by Crystal Jeffrey Rieger, will have you foaming at the mouth. You can make your own foam stamps from Cut-N-Dry Stamp Pad Foam by Ranger Industries. To do this, you'll need your favorite negative chipboard shapes (or shapes that will create cool indents, such as letter blocks) and a heat gun.

BONUS IDEA

Play with various chipboard shapes and textured items and see what kind of stamps you can add to your handmade collection. Here are a few ideas to get you going:

- Larger chipboard circles with smaller circles in the center
- Legos
- Wood letter blocks
- Name stamps, made with chipboard-letter negatives

HOW-TO: CREATE YOUR OWN FOAM STAMPS

1 Heat the reverse side of the foam mat momentarily with a heat gun to make it soft and pliable.

2 Push your negative chipboard shape into the foam and allow the foam to cool and set; remove chipboard. *Note:* With letters and direction-specific images, make sure to position the negative shape facedown so the finished image will face the correct direction when stamped.

Tip: Use the same piece of foam over and over again. Simply re-heat it and it will revert back to its original shape, and it will be ready for the next time you want to make a stamp.

5 STAMP AN ALPHABET BACKGROUND

Crystal used her one-of-a-kind stamp (see the how-to above) and acrylic paint to create a subtle background on her layout. Since she didn't use any patterned paper on her page, the stamped areas add nice interest.

Loveable Quirk *by Crystal Jeffrey Rieger.* **Supplies** *Cardstock:* **American Crafts and Core'dinations;** *Chipboard letters (negative):* **Fancy Pants Designs;** *Dies:* **AccuCut** (large scallop circle) and **Sizzix** (buttons); *Letter stickers:* **American Crafts;** *Talk-bubble stamp:* **Hero Arts;** *Paint, foam pad and brayer:* **Ranger Industries;** *Pens:* **American Crafts** (black) and Uni-ball Signo, **Newell Rubbermaid** (white); *Adhesive:* **Scrapbook Adhesives by 3L.**

FILE-FOLDER ORGANIZATION

Keep your patterned paper and cardstock within arm's length with the Memory Mate Hanging Folders and Racking System from Creative Memories. Whether you sort by color, company or theme, these handy folders are just the right size for your favorite sheets. You can also transform these folders into a savvy project system like the one here, which has folders for my pages in progress, folders for my printed photos to be scrapped and folders for my most recent product finds I want to use. You'll love this system whether you have only a small amount of space to work with or you often craft on the go.

The Memory Mate Daisy Wheeled Cart, also from Creative Memories, is designed to hold these folders so all you have to do is drop them in (Racking System and all) when it's time to clean up or hit the creative road.

BONUS IDEA

Dress up these basic white folders, like I did, with a little patterned paper for a more playful look.

SIMPLE SOLUTION: SEW A SUBTLE TEXTURE ON YOUR BACKGROUND

With the fall comes texture—knit scarves, wool sweaters and more. Inspired by the fashions of the season (and the theme of her page), Kim Watson added subtle detail to the background of her layout using her sewing machine. By selecting thread in the same color as her paper, Kim quickly filled in some of the white space on a page to create a stitched background that doesn't overpower her photos and journaling.

If you don't have a sewing machine or thread to match your design, you can create a similar look by paper-piercing holes in a line and then using a pen to add faux stitching that ties them together.

BONUS IDEA FROM KIM

Fashion changes with the season, and never is this more evident than with tweens and teens. Create a layout each season (or even once a year) describing your children's current fashion statements. It's a fun way to track their growth and watch as they find their own unique identity.

 Fall Fashion by Kim Watson. **Supplies** *Cardstock:* **Around The Block Products and Bazzill Basics Paper;** *Patterned paper and die-cut accents:* **Sassafras;** *Letter stickers:* **American Crafts;** *Buttons:* **Autumn Leaves and Making Memories;** *Butterfly pebble:* **Prima;** *Date stamp:* **Croxley Stationery;** *Ink:* **Clearsnap;** *Paper piercer:* **Making Memories;** *Adhesive:* **Scrapbook Adhesives by 3L and Mono Adhesive, Tombow;** *Other:* **Thread.** **ck**

dress up your
pages and gifts

GO TO TINSEL TOWN

Rather than use glitter to create a dazzling tree, Cindy Tobey cut up silver tinsel to cover the tree design in the background of her "Kitschy" page. Talk about a great way to further a theme! For additional sparkle, she filled an ornament accent with twinkling red gems. *Way to bring the bling, Cindy!*

6 handmade
holiday
ideas

Kitschy *by Cindy Tobey.* **Supplies** *Cardstock:* Bazzill Basics Paper; *Patterned paper:* BasicGrey (red) and Fancy Pants Designs (green and ledger); *Stamps, chipboard, felt, ribbon and rub-ons:* Fancy Pants Designs; *Letter stickers, paper border and stickers:* Doodlebug Design; *Metal star:* Nunn Design; *Gems:* me & my BIG ideas and Westrim Crafts; *Ticket:* Jenni Bowlin Studio; *Ink:* Stampin' Up!; *Pens:* Krylon (silver leafing) and Sakura; *Paint:* Making Memories; *Font:* Century Gothic; *Adhesive:* 3M (dimensional), Glue Dots International and Kokuyo; *Other:* Thread and tinsel.

BY MEGAN HOEPPNER

Snow Snack *by Keri Babbitt.* **Supplies** *Cardstock:* Bazzill Basics Paper; *Patterned paper:* BasicGrey (lace), Making Memories (music), October Afternoon (grid) and Webster's Pages (gingham); *Letter stickers:* Webster's Pages; *Mirrors:* Darice; *Pearls:* Kaisercraft; *Border punch:* EK Success; *Font:* Carbonated Gothic; *Adhesive:* Therm O Web; *Other:* Ribbon.

REFLECT YOUR CREATIVITY

You've heard the expression that "no two snow-flakes are alike." Well, that's certainly the case where Keri Babbitt's creative idea is concerned. She's created the look of glistening snow on her page using pearl stickers, strands of lovely ribbon and tiny mirrors. By using mirrors to house her pearl accents, her flawless flakes stand out on her page and up the elegance of her design. These reflecting glasses are full of creative potential. Use them to make a snowman or a shining ornament on a holiday layout.

Now What? *by Emily Pitts.* **Supplies** *Cardstock:* Prism Papers; *Letter stickers and patterned paper:* American Crafts; *Stamps:* Hero Arts, October Afternoon and Studio Calico; *Ink:* Stampin' Up!; *Pen:* Pigma Micron, Sakura; *Adhesive:* Scotch, 3M; Xyron; *Other:* Rickrack and thread.

CREATE A "TAKE TWO" WITH TAGS

Whether it's brown paper packages tied up with string or bright patterned paper topped with a bow, I love holiday packages. With an idea from Emily Pitts, I can prolong that beauty long after the presents are opened. She created a dangling border on her layout using the tags from her son's gifts.

These types of special "to" and "from" notes would also look great peeking out from under a photo or as a bit of journaling. As functional as this idea is, it's the idea of incorporating a piece of the holiday memorabilia onto the layout that makes this memorabilia tip one of my favorite things!

PIN IT ON

Make your packages shine brighter than any others under the tree with this trick from Beth Opel. Rather than spend beaucoup bucks on designer gift wrap, she threaded some sparkling beads on decorative pins and attached them in the shape of a snowflake using small spots of glue in the center. You can use this eye-catching technique to transform any basic bag, tag or piece of wrapping paper.

Don't fret if your craft supplies don't include beads; other accents such as gems, brads and eyelets will also add a little extra flair to your basic wrapping supplies.

Snowflake Gift Bag by Beth Opel. **Supplies** *Straight pins:* Papier Valise; *Beads:* Swarovski; *Large rhinestone brad:* Oriental Trading Company; *Velvet trim:* American Crafts; *Adhesive:* All Purpose Stik Glue Sticks, Surebonder; PeelnStick Adhesive Tape, Therm O Web; *Other:* Gift bag and hot glue gun.

MAKE A CHARMING GIFT

Personalized necklaces are all the rage right now, both in fashion and in scrapbooking. This trend makes sense because it takes nothing more than a little creativity and a few paper scraps—two things every scrapbooker has—to create an original fashion statement. You're sure to impress any sassy female on your gift list this year with a handmade bauble. Here are a few options available to you.

❶ Make a statement with your paper by using a glass pebble and some epoxy Dimensional Lacquer from Craft Fantastic (*CraftFantastic.com*).

❷ Contain eye-catching accents and paper inside one of these Memory Frames from Ranger Industries (*RangerInk.com*).

❸ Stamp your favorite image on a metal pendant from Nunn Design (*NunnDesign.com*). Use solvent ink like StazOn from Tsukineko so the stamped image won't smudge.

❹ Whether you want to make a small piece to wear around your neck or a larger glass ornament to hang from your tree, these Simply Adorned Charms from Stampin' Up! (*StampinUp.com*) make it easy and lovely.

SIMPLE SOLUTION: CREATE GLITTERED BUTTONS

The holiday elves at Close To My Heart have a dazzling idea for using clear buttons: add glitz with a layer of glitter. The touch of sparkle this adds to any project is just right, and this technique is an excellent way to create completely custom accents to accompany any project. Getting this look is a snap with the instructions below.

Pride & Joy *courtesy of Close To My Heart Studio.* **Supplies** *Album, patterned paper, felt accents, brads, letter stickers, buttons, ribbon and glitter: Close To My Heart; Other: Thread.*

HOW-TO: ADD GLITTER BEHIND BUTTONS.

❶ Adhere double-sided adhesive to the back of your clear or translucent buttons.

❷ Dip the buttons in glitter to coat the open side of the double-sided tape. Or, sprinkle glitter over the tape.

❸ For added flair, layer a small glitter button over a larger button.

25

SIMPLE
Shortcuts
to Save
You Time

Finish more layouts this season using these no-stress tips.

In December, you may be tempted to suspend all scrapbooking while you focus on shopping, baking, and decorating. You definitely should immerse yourself in the holiday hoopla, but you can also fit in some creative time for yourself in the midst of the preparations and celebrations. It's true. Use these 25 tips to help you focus and make the most of your busy schedule this season.

BY ALI EDWARDS

1 Follow this mantra: *I will not make things more complicated than they need to be.* Sometimes just saying this to yourself a few times as you embark on a project (or when you are knee deep in the middle of it) is enough to refocus you on keeping things simple.

25 *by Ali Edwards.* **Supplies** *Cardstock:* Bazzill Basics Paper; *Patterned paper:* American Crafts, Creative Imaginations, Fancy Pants Designs, Hambly Screen Prints, Scenic Route and Studio Calico; *Santa accent:* Creative Imaginations; *"25" accent:* Every Jot & Tittle; *Ticket:* Jenni Bowlin Studio; *Chipboard tag:* American Crafts; *Epoxy sticker:* KI Memories; *Other:* Brads, cork, pen, word stickers and punches.

2 Reuse your favorite design. There's no reason to reinvent the wheel when telling your stories. Focus more on the story and less on the design. You may achieve a more meaningful expression in the end because you dove into the story more than the design process.

3 Choose a consistent background. For me, that's light cardstock. It's my go-to background, and it has simplified my process tremendously. Not having to think about that choice means I can focus on other things.

4 Make a plan. If you want an easy recipe for more efficient creative time, spend a bit of time planning in advance before actually working on your project. Gather your materials and have your photos ready before you jump in.

5 Go with what you already have at home. Check your stash before picking up something new. Create pages that use a bunch of little accents grouped together, like I did on my "25" layout at left.

6 Use your scraps and a square punch. Combining a square punch with your scraps provides a fun and easy way to get a variety of images on a page—check out the grid design I created on my "25" layout.

7 Start a blog. These days, so many of my stories are recorded first on my blog and then later incorporated into my scrapbooks when I have the time. Documenting the stories on my blog when they are fresh makes a huge difference in the power of my stories. The stories are more in-depth and relevant and so much simpler to record than when trying to remember the details long after the fact.

8 Do what you can with the time you have. At this time of the year, odds are you won't be able to find uninterrupted spans of hours to work on your pages. When you do have a few minutes, do *something*. Upload or print a few photos, jot down a bit of journaling or pick out papers—you get the idea.

9 Think divided page protectors, especially ones that hold 4" x 6" photos and note cards. It's nice to be able to just slip a couple photos and a journaled note card inside the protector and call it good. You can always embellish a couple of the 4" x 6" spots for a quick creative release as well, like I did on my "Today" layout at right.

10 Use patterned papers as decorative elements that stand alone. So many of the patterned papers available have such cool designs that can stand on their own. These papers make great accents and help tell your story without adding anything else. I included one on the bottom-right corner of my "Today" layout.

11 Journal in a list. I find list journaling to be one of the quickest and easiest ways to tell a story. When you list journal, you're free to focus on the memories instead of worrying about connecting one sentence to the next.

12 Turn off the computer. The computer can be an awesome tool, but it can also be a major distraction during creative time. If you can't turn it off completely, at least avoid your e-mail and the Internet so you can focus on the task at hand.

13 Grab your stapler. Staples sometimes feel simpler to me than adhesive. Be flexible and use what is right in front of you rather than taking time to search for another element.

14 Don't worry whether your colors match exactly. When you find yourself stalled, try to stick down what's in your hand and let it be. It's likely just right.

15 Create a central location for your ideas. A regular three-ring binder works great for storing your ideas. Collect stories, design ideas and inspirational pages or techniques, and then store them all in one place rather than having them scattered around your house and creative space.

16 Stop trying to scrapbook every photo. Get picky and go for the ones that really mean something to you.

Today by Ali Edwards. **Supplies** Divided page protector: American Crafts; Cardstock: Bazzill Basics Paper; Patterned paper: Studio Calico; Rub-ons: Hambly Screen Prints; Stamp: Technique Tuesday; Mini staples: Tim Holtz; Journaling block and script words: DesignerDigitals.com; Fonts: Futura and Numbers; Other: Corner-rounder punch and ink.

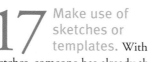

17 Make use of sketches or templates. With sketches, someone has already thought out the structure for you—you just need to fill in the content. If you're a digital scrapbooker, grab a favorite template to use. Either way, follow the sketch to quickly get down to business.

18 Create a compilation layout. Showcase a bunch of photos from a certain event rather than completing several separate layouts. You can even span one tradition over multiple years, like I did for my "Christmas Memories" layout below.

Christmas Memories by Ali Edwards. **Supplies** Software: Adobe Photoshop CS4; Patterned paper: Colbie Solids Paper Pack by Michelle Martin; LaCirque Solids by Katie Pertiet; The Traditionalist Paper Pack by Jesse Edwards; Ticket accents: Memorable Spots by Katie Pertiet; Title: Holiday Outline Word Art by Ali Edwards; Font: Numbers.

19 Go easy on yourself. Let go of unrealistic expectations and congratulate yourself on what you *are* able to accomplish.

20 Pick a theme. Instead of creating random pages over a period of time, choose sets of related photos. Maybe this is the time to scrap all your vacation pictures from last summer or all your birthday photos throughout the year. That way you won't have to switch gears mentally between layouts. Plus, all your themed product will already be at hand.

21 Whistle while you work. Or at least turn on some music that makes you happy. You'll be making progress on your layouts *and* recharging at the same time.

22 Set a timer. Only have an hour? Fire up your kitchen timer and make every second count. You may discover that you are more focused when your time is limited.

23 Take advantage of premade products. Instead of adding glitter to a paper or layering elements for a one-of-a-kind accent, look for embellishments or papers that already have a little extra something.

24 Keep it simple. It is perfectly okay to forego the fancy techniques and complicated designs when time is at a premium. There will be another day to experiment. If you do feel like playing, that's fine, too. There are no rules.

25 Remember why you are doing this in the first place. Let that knowledge inform all the choices you make, especially when your scrap time is limited this month. **ck**

100 Creativity Starters

BY BRITTANY BEATTIE

JUMP-START YOUR CREATIVITY TODAY WITH ONE OF THESE IDEAS!

Whether you're looking for a fun and innovative way to play at your next scrapbook night or you simply need help getting out of "scrapper's block," let one of these ideas get your creativity going. It's time to have a blast while letting your creativity shine!

CREATIVITY STARTERS: INSPIRATION **1.** Pick three colors you love and create a page with them. Don't try to match the photos to the colors—chances are, the photos will look fine with the color scheme. **2.** Browse an art book and find a piece to inspire your layout design. **3.** Rip a page from a non-scrapbooking magazine and create a layout using its color scheme, design or theme. **4.** Visit your local scrapbook or craft store and purchase a product you haven't tried before. Play! **5.** Use a fortune from a fortune cookie as a journaling prompt to record a to-be-scrapbooked event from a new perspective. **6.** Think about your scrapbook stash. Which product did you think of first? Create a page using it. **7.** Let the message on a Dove Promise chocolate wrapper inspire part of your page. For example, if you find the message (like I did) that "Life may change us, but we start and end with family," then create a layout where the first and last photos on the layout are pictures of your family. **8.** What colors are you wearing today? Use the colors as color-scheme inspiration on a page. **9.** Pack your camera bag in your purse, then pay attention to the signs you see throughout the day. Photograph a favorite and let it serve as inspiration for a design. **10.** Create a page using inspiration from the design on a fast-food cup or bag. **11.** Ask your child what shape would support the theme of your layout, then create the shape using your paper, tags or embellishments. **12.** Create a page using inspiration from a favorite website. **13.** Scraplift a layout from a recent issue of *Creating Keepsakes* magazine. **14.** Use a Becky Higgins sketch as a starter for a layout, but add an element you normally wouldn't include. **15.** Check out the page calls at *creatingkeepsakesblog.com*. Choose one that appeals to you and create a page. Scan or take a digital photo of your page and submit it for the call. **16.** Make a layout where the title is inspired by a corporate logo (either in theme or design or both). **17.** Use the color most prevalent in your closet as inspiration to create a monochromatic layout. **18.** Let the song you've listened to most this week inspire a page topic. **19.** Hang your favorite soon-to-be-scrapped photos (one photo representing each event) on a wall display so you can brainstorm ways to scrapbook them. **20.** Look through your album. Find a layout you've already finished, then rotate the design sideways or upside down and "scraplift" the layout using this new design approach.

CREATIVITY STARTERS: JOURNALING **21.** What made you laugh this week? Scrapbook the story and why it made you chuckle. **22.** When you come across a quote you love, use it to begin the journaling on a page. **23.** Journal using one of the five senses. **24.** Choose three adjectives that describe the event, then explain why you chose them. **25.** Create a mini album using the words from your favorite children's story, but replace the illustrations with your own photos. **26.** Start with a favorite movie quote that your family recites often. **27.** Include an applicable scripture on your layout. **28.** Pick a random date from 2005 through 2010. Got it? Use your diary entry from that date to create a layout. If you don't keep a journal, find your photos taken closest to that date and scrapbook them. **29.** Create a page about how the weather makes you feel. **30.** Take photos of your favorite object. Journal about why the piece is your favorite, what it means to you and any stories about it. **31.** Ask a family member to share a favorite memory from a week, month or year of their life. Summarize the story in your words, or write down what the person said verbatim. You'll record a great piece of family history! **32.** Think of a favorite advertising campaign (for example, MasterCard's "priceless" campaign) and use it as a starting point for your journaling. **33.** Carry a small notebook or calendar with you throughout the week to record the daily happenings. At the end of the week, use the details to create a summary of the week's happenings. **34.** Not sure what to scrapbook next? Write down your available themes and occasions, put them in a jar, and pull out a winner. **35.** Create a Mad Lib approach on a page about your kids: write down a basic story with some missing words and have your children fill in the blanks. **36.** Record your favorite recipe and the story behind it. **37.** Jot down how far in advance you knew about the event being scrapbooked, the preparations you made for it, the timeline of the event and who attended. **38.** Share how the topic you're scrapbooking reminds you of another experience. You could include how the previous event helped inspire or prepare you for this one. Or describe the fun times you had at both activities—you'll get two events scrapbooked on one layout! **39.** Ready to start journaling? Simply write nonstop for two minutes without worrying if your text makes sense. At the end of two minutes, read your thoughts. Pull out a couple sentences that best capture your memory of the event. **40.** If you were to have guessed five years ago what the event you're scrapbooking would have been like, what would you have expected? How does that compare to your expectations of the event the day before it happened? Write your thoughts about the event and use them to show how your perception has changed over time.

CREATIVITY STARTERS: TECHNIQUE **41.** Choose one color and create a layout where every element (except your photos) is in that color family. **42.** Re-create a favorite clothing pattern with paper, ink, ribbon or pen for a custom background. **43.** Paint a rectangle on your background to house your journaling. **44.** Create a 10" x 10" photo block with six cropped photos. **45.** Find a technique in *Creating Keepsakes* that you haven't tried before and give it a go. **46.** Glitter the edges of an accent. **47.** See how many designs, shapes or border styles you can create from ribbon scraps. **48.** Just bought a pair of jeans with a cool tag? Use the tag (or part of it) as an accent on your layout. **49.** Let your child's recent artwork cover the majority of one side of a two-page layout. **50.** Combine patterned papers that are all the same theme—such as dot, flower or stripe—even if they don't "match." **51.** Layer two accents from your stash for a new embellishment. **52.** Create a flower on your layout without using premade flower petals. **53.** Find a photo where the background scene is not showing. Scrapbook the photo by using your supplies to re-create the scene out of paper and accents, then add your photo to the appropriate location in your scene. **54.** Stamp using paint and a cooking utensil. **55.** Use embroidery floss to hand-stitch a shape. **56.** Have your teenager draw a "patterned paper" to use on a page about him or her. **57.** Hand-write your title in a more whimsical, formal or creative approach than you normally write. **58.** Use scissors to cut a large, random design from a patterned paper, then place it on a sheet of background cardstock and build a design around it. **59.** Moisten a paper accent, crinkle it, open it up and let it dry with an updated look. **60.** Place a shape or object on your layout, journal around it so your text forms the shape, then remove the object from your layout to leave only the shaped journaling.

CREATIVITY STARTERS: PRODUCT **61.** Looking for a journaling block? Try using a page from that new stationery set you received. **62.** Experiment with a free font from *1001FreeFonts.com, Dafont.com* or *UrbanFonts.com.* **63.** Actually use that paper you "love too much to use." **64.** Speed scrapbook by creating a page solely with 4" x 6" blocks placed in a divided photo page protector. Reserve one photo pocket for your title and journaling and fill the rest with photos or embellished accent blocks. **65.** Use gems and a ribbon to create a custom border. **66.** Grab a piece of patterned paper from your stash. Got it? Now grab the first three embellishments you see that go with it and start from there. Don't spend any more time searching your stash—just start the layout and see where your creativity takes you. **67.** Punch or cut circles in various sizes, then use them as the only accents on your page. See what you can come up with by playing creatively with the arrangement of the shapes. **68.** Close your eyes and reach your hand into a drawer of supplies. Pull out one or two pieces and make a layout with them today! **69.** Don't be afraid to use nontraditional colors with a theme. Blue isn't against the law when it comes to baby-girl pages. **70.** Find nonscrapbooking products around your home and see how you can use them on your layouts. **71.** Cover chipboard letters with patterned paper for a title look that perfectly matches your layout. **72.** Have lots of tags in your stash? Use only photos, plain cardstock and the tags to create a page. **73.** Punch one small shape (circles, squares, butterflies, etc.) thirty times, then use the shapes to frame your focal-point photo. Place most of them partially behind the photo so the shapes and colors don't overpower your picture. **74.** Replace a letter in your title with a decorative accent (of similar shape to the letter) that ties into your page theme. **75.** Create a frame or border with word and phrase stickers. **76.** Use an art medium like watercolor or chalks to create and color a journaling block or photo mat. **77.** Stamp a design on three colors of paper or cardstock. Cut a square around each shape and use them to create a row of coordinating accents on your page. **78.** Have an older paper in your stash that you haven't used yet and aren't sure if you will? Trim it into strips and see what types of border designs you can create with the smaller pieces. **79.** Layer multiple rub-ons on top of each other for a more intricate design. **80.** See what shapes you can create with photo corners. Scalloped photo corners, for example, could easily be turned into butterfly or bird wings.

CREATIVITY STARTERS: PHOTO **81.** Line the top and bottom of a layout with small photos. **82.** Find a picture of your mother at the age you are now and a current photo of you, then scrapbook them with journaling about the differences in your lives at that age. **83.** Open the folder with digital photos stored on your computer. Now click on the third folder from the left and select the twelfth photo in that folder and scrapbook it. If you've already scrapbooked it, ask someone in your home for two new numbers, then use them to direct the folder you open and the photo from that folder that you scrapbook. **84.** Crop several photos into letters to spell out your title. **85.** Round one or more corners of a photo for a softer look. **86.** Adhere a photo to a painted chipboard block to help it stand out, literally, on the page. **87.** Use a small hole punch to create a border of holes around the inside edges of your photo, then adhere the photo to a block of cardstock to back the holes with color. **88.** Trim a landscape or still-life photo into three sections, then adhere them to your layout with 1/8" or 1/4" between the pieces to create a cool tiled effect. **89.** Paint the edges of your photo for a handmade, artistic "frame." **90.** Print a photo twice. Adhere the first photo to your layout. Cut out your main subject in the second photo, then adhere it over the first photo with dimensional adhesive to let the main subject draw even more attention. **91.** Add a photo frame inside your photo—use a pen designed for nonporous surfaces to draw a thin line 1/8" or 1/4" inside the edges. **92.** Stamp a phrase or design in the white space of a photo (be sure to use a solvent ink, like StazOn from Tsukineko). **93.** Frame a photo with brads. **94.** Write your journaling or photo captions around the inside edges of your photo. **95.** Layer photos that show a sequence of action shots. Secure them together on one side to create a "flip book" that reveals the subject in motion. **96.** Crop a favorite digital photo into a square, then print it at 12" x 12" (use an online service) and let it fill an entire page of a two-page layout. **97.** Mat your photo on white or black cardstock, then cut out the mat to look like an old Polaroid print. **98.** Print a photo on vellum or canvas. **99.** Crop multiple photos into various shapes to build a larger shape. For example, cut squares, rectangles and a triangle to form a house. **100.** Trim a scallop border on one edge of your photo. **ck**

{photo highlights}

I love looking for ways to creatively display my photos on layouts. I'm a big fan of leaving a photo in context and not cropping out all the detail—but sometimes context can be overwhelming and make it hard to see the focal point. One cool way to call attention to a photo subject *without* losing any context is to create a double-photo effect with a single photo.

THIS TECHNIQUE is all about focal points. Adding this pop of color and a shaped digital frame provides instant focus without losing any photo context. I got lucky with this picture at left—it is so fun to see my daughter taking a photo of what she loves. I wanted to make sure the layout's focus was on my daughter instead of the bright fire truck in the background. This technique helps me accomplish that. **>>**

Create a
double-photo
effect with
one photo

BY JESSICA SPRAGUE

Seeing by Jessica Sprague. **Supplies** *Cardstock:* Bazzill Basics Paper; *Patterned paper and flower die cut:* BasicGrey; *Chipboard bracket:* My Mind's Eye; *Ink on bracket:* ColorBox, Clearsnap; *Digital frame:* Katie Pertiet, www.designerdigitals.com; *Cutting machine:* Silhouette, QuickKutz; *Fonts:* P22 Cezanne (title), www.myfonts.com; Century Gothic (journaling), Microsoft Word; *Other:* Buttons and thread.

the technique

You can create a double-photo effect with one photo through both traditional and digital methods. Here's how:

traditional scrapbooking method:

1. Print two copies of the photo—one in black-and-white and one in color.
2. Crop the color photo and place it inside a premade frame.
3. Stack the two photos.

Try this technique on some of your favorite photos. It's effective for a variety of shots.

digital technique using photoshop:

1. Open your photo and duplicate it onto a second layer.
2. Change the bottom layer to black and white, or desaturate it.
3. Add a digital frame above the color-photo layer.
4. Cut away the portion of the photo that falls outside of the frame, revealing the desaturated layer.

variation 1:
working with still-life photos

This technique is great for highlighting photo subjects, but it's also useful with still-life pictures. I collected this fast-food bag a couple of months ago, thinking, "Wow, I could really use this advice today!" When I finally got around to taking photos, I realized that I wanted to capture the entire bag but needed a way to place the focus squarely on the important detail in the center. With the double-frame technique, I preserved the photo's context and still highlighted the important details.

Wisdom from a Fast-Food Bag *by Jessica Sprague.* **Supplies** *Cardstock:* Bazzill Basics Paper; *Digital frame:* Katie Pertiet, www.designerdigitals.com; *Cutting machine:* Silhouette, QuicKutz; *Swirl die cut:* QuicKutz; *Fonts:* Impact and Century Gothic, Microsoft Word; Studio, QuicKutz.

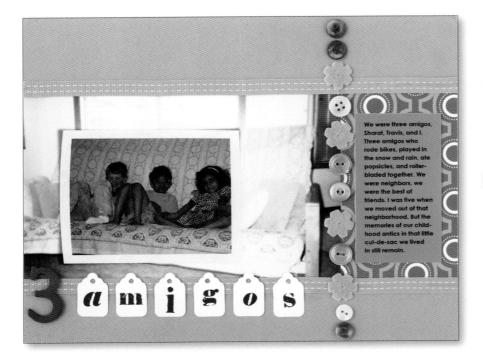

We were three amigos, Sharat, Travis, and I. Three amigos who rode bikes, played in the snow and rain, ate popsicles, and roller-bladed together. We were neighbors, we were the best of friends. I was five when we moved out of that neighborhood. But the memories of our child-hood antics in that little cul-de-sac we lived in still remain.

variation 2:
older color photos

Experiment with this technique on older photos to highlight the sub-jects. Says Vidya, "This works great for old photos, especially those with a lot of background clutter."

3 Amigos by Vidya Ganapati. **Supplies** *Patterned paper:* Scenic Route; *Rub-on letters:* Making Memories; *Ribbon:* Stemma; *Chipboard number:* Crate Paper; *Felt flowers:* American Crafts; *Font:* Century Gothic, Microsoft Word; *Other:* Buttons and tags.

The Magic of Soulmates by Jamie Harper. **Supplies** *Cardstock:* Bazzill Basics Paper; *Rub-on words:* Scenic Route; *Chipboard letters ("bear"):* Scenic Route; *Digital frame:* Katie Pertiet, www.designerdigitals.com; *Font:* Abadi MT Condensed Light, downloaded from the Internet.

variation 3:
photos in a series

Use this technique to highlight a single photo in a series of shots. Says Jamie, "I'm a multi-photo kind of girl, and some-times it's hard to emphasize the focal-point photo. This is a perfect way to accomplish that." **ck**

····{ # altered *clip* art }····

Looking for a cool way to boost your supply stash and add custom touches to your pages . . . all for free? My secret? Altering clip art to create unique page accents! Most clip art you find on the Internet is free for personal use. The only drawback is that most of it isn't the print quality you need for a scrapbook layout. I'll show you some techniques for re-coloring, resizing, customizing and printing downloaded clip art to help it look great *and* tell the story you want to tell.

Make *customized* **images for free**

TECHNIQUE 1

Add texture to your page by transferring clip art to fabric or muslin as Kendra did here. Print the image on an inkjet iron-on sheet, then iron it onto fabric.

Says Kendra, "These paper dolls were exactly what I was looking for! But they are only 72 dpi, so the print quality decreased significantly when I increased the resolution for printing (300 dpi). Fortunately, I found a way to make these work—I reduced the image dimensions from 4" to 2.5" and applied the high pass filter at a radius of 4 pixels. In less than 15 seconds, I had perfect print-quality images." **>>**

Dreams Crumpled *by Kendra McCracken.* **Supplies** *Patterned paper:* Bo-Bunny Press; *Clip art (paper dolls and dresses):* Karen Whimsy, *karenswhimsy.com/paper-dolls.shtm; Chipboard letters:* American Crafts; *Ribbon, rubbons, chipboard buttons and tag from packaging:* Love, Elsie for KI Memories; *Snaps:* Tim Holtz, Junkitz; *Font:* 1942 Report, *dafont.com; Other:* Lace, fabric and thread.

BY JESSICA SPRAGUE

the technique

You can have fun with altered clip art with both traditional and digital methods. Here's how:

traditional scrapbooking method:

❶ Print out clip art.

❷ Cut out design.

❸ Alter to fit layout by hand-coloring, adding stickers, brads or rub-ons, layering under a premade transparency and more.

This technique is an ideal way to create an accent for pages or themes where products are hard to come by.

digital technique using Adobe Photoshop Elements:

❶ Locate and download a clip-art image from the Web. (*Note:* A search on Google is usually the most effective.)

❷ If the image is not set on a transparent background, erase the background around the image using the Magic Eraser Tool. (This allows you to print out just the image, not the background.)

❸ Alter your clip art. Some examples: (a) use the Paint Bucket Tool to re-color the image, (b) add text with the Horizontal Type Tool or (c) blend the image with your background by adjusting the opacity and hue saturation.

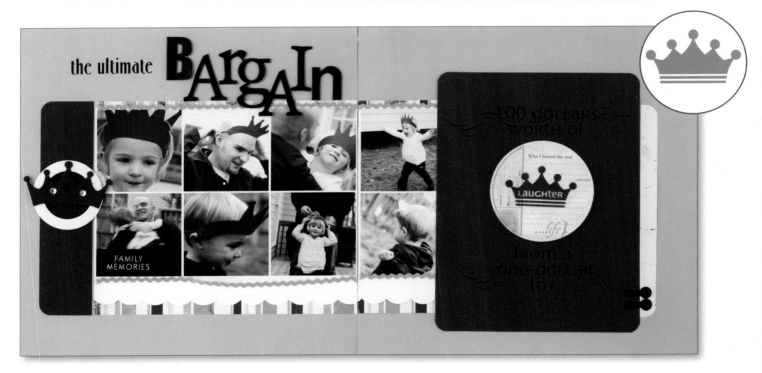

The Ultimate Bargain by *Jessica Sprague.* **Supplies** *Software:* Adobe Photoshop Elements 6.0, Adobe Systems; *Cardstock:* Bazzill Basics Paper (red) and WorldWin (green); *Patterned paper and cardstock journaling circle:* Daisy D's Paper Co.; *Scalloped border stickers:* Martha Stewart Crafts for Michaels; *Chipboard letters:* Heidi Swapp for Advantus; *Chipboard accent:* Technique Tuesday; *Chipboard crown:* Maya Road (as seen in Latest & Greatest on page 30); *Photo turns:* 7gypsies; *Mini brads:* Doodlebug Design; *Clip art:* fundraw.com; *Paint:* Making Memories; *Fabric tab:* me & my BIG ideas; *Rickrack:* Bazzill Basics Paper; *Font:* Migraine, Internet; *Other:* Rhinestones and transparency.

TECHNIQUE 2
Alter clip-art color, add text and print the results onto a transparency

Until I started this month's column, I hadn't realized just how many photos I had of the afternoon my family spent playing with this $1 crown from the craft store—or just how fond my memories were of that time. So I gathered the photos into two lines across my pages and downloaded (what else?) a clip-art crown. I re-colored it to match my page, customized it with text, and printed it onto a transparency for a great, custom embellishment that was practically free. Best of all, now I have this layout to remember our "Ultimate Bargain."

The Pink Panther by Summer Fullerton. **Supplies** Cardstock: Bazzill Basics Paper; Patterned paper and paint: Making Memories; Rhinestones and acetate arrow: Heidi Swapp for Advantus; Clip art: www.andyfilm.com/ppcartoon06.jpg; Stickers: American Crafts; Chipboard coaster circle: Imagination Project; Brads: Queen & Co.; Fonts: Headline Two (journaling and accent) and Potrzebie (title), Internet; Other: Transparency.

TECHNIQUE **3**

Alter clip art to "hold" an accent

This Pink Panther clip-art image added the perfect touch to enhance Summer's layout. Says Summer, "I loved the circle the character was holding. I decided it would be a great spot for a subtitle I could create with traditional scrapbooking products (I used a chipboard circle covered with gems). This gave my subtitle extra pop and dimension."

TECHNIQUE **4**

Use altered clip art to create an album background

My husband loves playing computer games. When he took a trip out to the Blizzard Convention in Anaheim last summer, he brought home several dozen pictures and wanted me to make an album for him. I knew I needed something quick but cool and masculine with a little geeky flair.

I turned to one of the default templates in Adobe Photoshop Elements to create my album. The templates actually have clickable photo spaces for you to add pictures to, so an album couldn't be easier to create. I embellished the blank brown pages with a stripe and a journaling spot, as well as a clip-art image of a dragon, then I uploaded the finished pages to Shutterfly. In just a few days, I received this gorgeous leather album back in the mail. Success!

BlizzCon 2007 by Jessica Sprague. Photos by Jared Sprague. **Supplies** Software and background page template: Adobe Photoshop Elements 5.0, Adobe Systems; Album: Shutterfly; Striped paper: Echoes of Asia kit by Jessica Sprague, www.creatingkeepsakes.com; Journaling block: Journal Spots No. 4 Curled and Flat kit by Katie Pertiet, www.designerdigitals.com; Date stamp: Digital Date Stamps Vol. 4 by Katie Pertiet, www.designerdigitals.com; Dragon clip art: www.webweaver.nu; Font: CBX Piguet, "Font CD Vol. 2," Chatterbox.

photo collage
templates

I talk to scrapbookers all the time who say they'd like to learn more about using Photoshop Elements as a scrapbooking tool. There's never been a better time to learn than right now! On the following pages, I'll cover the basics of Adobe's Photoshop Elements as I use it most often to make my layouts.

new year's resolution: *learn* photoshop elements!

Everyone needs an accessory that makes him feel like a rockstar. Somehow flip-out lizard glasses are the thing for you, and I must say, you are rocking them. You have perfected the perfect "Rockstaaaar!" shout, with your finger pointed in the air, and I think I've spotted a little head-banging to our nightly mix of Ralph's World and Dan Zanes. It's been tough to get you to take them off even for bath-time or bed. But you know when you're rocking a good thing. I get it.

Rock Star *by Jessica Sprague.* **Supplies** *Software:* Adobe Photoshop Elements 6.0; *Printer:* Epson R1900; *Photo paper:* Premium Photo Paper (Semi-Gloss), Epson; *Cardstock:* Bazzill Basics Paper; *Letter rub-ons:* Making Memories; *Letter stickers:* American Crafts; *Chipboard star:* BasicGrey; *Punches:* EK Success (corner rounder) and Stampin' Up! (star); *Glitter and ink:* Ranger Industries; *Date tag:* Creative Imaginations; *Date stamp:* Technique Tuesday; *Digital patterned paper:* Benjamin's Laundry Line by Jen Wilson and Dirty Shirt by Kim Christensen; *Font:* Century Gothic.

WE'RE STARTING with the most fundamental use of Photoshop—arranging photos in a printable grid. Imagine how long this configuration would take if you cut each photo by hand. I'll show you how to make this photo collage in minutes using Elements.

The best part about this template is that you can get up to eight photos on a single page. Simply print your photo block onto letter-sized photo paper, adhere it to your layout, add a few embellishments and you're layouts are done! **>>**

BY JESSICA SPRAGUE

the technique

You can have fun with this technique traditionally and digitally!

traditional scrapbooking method:

1. Arrange several photos in a grid shape on your scrap table, with one photo overlapping the others in the center.

2. Use a circle-cutting template to trace and cut around one of the photos.

3. Trace lightly with pencil around the circle onto the arranged photos. Cut the circular pieces out of each photo and adhere to the background cardstock. You're all set!

digital technique using Photoshop Elements:

With one simple key command, you can instantly "cut" your photos into the shapes that you see. Here are the steps (watch my online video at *CreatingKeepsakes.com/issues/january_2009*):

1. Download and open the photo template in Photoshop Elements. Open eight photos or a mix of photos and digital patterned papers to fill the eight spaces.

2. In the template, click on the photo space you'd like to work with. Switch over to your first photo, and with the Move Tool selected, click and drag it down onto the thumbnail of the template in the Project Bin.

3. Arrange the photo over the photo space. In the Layers palette, hover your mouse over the line between the photo and the layer below it, and Alt-click to join them together.

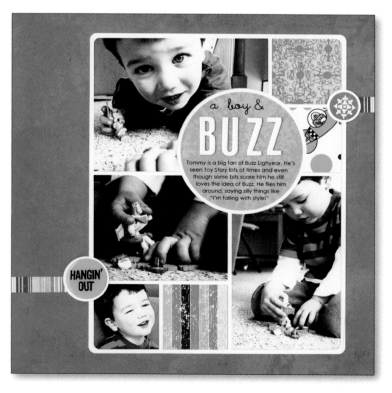

variation 1:

Add your title and journaling to the circle space.

Paula Gilarde used the circle space for her title and journaling. Notice how she matted her circle stickers on white cardstock to mimic the look of the circle portion of the template. Paula says, "This was the first time I've tried this technique, but it definitely won't be the last! I loved getting all the photos printed at once and how easy it was to finish the layout by adding some embellishments and papers."

A Boy & Buzz *by Paula Gilarde.* **Supplies** *Software:* Adobe Photoshop CS2; *Template:* Jessica Sprague, *Digital patterned paper:* Soft and Snow Solids Paper Pack (green) and Mango Shakes (blue and green) by Jesse Edwards and Robot Dudes by Pattie Knox (robot); *Patterned paper:* My Mind's Eye (blue) and October Afternoon (stripe); *Stickers:* me & my BIG ideas (epoxy) and Scenic Route (snowflake); *Chipboard letters:* Heidi Swapp for Advantus; *Rub-on letters:* American Crafts; *Font:* Century Gothic.

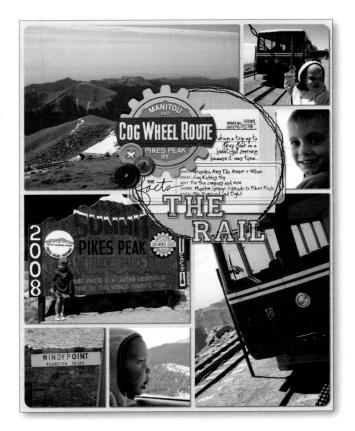

variation 2:

Finish it as an 8½" x 11" page.

Like Paula, Amy Martin used the circle space to hold her page title and journaling. She used the remaining spaces to hold photos and added a background design to the template before printing. Amy comments, "I didn't alter the original template at all for this layout. I simply filled in the blanks. Sometimes it's just as easy to take inspiration and not modify it to complicate it. In this case, the layout contained enough photos to make it interesting without adding much in the way of embellishments."

The Rail by Amy Martin. **Supplies** *Software:* Paint Shop Pro Photo X2, Corel; *Digital paper:* Cherry Crush Kit by Kasia Designs; *Journaling tag:* Title + Journal Blocks No. 01 by Ali Edwards; *Stitching:* Triple Dipped Stitches by Chere Edwards; *Buttons:* Michelle Godin, Karah Fredricks and Natalie Braxton; *Title letters:* Game Time by Lori Barnhurst; *Fonts:* Pea Breathe Easy and Susie's Hand.

Winter Delicacy by Cindy Tobey. **Supplies** *Software:* Adobe Photoshop Elements 6.0; *Digital paper:* Christmas Fancy Paper by Dianne Rigdon; *Digital elements:* Prima Hybrid (frame and journaling doodle); Thrift Chic Element Pack by Kim Christensen; *Cardstock:* Bazzill Basics Paper; *Patterned paper, chipboard swirl, ribbon and flower:* Prima; *Brads:* Doodlebug Design (white glitter) and Queen & Co. (white); *Letter stickers:* American Crafts; *Colored pencil:* Newell Rubbermaid; *Paint:* Heidi Swapp for Advantus (blue) and Pebbles Inc. (white); *Pen:* Sakura; *Thread:* Gutermann; *Font:* Century Schoolbook; *Other:* Buttons.

variation 3:

Stretch it out across a two-page spread.

If you like to scrapbook with the 8½" x 11" format but want a little additional space for your title and embellishments, consider Cindy Tobey's spin on this template. "I used the template horizontally at 100% size," explains Cindy. "I placed it on a two-page spread so that the photo block spans across both pages." **ck**

justify your type

Fully justified type lends a structured flair to any journaling. You can use this easy but little-known technique in Adobe Photoshop Elements to create newspaper-style columns of journaling, to tell a long story on your page, or to create gorgeous home decor using your favorite quotations.

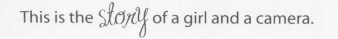

create fully justified text with ease

Every now and then I have a really long story I'd like to tell, and I want the journaling to take center stage. By justifying the text (making sure to keep my paragraph box wide enough that I don't get too many hyphens at the end), I create a cool architectural style that allows the simple lines of the page to shine through, placing focus on the story I'm telling.

This Is the Story . . . *by Jessica Sprague.* **Supplies** *Software:* Adobe Photoshop Elements 6.0, Adobe Systems; *Printer:* Epson R1800; *Cardstock:* Bazzill Basics Paper; *Flourish die cuts:* me & my BIG ideas; *Chipboard circle:* Scenic Route; *Acrylic number stamps:* My Sentiments Exactly; *Ink:* Distress Ink, Ranger Industries; *Corner-rounder punch:* EK Success; *Mini brads:* Chatterbox; *Fonts:* Myriad, Adobe; Ma Sexy, dafont.com.

BY JESSICA SPRAGUE

the technique

You can have fun with this technique traditionally and digitally! Here's how:

traditional scrapbooking method:

❶ Use a pencil to draw light vertical guidelines down the sides of your journaling area.

❷ Hand journal, being careful to begin at the left guideline and spacing your words and letters so you'll either end with a word or a hyphen at the right-hand guideline.

❸ Erase your guidelines to show off your "justified" journaling.

digital technique using Adobe Photoshop Elements:

❶ Select the Horizontal Type tool and draw a text box on your document.

❷ Type your journaling, then select the Horizontal Type tool again and highlight all of your text.

❸ Type Ctrl+Shift+j to fully justify your paragraph of journaling. Print your journaling, or even add a stamp to the journaling block to decorate your text before printing.

VARIATION 1
Create a framed quote with justified text.

Justified type doesn't have to be boring! By playing with the font sizes and adding in a couple of extra line breaks for the focal area of my text ("do what is in us"), I easily created a beautiful, dynamic wall hanging that's full of interest.

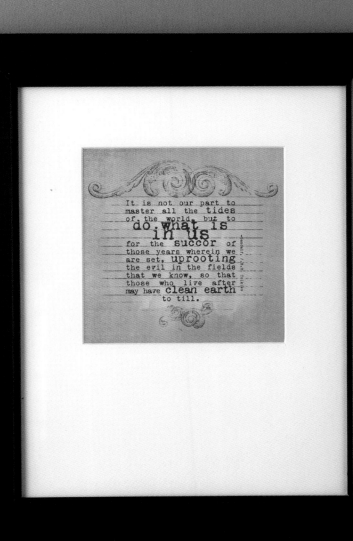

Quote Wall Decor *by Jessica Sprague.* **Supplies** *Software:* Adobe Photoshop Elements 6.0, Adobe Systems; *Printer:* Epson R1800; *Photo paper:* PremierArt Matte Scrapbook Photo Paper, Epson; *Digital patterned paper:* Living - Being Papers by Jen Wilson, *www.jen-wilsondesigns.com; Digital journaling stamp:* By Nancie Rowe Janitz *Watercolor brush stamps:* Michelle Coleman, *www.littledreamerdesigns. com; Font:* VT Portable Remington, *www.dafont.com; Frame:* Michaels.

VARIATION 2

Justify journaling in a shaped journaling tag.

Paula picked a fun, whimsical journaling tag to match the lighthearted feel of her layout. By justifying her journaling text within the tag, she created a perfect balance between the photos on the left of her page and the block of journaling and title on the right.

Pink by Paula Gilarde. **Supplies** *Software:* Adobe Photoshop CS2, Adobe Systems; *Cardstock:* Bazzill Basics Paper; *Patterned paper:* Adornit - Carole's Creations (floral), BasicGrey (small dot), Daisy D's Paper Co. (plaid), KI Memories (pink flowers and dot) and SEI (colored dots); *Rub-ons:* Autumn Leaves; *Journaling brush:* Love Frames Brushes-n-Stamps by Jesse Edwards, www.designerdigitals.com; *Font:* Century Gothic, Microsoft.

VARIATION 3

Balance text within a circular journaling tag.

Combining different shapes on a layout based on a grid can be tricky, but Paula figured out an easy workaround. Says Paula, "I like the circular journaling shape and thought it would be an interesting addition to this grid. By justifying my journaling within the circle, I maintained the style of the square photos and the grid on my layout."

B&A by Paula Gilarde. **Supplies** *Software:* Adobe Photoshop CS2, Adobe Systems; *Cardstock:* Bazzill Basics Paper; *Patterned paper:* me & my BIG ideas; *Felt flowers:* American Crafts; *Chipboard letters:* Crate Paper; *Brads:* Jo-Ann Stores; *Rub-ons:* Doodlebug Design; *Digital journaling stamp:* By Nancie Rowe Janitz; *Font:* Century Gothic, Microsoft.

scrap 9 photos in a *snap*

Want a super-easy way to get a lot of photos on a scrapbook page? Create a regular grid of equally sized, equally spaced photos and watch how quickly your layout comes together! Grids lend structure and graphic appeal to a page, and they make designing a snap.

I'll show you how to create perfect grids in Photoshop in just a few quick steps. You can print your entire grid on a single sheet of photo paper, adhere it to your layout and have a gorgeous page in minutes. Best of all, you can swap out one or more of the

create this grid for an *instant* layout

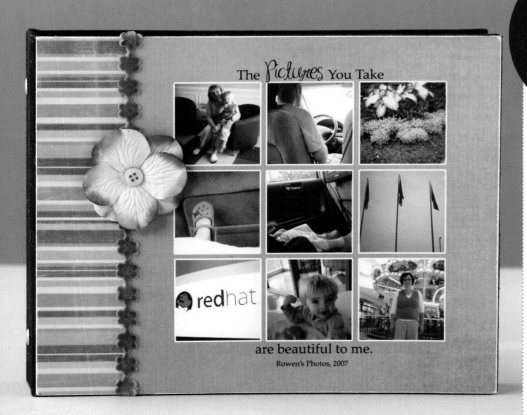

The Pictures You Take (album cover) *by Jessica Sprague.* **Supplies** *Digital patterned paper:* Living - Being by Jen Wilson; *Striped patterned paper:* Fancy Pants Designs; *Flower ribbon:* Doodlebug Design; *Flower:* Prima; *Button:* Autumn Leaves; *Photo paper:* Premier Art Matte Paper, OfficeMax; *Adhesive:* Xyron 900; *Printer:* Epson R1800; *Fonts:* Palatino Linotype, Microsoft; Ma Sexy, www.dafont.com.

photos for a title block, a journaling block or even squares of patterned paper. Grids are flexible and fast!

I created a nine-photo grid for an album cover I've made to capture and highlight some of the photos my daughter took with her "toddler-size" digital camera. I love seeing the photos from her angle and point of view, and since the photos aren't the greatest quality, a 2" x 2" square was the perfect size for them, both on the cover and inside the album itself. Because I was designing a grid to fit over a kraft-colored digital paper, I added a white outline around each photo.

BY JESSICA SPRAGUE

the technique

You can have fun with this technique traditionally and digitally! Here's how:

traditional scrapbooking method:

❶ Use your trimmer or a 2″ square punch to cut or punch out nine photos or a combination of photos and patterned paper.

❷ Lightly draw guidelines for your grid on your paper using a ruler and pencil. Adhere your photos in an evenly spaced grid.

❸ Erase your guidelines and optionally swap out one of your blocks to use for journaling or an accent.

digital technique using Photoshop:

❶ Set your Crop tool to 2″ x 2″ and crop nine photos.

❷ Drag your photos into a new blank document.

❸ Use the Grid (View > Grid in Photoshop Elements, or View > Show > Grid in CS3) and Snap to Grid (View > Snap to > Grid) features to line up your photos. Print onto letter-sized matte photo paper.

VARIATION **1**
Create two grids for an 18-photo display.

Allison Davis had a lot of photos from her family's Fourth of July celebration, so she repeated the technique to create an 18-photo grid that stretches across a two-page layout. Says Allison, "I always take so many pictures at events, and then I have a hard time narrowing down my selection for a layout. With this technique, I end up with a layout full of all my favorite pictures!"

Fun on the Fourth *by Allison Davis.* **Supplies** *Software:* Adobe Photoshop 4.0, Adobe Systems; *Cardstock:* Bazzill Basics Paper (white) and Prism Papers (blue and red); *Patterned paper:* My Mind's Eye; *Chipboard accents:* Rusty Pickle; *Chipboard letters:* Heidi Swapp for Advantus ("on") and Tim Holtz for Ranger Industries ("Fun"); *Stamps:* Autumn Leaves; *Letter stickers:* Doodlebug Design ("the") and K&Company ("fourth"); *Stickers:* Doodlebug Design; *Ink:* ColorBox, Clearsnap; *Glimmer mist:* Tattered Angels; *Pen:* Gelly Roll, Sakura; *Font:* CK Peace Out Filled, www.scrapnfonts.com; *Other:* Epoxy stickers and beads.

VARIATION **2**
Replace one square with your title.

It should come as no surprise that I took a *lot* of pictures on Rowen's fourth birthday. Rather than picking out one or two focal-point photos, I chose to scrap eight pictures on this single page and let the structure of the grid guide the viewer through all of the day's moments. I swapped out one photo for a two-color title treatment, printed the entire grid on letter-sized photo paper, and had the foundation of a great layout as soon as I sat down to add my traditional elements.

Happy Birthday *by Jessica Sprague.* **Supplies** *Patterned paper:* BasicGrey; *Flourish brush (printed onto page background before adhering the photo grid):* Ledger Frames by Katie Pertiet; *Flourish chipboard and artist trading card:* Fancy Pants Designs; *Paint:* Ranger Industries; *Chipboard letter:* Cosmo Cricket; *Chipboard flowers:* K&Company; *Printer:* Epson R1800; *Font:* VT Portable Remington, dafont.com.

VARIATION **3**
Add accents to photo spaces.

Noel Culbertson wanted to showcase the activities from one sunny, summer afternoon and also seamlessly add an accent and title to her design. To do this, she simply left two grid squares blank so that she could place her patterned-paper accent and her title in those spaces. "I also wanted to add a little something to highlight two of the pictures," she explains. "I added a digital frame to two photos of my daughters in a color that matched my patterned paper and embellishments." **ck**

Sun Luv *by Noel Culbertson.* **Supplies** *Software:* Adobe Photoshop Elements 5.0, Adobe Systems; *Digital frame brush:* Ledger Frames by Katie Pertiet; *Photo paper:* Professional Photo Paper—Brilliant Matte, Office Depot; *Patterned paper:* BasicGrey (blue), Making Memories (red) and Stampin' Up! (brown); *Lace paper :* KI Memories; *Felt:* Fancy Pants Designs (blue), Making Memories (heart) and Queen & Co. (red flowers); *Letters:* Making Memories; *Chipboard heart:* Doodlebug Design; *Font:* Garamond, Microsoft.

photos + type + *brushes*

My three favorite items to play with in Photoshop are photos, type and brushes. I like placing text on and around my photos. It helps keep the viewer centered in the most important parts of the layout. In addition to text and photos, I love to dress up my photo blocks with digital rubber stamps, called "brushes" in Photoshop. If you've never played with Photoshop brushes before, you're in for an awesome treat!

combine **all 3 for a fast approach**

I CREATED a vertical block with my photo on top and journaling in a red block on the bottom. The brush overlaps the bottom of the photo and extends over the side of the journaling block, tying the entire "photo and journaling" block together. I added the title up the side of the block, and after printing I only needed to add some cardstock, patterned paper and a few embellishments and I was done with my page!

BY JESSICA SPRAGUE

Stopped in My Tracks *by Jessica Sprague.* **Supplies** *Software:* Adobe Photoshop Elements 6.0; *Printer:* Epson R1800; *Photo paper:* Premium Semigloss Photo Paper, Epson; *Cardstock:* Bazzill Basics Paper; *Patterned paper:* 7gypsies (words) and Cosmo Cricket (blue); *Ribbon:* Cosmo Cricket; *Mini brads:* American Crafts; *Digital brush:* Cluster Brushes-n-Stamps by MaryAnn Wise, www.designerdigitals.com; *Fonts:* 2Peas Stopsign, www.twopeasinabucket.com; CK True, www.scrapnfonts.com.

the technique

You can have fun with this technique traditionally and digitally!

Traditional scrapbooking method:

1. Print out your photo and cut a journaling block from paper or cardstock.

2. Adhere your photo and journaling block to the same cardstock or patterned-paper background so their sides touch.

3. Bust out your rubber stamp collection and stamp some embellishments or images that overlap both your journaling block and your photo.

Digital technique using Photoshop Elements:

1. Create a new blank document. Add in your photo and create a space for journaling either on or near your photo.

2. Add a brush embellishment that overlaps or surrounds your entire block.

3. Print your photo + text + brush onto letter-sized photo paper and complete your layout with traditional supplies.

VARIATION 1
Replace the single photo with a photo-block collage.

I wanted to celebrate finally finding a toy that my daughter will play with (and snuggle with, sleep with and take in the car). I created a block of three photos and added my title into a fourth black block (which I drew and filled with the Rectangular Marquee Tool), then I framed the entire block with a white brush frame to soften up the clean, graphic lines a bit. My journaling went on the large focal photo, and I printed the whole thing onto a letter-sized sheet of photo paper. I was nearly done with this layout from the moment it left my printer!

Finally *by Jessica Sprague.* **Supplies** *Software:* Adobe Photoshop Elements 6.0; *Printer:* Epson R1800; *Photo paper:* Premium Semigloss Photo Paper, Epson; *Cardstock:* Bazzill Basics Paper; *Patterned paper and chipboard letter:* Cosmo Cricket; *Brush frame:* Artistic Photo Frames 1 by Gypsy Chick, *www.scrapartist.com; Cardstock circle sticker:* EK Success; *Heart transparency:* Fancy Pants Designs; *Clip:* Making Memories; *Font:* Myriad, Adobe Systems..

VARIATION 2

Try a horizontal format.

Sheri placed her digital patterned paper and journaling to the left of her focal photo, leaving the bottom portion free to include additional accent photos. Sheri says, "The flourish brush gives the illusion of flow and movement, tying in perfectly with the lighthearted feel of happiness and floating bubbles. This technique is a simple, wonderful way to achieve a classic, uniform look without taking too much time or effort."

Sweet Bubble Love *by Sheri Reguly.* **Supplies** *Software:* Adobe Photoshop Elements 3.0; *Cardstock:* Bazzill Basics Paper; *Patterned paper:* BasicGrey and Making Memories; *Flowers and letter stickers:* Making Memories; *Butterfly stamp:* Hero Arts; *Ink:* StazOn, Tsukineko; *Chipboard button:* BasicGrey; *Brads:* BasicGrey and SEI; *Digital patterned paper:* The Shabby Princess, www.theshabbyshoppe.com; *Digital flourish:* Rhonna Farrer, www.twopeasinabucket.com; *Fonts:* Baskerville Old Face, www.myfonts.com; Times New Roman, Microsoft; *Other:* Thread and string.

VARIATION 3

Place your photos and journaling inside a brush.

Joanna enlarged her brush to hold her photo and journaling (she used the .png file). Joanna comments, "A thought bubble was a perfect fit for my partial list of Harper's words and phrases . . . to indicate the fact that she talks a lot! I've used journaling boxes before, but this was the first time I used a large brush. It's a handy technique because it made my page design go very quickly." **ck**

Talkative *by Joanna Bolick.* **Supplies** *Software:* Adobe Photoshop Elements 5.0; *Cardstock:* Bazzill Basics Paper; *Craft knife:* Fiskars; *Fonts:* 2Peas Fancy Free, www.twopeasinabucket.com; Donata, Internet; Impact, Microsoft; *Digital brush:* Think About It Brush Set by Erica Hernandez, www.twopeasinabucket.com. *Idea to note:* Joanna hand cut the title using the Impact font as a guide

reversed-out *journaling*

Nothing adds a graphic touch to a layout better than white type! This technique involves creating a solid fill of color and typing over it in white. When you print your document on white cardstock or photo paper, your printer will leave spaces where your letters are, allowing the white paper to show through and giving the illusion of white printed type. Here are some examples of this great technique!

learn how to print *white* text

A LARGE brown block is the home to my title (in a combination of type and chipboard letters) and fully justified journaling. The rounded corners and the way the block extends all the way to the edge of the page add interest to a basic, four-square grid page. I printed the journaling onto matte photo paper for a crisper edge to the lettering and a richer color to the brown block, then I trimmed it to size for my page.

BY JESSICA SPRAGUE

The World's Smallest Jedi *by Jessica Sprague.* **Supplies** *Software:* Adobe Photoshop Elements 6.0; *Printer:* Epson R1900; *Photo paper:* PremierArt Matte Scrapbook Photo Paper, Epson; *Cardstock:* Bazzill Basics Paper; *Patterned paper:* American Crafts (background) and KI Memories (stripe); *Chipboard letters:* Heidi Swapp for Advantus; *Nested star chipboard:* Deluxe Designs; *Font:* Century Gothic (journaling) and Impact (title), Microsoft; *Other:* White acrylic paint.

the technique

You can have fun with this technique traditionally and digitally! Here's how:

traditional scrapbooking method:

1. Add a large block of black or brown cardstock to your layout.

2. Use a white pen, such as a Uni-ball Signo from Newell Rubbermaid, or a white inkpad, such as the StazOn opaque inkpad from Tsukineko, with rubber or acrylic stamps to create white journaling and accents.

digital technique using Adobe Photoshop Elements:

1. Create a new blank document. With the Rectangular Marquee Tool, draw a selection on its own layer and fill the selection with black or another dark color.

2. Select your Horizontal Type Tool and set your font color to white.

3. Type your journaling, title or accent type in white. Print onto white cardstock or matte photo paper.

Note: You can easily achieve this same look in Microsoft Word. Simply create a text box, change the fill color to your desired hue, and type your text with a white font color.

variation 1:

Create a mini album with white text.

A premade, ring-bound mini book became home to a cool album-in-progress. Because I kept the template simple, I can take five minutes each year to add a photo and label, change the year, then print the pages to keep my album updated.

Spooks Mini Album *by Jessica Sprague.* **Supplies** *Cardstock and chipboard circle:* Bazzill Basics Paper; *Digital patterned paper:* Fairy Dreamer Kit by Katie Pertiet, *www.designerdigitals.com; Digital photo frame (black):* Grunged Up Photo Blocks No. 2 by Katie Pertiet, *www.designerdigitals.com; Patterned paper (stripe):* Cosmo Cricket; *Letter stickers:* American Crafts; *Scallop-oval punch and oval punch:* EK Success; *Font:* Impact, Microsoft (year) and Sidewalk, *www. dafont.com* (label).

variation 2:

Create an informal look with white script text.

You can also create a more informal look with reversed text using a script font in your journaling and title. Marcia Bettich also created white-pen pumpkin designs to emphasize the white text in the layout.

You & a Pumpkin Patch Adventure by *Marcia Bettich*. **Supplies** *Software:* Adobe Photoshop Elements 6.0; *Patterned paper:* Samantha Rose Paper Pack by Katie Pertiet; Color My World (Free Digital Kit June 2007) by Rhonna Farrer, *www.twopeasinabucket.com; Love-ly Paper Pack by Jesse Edwards; Flourishes:* 2nd Hand Titles {Love} Brushes-n-Stamps and On the Edge Flourishes by Katie Pertiet; *Transparencies:* 3M; *Paint pen:* Sharpie, Newell Rubbermaid; *Felt shapes:* Fancy Pants Designs; *Ribbon:* American Crafts; *Chipboard letters:* Heidi Swapp for Advantus, *Fonts:* Century Gothic, Microsoft; CK Classic, *www.scrapnfonts.com; Other:* Thread. *Note:* Unless listed otherwise, all digital elements are from *www.designerdigitals.com.*

FRESH FACE

You a pumpkin patch adventure

Every year in early October we visit Burt's Pumpkin Patch in the Georgia Mountains to find our prime pumpkins and gourds for the Halloween and Thanksgiving season. The highlight of the trip is always the hayride through the actual pumpkin patches.

MAY YOU ALWAYS **SEE THE** FOREST FOR THE **TREES**

Forest for the Trees by *Noel Culbertson*. **Supplies** *Software:* Adobe Photoshop Elements 5.0; *Cardstock:* Bazzill Basics Paper; *Patterned paper:* Scenic Route; *Lace paper:* KI Memories; *Flowers and journaling block:* Making Memories; *Foam letters:* American Crafts; *Printed tape:* Prima; *Stamp:* Impress Rubber Stamps; *Brad and ink:* Stampin' Up!; *Font:* Arial, Microsoft.

variation 3:

Use reversed text to add extra color.

Noel Culbertson used reversed text on a green background for her title and journaling strips. By putting white text on a green background, she was able to add an extra element of color—the green—which brings out another color in her photos and papers. **ck**

going in circles

One of the questions I'm asked most is "How do you create journaling that flows inside of a shape?" While you can't create filled journaling shapes in Photoshop Elements alone, you can do it with shaped text templates. Most online digital stores sell these templates (which must be created in the full version of Photoshop). To help you get started, I've created four free journaling templates for you—available at *www.creatingkeepsakes.com*.

Journal *"in the round"*

I LOVE balancing a large photo at right right with journaling on the left. This arrangement ensures that the text gets equal visual treatment with the photo yet allows your eyes to linger on it.

To create this look, I placed my circle template over a digital patterned paper on a new document. I typed my journaling and hit Enter a few times between paragraphs to leave space for a title. I added a digital ampersand brush, placed it in a layer below the type, then printed the entire journaling block/ brush/patterned paper combo on matte photo paper. For my title, I added chipboard letters on top.

You & Me *by Jessica Sprague.* **Supplies** *Cardstock:* Bazzill Basics Paper; *Digital patterned paper:* Dirty SunPrints Paper Pack by Katie Pertiet, *www.designerdigitals.com; Patterned paper:* Scenic Route; *Chipboard swirl:* Maya Road; *Paint:* Paint Dabbers, Ranger Industries; *Chipboard letters:* Cosmo Cricket; *Date stamp:* Rhonna Farrer, Autumn Leaves; *Ink:* Cat's Eye, Clearsnap; *Font:* Nimbus Sans, *www.myfonts.com.*

BY JESSICA SPRAGUE

the technique

You can create shaped journaling with both traditional and digital methods. Here's how:

traditional scrapbooking method:

1. Using a circular template or a large circular object (like a dinner plate), trace a shape onto cardstock.
2. Cut out the shape.
3. Hand-write your journaling.

This technique is a perfect alternative to the typical journaling block. It's great for experimenting with different nonlinear designs on your scrapbook layouts!

digital technique using photoshop:

1. Open the half-circle (or other shape) text template (a .psd file) in Photoshop.
2. Drag the path onto your layout or a blank canvas.
3. Replace the mock-up type with your own journaling.
4. Print.

variation 1:
journaling under the main photo

The 6″ half-circles create visual interest on layouts with a traditional rectangular photo collage. Here, I created the collage, then added the journaling template and cutting guide below it. I opened and re-colored a digital patterned paper, added it below the text and changed my font to white.

Geek Is Love *by Jessica Sprague.*
Supplies *Patterned paper:* Cosmo Cricket (cream background) and KI Memories (stripe); *Digital patterned paper (re-colored) and digital "love" brush:* Eternal Love Kit, designed exclusively for *Creating Keepsakes* by ScrapGirls.com; *Transparency flourish:* Hambly Studios; *Chipboard letters:* Heidi Swapp for Advantus; *Rub-on letters:* Making Memories; *Cnipboard circle:* Bazzill Basics Paper; *Font:* Century Gothic, Microsoft; *Other:* Mini brads and metal brad jackets.

I Am Divided *by Karen Wilson-Bonnar.*
Supplies *Software:* Adobe Illustrator and
Adobe Photoshop, Adobe Systems; *Rub-ons:*
Daisy D's Paper Co.; *Alphabet letters:* Heidi
Swapp for Advantus; *Ink:* StazOn, Tsukineko;
Clip art: Dover Electronic Clip Art; *Fonts:* ITC
Eras Std, Adobe; Symbol Glyph, Apple.

variation 2:
unifying a two-page layout

Pair a semicircle of journaling with a photograph cut into a semicircle and use it to unify
a two-page spread. Embellish the page with a mix of rub-ons and digital embellishments. Says Karen, "If you use up your rub-ons and don't have a matching one to complete your page, substitute with a similar digital element for a perfectly hybrid page!"

What I Love About *by Shannon Taylor.* **Supplies**
Patterned paper: Crate Paper; *Letter stickers:*
American Crafts; *Chipboard letters:* K&Company
and Kurio; *Heart sticker patch:* Memories Complete;
Plastic hearts: Heidi Grace Designs; *Font:* Franks,
Internet; *Adhesive:*
Therm O Web.

variation 3:
combining horizontal and vertical templates to create a scalloped effect

Combine shaped templates to create a scalloped frame around your
photos. Says Shannon, "I created each journaling section separately. I
printed and cut each piece of shaped journaling before matting it with
red cardstock and adhering it to my page. Once you put them together,
it looks like one cohesive piece." **ck**

column *journaling*

As scrapbookers, most of the time we allow our photos to take center stage on our pages. The pictures tell most of the story, and our journaling, title and embellishments play a supporting role. Every now and then, though, it's great to switch things up and let your words lead the way—especially if you have a great story to tell. To help you create a beautiful, striking page filled with words, I'll show you how to create journaling in even-sized columns using Photoshop Elements (this works in the full version of Photoshop, too!).

let your *words* be the star

Wonder by Jessica Sprague. **Supplies** *Software:* Adobe Photoshop Elements 6.0; *Printer:* Epson R1900; *Photo paper:* Premium Photo Paper (Semi-Gloss) and Premium Presentation Paper (Matte), Epson; *Cardstock:* Bazzill Basics Paper; *Chipboard star:* Chatterbox; *Circle accent:* Heidi Swapp for Advantus; *Digital patterned paper:* Office Girl, Trish Jones; *Fonts:* Myriad (text) and Ornament Scrolls (swirl accent).

I AM AMAZED at how much my son Elliott loves space, and I wanted to tell him about our experiences with my journaling, accompanied by photos. I arranged my photos in a strip across the bottom of my page, then arranged my journaling in irregular columns. The key to getting the look on this page is making sure to zoom in and line up the journaling lines within the columns. >>

BY JESSICA SPRAGUE

the technique

Be sure to check out the video tutorial for Photoshop Elements at *creatingkeepsakes.com*.

traditional scrapbooking method:

1. Crop your photos and arrange them on the background page, leaving a large space for journaling.
2. With a pencil and a ruler, lightly draw guidelines, either in even columns or in irregular columns (as I did in my "Wonder" layout on page 139).
3. Write your journaling in the columns you've drawn, then erase the guidelines.

digital technique using Photoshop:

1. Write your journaling in a separate program, such as Microsoft Word. That way you can get down what you want to say independent of the formatting. Divide your journaling into even thirds (I just hit Enter in between paragraphs).
2. In Photoshop, create a long, narrow text box with the Horizontal Type Tool. Paste the first third of your journaling into this box.
3. Duplicate the text box, and copy and paste the second third of your journaling to replace the text. Repeat for the last third of your journaling.

variation 1:

Use different columns for journaling from different people.

Cindy Tobey used the column journaling technique to represent two different voices on her layout. "I wanted to include the letter my husband wrote to our son as well as some journaling," explains Cindy. "This easy technique was the perfect solution to fit all that journaling without it becoming overwhelming. Plus, it gave me a great way to separate the letter from the journaling. They are each in their own column."

free video tutorial and download!

Go online to see the free video tutorial of this technique at *creatingkeepsakes.com* (click on "Magazines" and February 2009). Follow a link to download some patterned papers I created for you.

tip: Need instructions on how to create white text on your layout like Cindy did here? To find an article and a tutorial I created on reversed text, go to *creatingkeepsakes.com*/articles/ Computer_Tricks_Learn_to_Print_ White_Text.

Guy's Weekend *by Cindy Tobey.* **Supplies** *Software:* Adobe Photoshop Elements 6.0; *Patterned paper, chipboard, brad and buttons:* Fancy Pants Designs; *Letter stickers:* American Crafts (orange) and Doodlebug Design (brown); *Rub-ons:* Fancy Pants Designs (large green circles) and Love, Elsie for KI Memories (small green circles); *Charms:* Love, Elsie for KI Memories; *Embroidery floss:* DMC; *Font:* Calibri; *Other:* Staples and thread.

variation 2:

Group your columns for a classic, clean look.

Ingunn Markiewicz sized the column journaling in equal proportions on the right side of her layout to balance the photos she placed on the left side. "I had lots and lots of journaling to get down, so I chose to use three columns," comments Ingunn. "I mirrored the design of the three square photos on the facing page. So much is happening in the different photos that I wanted to keep this layout as simple as possible."

Alpine Adventure by Ingunn Markiewicz. **Supplies** *Software:* Adobe Photoshop Elements 7.0; *Patterned paper:* My Mind's Eye; *Die-cut circles:* QuicKutz; *Epoxy stickers:* Love, Elsie for KI Memories; *Font:* Traveling Typewriter.

variation 3:

Let each column represent a different piece of the story you're telling.

In this layout, Noel Culbertson had three different stories she wanted to share. Noel remarks, "I love this technique for telling a story within a story. You can write out each section of the story and compile the paragraphs into columns for easy reading. I also love that the columns work as page elements. Your journaling actually becomes part of the graphic design of your page."

Crazy Fun by Noel Culbertson. **Supplies** *Software:* Adobe Photoshop Elements 5.0; *Patterned paper:* Autumn Leaves (yellow) and Dream Street Papers (green); *Felt letter stickers:* American Crafts (red) and Making Memories (blue); *Chipboard circles:* Scenic Route; *Digital patterned paper:* Katie Pertiet; *Font:* Century Gothic. **ck**

punch cool custom designs

I love the opportunity that my computer gives me to create custom, one-of-a-kind embellishments and titles. Combining computer-generated elements with punches is a great way to explore this technique. To create this look using Photoshop Elements, simply create a colored circle or block with accompanying text and graphics in the size of the punch you intend to use, print it onto white cardstock or photo paper, and adhere it to your layout. It's a great way to add a beautiful, custom feel to any page!

create "one of a kind" *looks* today

No Small Thing by Jessica Sprague. **Supplies** *Software*: Adobe Photoshop Elements 6.0; *Cardstock*: Bazzill Basics Paper; *Patterned paper*: BasicGrey; *Brads*: American Crafts; *Chipboard sticker*: Chatterbox; *Punch*: EK Success; *Ribbon clips*: Heidi Swapp for Advantus; *Ribbon*: Fancy Pants Designs (blue) and unknown (red); *Fonts*: 2Peas Stop Sign, Century Gothic and Seeing Stars.

EVERY NOW AND THEN when I'm looking through my pictures, a thought goes through my head that becomes the theme for a layout. As I looked at these sweet pictures, I thought to myself, "Moving to North Carolina was no small thing. Look what we're able to do that we couldn't do before." And then I knew I had the basis for this page. I created three separate blue blocks for my title, then I printed and punched them with a square punch and rounded the top- and bottom-left corners of the set. I adhered them to the layout with foam tape.

BY JESSICA SPRAGUE

the technique

You can have fun with this technique traditionally and digitally! Here's how:

traditional scrapbooking method:

1. Punch circles or squares from cardstock or patterned paper.
2. Use letter stickers, rub-ons and other small accents to create custom blocks.
3. Adhere the custom blocks to your layout with dimensional adhesive.

digital technique using Photoshop:

1. Create a new blank document. Use the Elliptical or Rectangular Marquee Tools to draw a circle or square selection in the size of the punch you intend to use.
2. Create a new layer. Fill the selection with the color of your choice.
3. Add text, dingbats and lines to complete your design. Print onto white cardstock. Punch. Adhere to your layout with dimensional adhesive.

variation 1:

Punch a circle shape with a scallop punch.

We bought Rowen her first camera a while ago, and it has continued to hold her interest. This, of course, couldn't make me happier. I came downstairs one morning to find that she had lined up all her "friends" on the table behind our sofa for a photo shoot and was happily chatting with them as she snapped away. I created the title circle to fit a 2" circle punch and the small circles for a 1¼" punch. For added interest, I punched each of the small circles with a scalloped punch, which left a little white edge around them.

Photo Shoot *by Jessica Sprague.* **Supplies** *Software:* Adobe Photoshop Elements 6.0; *Cardstock:* Bazzill Basics Paper; *Patterned paper:* BasicGrey (blue), Fancy Pants Designs (stripe) and Making Memories (heart); *Sticker:* me & my BIG ideas; *Punches:* EK Success (circle), Fiskars (heart) and Martha Stewart Crafts (scallop); *Fonts:* 2Peas Tasklist and Downcome.

free video and downloads online!

Check out my online March 2009 tutorial at CreatingKeepsakes.com to learn more about creating your own punchable accents. While you're there, check out the downloadable, punchable journaling shapes I have waiting for you. Download each of them and try creating your own custom punchable accents today!

variation 2:

Highlight one large punched accent.

Maggie Holmes accented her punched shape with traditional and dingbat fonts and a digital brush before punching it out. "I used my punched accent as my title and as a start to my journaling," Maggie explains. Mounting the accent on top of a mirrored embellishment helps her title stand out. Maggie tells us, "I have created things like this before, but not with the idea of punching them out to use as accents. This could be a great technique for making your own Christmas cards or other projects. You could print out a bunch of accents and punch them—a great low-cost idea."

Today You *by Maggie Holmes.* **Supplies** *Software:* Adobe Photoshop CS2; *Patterned paper:* Anna Griffin, BasicGrey and The Scarlet Lime; *Lace paper:* Creative Imaginations; *Rub-ons:* BasicGrey; *Mirrors:* Heidi Swapp for Advantus; *Corner-rounder punch:* Zutter Innovative Products; *Word stickers, brads and border strip:* Making Memories for Michaels; *Buttons:* Making Memories; *Brush:* Everyday Hand-Drawn Brushes by Ali Edwards; *Pen:* Precision Pens, American Crafts; *Fonts:* Cairo and Hearts For 3DFX.

variation 3:

Add a patterned paper to your shape for dimension.

Brittany Laakkonen mixed things up a bit and added a digital patterned paper to her circle shapes along with a digital brush and glossy accents for interest. "I had so much fun with this technique!" says Brittany. "After printing and punching the shape out, I applied some glossy accents to my letters to make my own epoxy accent." Brittany tells us that she will definitely use this technique in the future, because "there are so many ways you can make it your own!"

Now *by Brittany Laakkonen. Photography by Breanna Laakkonen.* **Supplies** *Software:* Adobe Photoshop Elements 2.0; *Patterned paper:* Making Memories and Prima; *Digital patterned paper:* Damask Dreams by Dianne Rigdon; *Digital brush:* A Little Magic Vol. 1 by Vera Lim Design; *Buttons:* foof-a-La, Autumn Leaves; *Journaling stickers and photo corner:* American Crafts; *Ribbon:* Jenni Bowlin Studio; *Sticker and felt flowers:* Prima; *Ink:* StazOn, Tsukineko; *Pen:* Zig Writer, EK Success; *Font:* Porcelain; *Other:* "We Can Do It" image. **ck**

create a grid background

I'm one of those line-them-up kinds of scrapbookers. I rarely put elements at angles, and I prefer to have things look organized on my page. Enter the grid. I've found that I can actually use Photoshop Elements' drawing tools to create a grid shape, print it onto my background cardstock, then measure and cut photos and patterned paper to fit my grid shapes. I end up with a clean, organized page that comes together in a snap. I'll show you how!

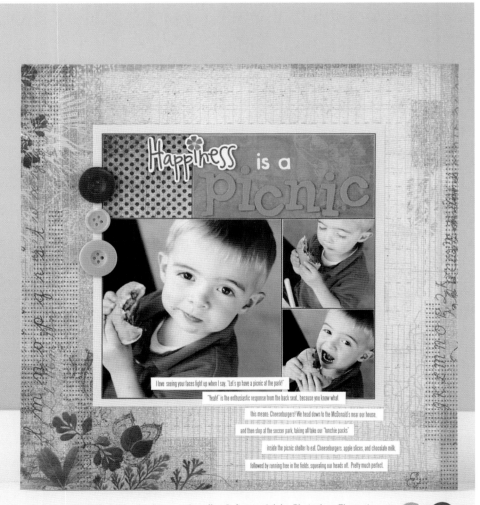

Happiness Is a Picnic *by Jessica Sprague.* **Supplies** *Software:* Adobe Photoshop Elements 7.0; *Printer:* Epson R1900; *Photo paper:* Epson Premium Semi-Gloss Photo Paper; *Cardstock:* Bazzill Basics Paper; *Patterned paper:* 7gypsies (brown) and BasicGrey (background and brown dot); *Chipboard "happiness" word and buttons:* Fancy Pants Designs; *Letter stickers:* American Crafts; *Rub-on letters:* Making Memories; *Font:* Steelfish.

line things up for a **clean** *look!*

FEW THINGS bring a smile to my face faster than my kids' excited "Yeah!" when I surprise them with something simple and fun. We love grabbing a few cheeseburgers and heading to the park for a picnic. I snapped Elliott in action eating his burger, and I organized three of the photos in a five-space grid.

Have a letter-sized printer instead of a wide-format printer? No worries! I printed this grid onto 8½" x 11" paper, cut it down and mounted it to the patterned-paper background.

BY JESSICA SPRAGUE

the technique

You can have fun with this technique traditionally and digitally! Here's how:

traditional scrapbooking method:

1. Use a pencil and a ruler to mark grid lines on a light-colored sheet of cardstock.

2. Trace over the pencil lines with a fine-tip marker.

3. Measure and cut photos and patterned paper to fit the grid shapes, then embellish.

digital technique using Photoshop elements:

1. Create a new layer, then select the Rectangular Marquee Tool and click and drag the cursor on your canvas to create the outer box for the grid. While the box is selected, click on the Edit menu, then select "Stroke [Outline] Selection." Set your stroke width and color, then click "OK."

2. Use the Line Tool, set to the same pixel width as the stroke, to draw the grid lines inside the box. (Hold down the Shift key while you draw your line to ensure it's straight.) Place each line on its own layer. Print onto cardstock.

3. Measure and cut photos and patterned paper to fit the grid shapes, then embellish.

variation 1:
Combine two grids.

Almost all the grids I've seen are single-piece grids basically printed out in one big "chunk." I wanted to mix things up a bit by creating two separate but complementary grids for this page. I adhered the two grids to a solid sheet of patterned paper to anchor them together, then I placed a vertical title between them. It was a unique way to change up the layout design but still keep things clean, organized and perfect for scrapping multiple photos!

Splash by Jessica Sprague. **Supplies** *Software:* Adobe Photoshop Elements 7.0; *Cardstock and chipboard circle:* Bazzill Basics Paper; *Patterned paper, circle accent and buttons:* Fancy Pants Designs; *Brown patterned paper:* BasicGrey; *Chipboard letters:* Heidi Swapp for Advantus; *Ink:* ColorBox, Clearsnap; *Font:* Century Gothic.

free online video tutorial and download

Go to CreatingKeepsakes.com to check out my April 2009 online tutorial and learn more about creating a grid using Photoshop Elements. While you're there, download some fun grids I've created for you!

variation 2:

Let your embellishments guide your design.

Deena Wuest's embellishments were the inspiration for creating this layout. To create the appropriate-sized grid, she had to be sure she was creating a grid large enough to house the elements.

Deena tells us, "Sometimes it's difficult to get an accurate reading of how the space relates between the digital page and paper products." To create this page, Deena held an 11" x 8½" sheet of paper up to her screen and adjusted her view percentage (located in the bottom-left corner of Photoshop Elements) until it matched her paper size. Deena said, "Once you determine the percentage setting, you can use it for every project no matter what the size."

Proof Positive by Deena Wuest. **Supplies** *Software:* Adobe Photoshop Elements 4.0; *Cardstock:* Wausau Papers and WorldWin; *Patterned paper and embellishments:* CKU Album in a Box, CK Media; *Chipboard letters:* Heidi Swapp for Advantus; *Font:* Avant Garde.

variation 3:

Try different shapes.

Using a grid doesn't mean you're limited to using only squares and rectangles! Here, Marcia Bettich decided to place her grid inside a circle shape. She first created a 12" x 12" circle in Photoshop Elements. Marcia explains, "After making the circle, I created a grid of several 2" x 2" boxes. I used a clipping mask to make my boxes conform to the circle shape, then I was ready to print and go!" Follow Marcia's lead and try a different shape for a fun effect.

Pirates by Marcia Bettich. **Supplies** *Software:* Adobe Photoshop Elements 6.0; *Cardstock:* Bazzill Basics Paper; *Patterned paper:* Chatterbox, Daisy D's Paper Co., Déjà Views by The C-Thru Ruler Co., KI Memories and Scenic Route; *Flowers:* Bazzill Basics Paper and Prima; *Chipboard flourish:* Maya Road; *Letters:* American Crafts; *Brads and arrows:* 7gypsies; *Die cuts:* Fancy Pants Designs; *Transparencies:* Hambly Screen Prints and My Mind's Eye; *Stamps:* Stampin' Up!; *Ink:* Colorbök; *Paint:* Making Memories; *Pen:* Sharpie, Newell Rubbermaid; *Other:* Thread. **ck**

frame a photo

Do you have all your photos printed in a lab? Don't worry! It doesn't need to stop you from dipping your toes into the great world of computer-infused scrapbooking! In this column, I show you how to add a frame to a photo before printing it. Best of all, each photo used in this month's column is standard size (4" x 6" or 5" x 7"), which you can easily print at your lab or on the smaller (and less expensive!) sheets of photo paper at home.

How Does This Garden Grow? *by Jessica Sprague.* **Supplies** *Software:* Adobe Photoshop Elements 7.0; *Digital frame:* Split Pea Digital Kit by Rhonna Farrer; *Cardstock:* Bazzill Basics Paper; *Patterned paper:* BasicGrey; *Chipboard circle, letters and ribbon:* Fancy Pants Designs; *Printer:* Epson R1900; *Photo paper:* Epson Premium Photo Paper Semi-Gloss; *Font:* LL Rubber Grotesque; *Other:* Buttons and chipboard leaves.

add a *frame* **for definition and interest**

I AM NOT someone with a green thumb. I will freely admit that. So it feels like a miracle that anything I plant grows in my front yard. I wanted to place the focus of my layout firmly on the delicate pink and white blossom I photographed, so I used a premade digital border to frame a standard 4" x 6" photo. By adding a few embellishments and a title that playfully surrounds the photo, I created a page that celebrates my unlikely garden.

BY JESSICA SPRAGUE

the technique

You can have fun with this technique traditionally and digitally! Here's how:

traditional scrapbooking method:

1. Print a digital frame onto a transparency, or purchase a premade transparency frame.
2. Staple the transparency frame over your photo.
3. Alternatively, you can construct a frame for a photo using rub-ons.

digital technique using Photoshop:

1. Crop your photo to the final size you would like it to be.
2. Open a digital frame, and drag it onto your photo.
3. Save and print, or upload to your favorite photo lab for printing.

variation 1:

Place two framed photos on one standard sized print.

I mentioned in last month's column that I'm a liner-upper. As I thought more about that, I figured, why not line everything up and then give the *whole thing* a little tilt? I really love the results here, and the best part is that all my photos are printed on standard-size papers. The focal photo is a 5" x 7", and the two smaller photos were printed together on a single 5" x 7" document. I framed the focal photo with both a black and a white frame to add extra interest to the photo edges.

Today by Jessica Sprague. **Supplies** *Software:* Adobe Photoshop Elements 7.0; *Cardstock:* Bazzill Basics Paper; *Patterned paper and heart tag:* Colorbök; *Decorative border punch:* Fiskars; *Chipboard:* American Crafts; *Bookplate tab:* 7gypsies; *Digital frames:* Artistic Photo Frames by Gypsy Chick; *Rhinestones:* My Mind's Eye; *Stamp:* Heidi Swapp for Advantus; *Printer:* Epson R1900; *Photo paper:* Epson Premium Photo Paper Semi-Gloss; *Ink:* StazOn, Tsukineko; *Font:* Century.

free video tutorial

Check out my free online May 2009 video tutorial and learn more about adding digital frames using Photoshop Elements. Go to CreatingKeepsakes.com to learn more!

variation 2:

Use multiple photos within one frame.

Instead of using just one photo in this funky frame, Kelly Noel created one canvas for two photos and placed the frame around both of them. Kelly tells us, "I think the frame's scalloped border really sets off my photos and creates a fun and cute look."

To make the frame even more colorful, Kelly added a frame made from patterned paper, which makes the photos jump off the page. Kelly adds, "This might be a fun technique to use to create a journaling block, too!"

8 Months *by Kelly Noel.* **Supplies** *Software:* Adobe Photoshop Elements 3.0; *Digital frame:* 12X12 Funky Scalloped Frame by Crystal Wilkerson; *Cardstock:* Bazzill Basics Paper; *Patterned paper and stickers:* BasicGrey; *Chipboard:* American Crafts ("8") and Making Memories ("months"); *Buttons:* American Crafts and Autumn Leaves; *Font:* National Primary.

variation 3:

Define your photo's edges.

Greta Hammond chose a subtle, light-blue paper for the right-hand side of her layout, but when she added the photo, the gray color of the concrete seemed to fade away into the paper. "I used these grungy digital frames to give my photos' edges more definition," Greta explains. "It actually makes the subject in the photos more of the focal point of my layout."

Simple Joys *by Greta Hammond.* **Supplies** *Software:* Adobe Photoshop Elements 5.0; *Digital frame:* Rhonna Farrer; *Cardstock:* Bazzill Basics Paper; *Chipboard, felt, patterned paper, pin, ribbon and rub-on:* Fancy Pants Designs; *Stickers:* EK Success; *Font:* Shutri.

free frame downloads

Ready to try this technique? Download cool frames from the May 2009 issue at *CreatingKeepsakes.com*! ck

play with huge *punctuation*

Next time you're stuck with scrapper's block, try this quick trick: upsize! Creating one huge element for your layout helps focus your story and provides hierarchy and visual interest. When we look at a page, we tend to glance first at what-ever's biggest (or highest contrast) on the layout. This can be a huge photo (like I've done with my "Just This Big" layout on page 152), or it can be another huge element, such as the large ampersand I included on my "8 Years & Counting" layout below. I love the way the huge punctuation in these pages turned out. Here, I'll show you how to add some playful focus to your layouts by supersizing your type!

8 Years & Counting by Jessica Sprague. **Supplies** Software: Adobe Photoshop Elements 7.0; Cardstock: Bazzill Basics Paper; Patterned paper: Cosmo Cricket (stripe) and My Mind's Eye (floral); Chipboard letters: BasicGrey; Tag die cut: Daisy D's Paper Co.; Printer: Epson R1900; Photo paper: Epson Premium Photo Paper Semi-gloss; Fonts: Georgia and LL Rubber Grotesque; Adhesive: Mono Adhesive, Tombow.

add *impact* to your pages

I PRINTED THE huge ampersand for this layout onto the front of a sheet of patterned paper. I then carefully cut around it, leaving about a 1/8" border as I went. It created a great die-cut shape that I could use on either dark or light colors. The sheer size of the ampersand creates dramatic visual impact, while the curling font I used adds some contrast to the lines and rectangles in the rest of the page.

BY JESSICA SPRAGUE

the technique

You can have fun with this technique traditionally and digitally! Here's how:

traditional scrapbooking methods:

1. Choose large die-cut or chipboard accents in punctuation shapes to complement your designs and add visual impact. Or . . .

2. Hand-draw some punctuation of your own—it'll give a great handmade feel to your page!

digital technique using Photoshop:

1. Create a new blank document.

2. Select your Horizontal Type Tool, and type your punctuation.

3. Resize the punctuation with the Move Tool, and print it on cardstock or paper.

   Note: You could also add it to a photo before printing, and then print them as a set.

Just This Big *by Jessica Sprague.* **Supplies** *Software:* Adobe Photoshop Elements 7.0; *Cardstock:* Bazzill Basics Paper; *Patterned paper:* BasicGrey (blue) and Daisy D's Paper Co. (red); *Chipboard elements:* BasicGrey (star) and Chatterbox (tag); *"Celebrate" tag and rhinestones:* My Mind's Eye; *Rub-on letter:* American Crafts; *Sequins:* Doodlebug Design; *Scalloped circle punch:* Marvy Uchida: *Printer:* Epson R1900; *Photo paper:* Epson Premium Photo Paper Semi-gloss; *Fonts:* Bernhard Modern and Century Gothic; *Adhesive:* Memory Dots, Glue Dots International; Mono Adhesive, Tombow.

variation 1:

Add your punctuation to your photo and enlarge both elements.

As Elliott celebrates his fourth birthday this month, I've taken the opportunity to look back at some of his newborn pictures, and I'm amazed at his *smallness*. I enlarged a photo of him to as close to life-size as I could, and then I added my text directly to the photo. I enlarged an open-bracket shape to set off the type and lead the eye into the focal area of the photo. The bracket adds direction, but because it's only outlined, it doesn't add much visual weight.

free online video tutorial and download

Want to watch a step-by-step video tutorial on creating oversized punctuation in Photoshop Elements? Simply visit CreatingKeepsakes.com today. While you're there, check out my June 2009 download to use on your pages!

variation 2:

Add journaling around the punctuation for a unique border.

In Deena Wuest's "Mom!" layout, you can almost hear her kids calling her, can't you? Deena tells us, "I repeated the word 'mom' inside the exclamation point to portray the numerous times I hear this word." She explains, "I used different fonts to represent my kids' different voices (and different tones)." She placed her journaling around the exclamation point to create a unique border.

MOM! *by Deena Wuest.* **Supplies** *Software:* Adobe Photoshop Elements 4.0; *Patterned paper:* Sayge Paper Pack and Caron Paper Pack by Michelle Martin; *Digital frames:* DoodleDo Frames No. 03 Brushes and Stamps by Katie Pertiet; *Circle text path:* Text Bytes: Shaped Text Templates No. 15 by Pattie Knox; *Fonts:* Avenir, CK Ali's Handwriting, CK Deena, Rockwell and Steelfish.

variation 3:

Use punctuation to frame a photo.

Paula Gilarde used an oversized question mark to represent all the questions her daughter asks. She also used it to frame the top photo on her layout. "I created the question mark in Photoshop by typing the symbol at 850 points and outlining it," Paula says. The outline gives the punctuation definition, and the placement is perfect.

Why? *by Paula Gilarde.* **Supplies** *Software:* Adobe Photoshop CS2; *Photo frames:* Little Vintage Frames by Katie Pertiet; *Cardstock:* Stampin' Up!; *Patterned paper:* October Afternoon (floral and stripe), Scenic Route (grid) and SEI (dot); *Stamps:* Imaginisce (bird) and Studio Calico ("faq"); *Sticker:* Jenni Bowlin Studio; *Ink:* StazOn, Tsukineko; *Font:* SS Whimsy. **ck**

scrapbook a *screenshot*

Have you ever stopped to think about how much you're influenced by the Internet? There are numerous destinations we visit online every day, and there are also great online tools you can use to help complete your stories. Here, I'll show you how easy it is to include screenshots on your pages and in your albums!

use online **images** *to tell your stories*

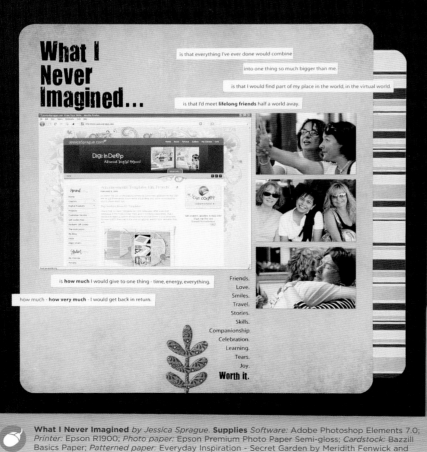

What I Never Imagined by *Jessica Sprague.* **Supplies** *Software:* Adobe Photoshop Elements 7.0; *Printer:* Epson R1900; *Photo paper:* Epson Premium Photo Paper Semi-gloss; *Cardstock:* Bazzill Basics Paper; *Patterned paper:* Everyday Inspiration – Secret Garden by Meridith Fenwick and Scenic Route (stripe); *Chipboard accent:* BasicGrey; *Fonts:* Myriad Pro and You Are Loved.

AS YOU MIGHT imagine, I spend a huge amount of my time online—both working time and free time. Over the past couple years, work time and free time have blended together at a website I created, *JessicaSprague.com*, that has grown into much more than I ever imagined. I scrapped some photos of a get-together that the members of the website had in 2008, along with a screenshot of my site's home page. Do you have an online destination that feels like home? A screenshot would be the perfect focal point for a layout about it!

BY JESSICA SPRAGUE

the technique

Since this technique requires a screenshot on a computer, we'll only discuss a digital technique this time. Here are the details:

Digital technique using Photoshop Elements:

1. Create a new blank document in Photoshop Elements or Microsoft Word.

2. Launch your web browser and navigate to the web page you would like to capture.

3. Press the Alt + Print Screen buttons on your keyboard, and then paste your screenshot into your new document.

4. Print the screenshot onto cardstock or photo paper, and use it just like you would a photo!

Hello, Home *by Jessica Sprague.* **Supplies** *Software:* Adobe Photoshop Elements 7.0; *Printer:* Epson R1900; *Photo paper:* Epson Premium Photo Paper Semi-gloss; *Cardstock:* Bazzill Basics Paper; *Patterned paper:* Cosmo Cricket; *Ribbon and "Hello" rub-on:* American Crafts; *Transparent letters:* Making Memories.

variation 1:

Print a map of your neighborhood.

I recorded some shots of my home in a layout with a bit of a whimsical feel—the journaling reads like a poem, and the title is punctuated by a large Google map of my neighborhood, which I captured and then printed on white cardstock.

Bonus idea: Create a mini album containing maps of all the homes you've lived in!

variation 2:

Use screenshots in place of missing photos.

During Jackie Stringham's trip to New York City with her husband, her camera broke. She wasn't able to take pictures while on her trip—a scrapbooker's worst nightmare! Jackie tells us, "Using a screenshot was a fun and easy way to document my vacation when I didn't have photos to go along with my journaling."

 New York City *by Jackie Stringham.* **Supplies** *Cardstock:* Bazzill Basics Paper (black) and Die Cuts With a View (silver); *Patterned paper:* KI Memories, October Afternoon and Scenic Route; *Chipboard circles:* Imagination Project; *Photo of subway:* Urban75.org; *Font:* Adobe Jenson; *Other:* Brads and glitter.

variation 3:

Capture your blog and put it on paper.

Have you joined the blogging world? You can take a screenshot of your blog and include it on a page, like Kelly Purkey did here. "Blogging has become a popular trend, and I wanted to get my thoughts about it down on a page," says Kelly. "Working with a screenshot of my blog is a fun way to remember what my blog looked like." If you don't blog but have favorite blogs that you visit, incorporate screenshots of those sites and record your thoughts about them.

Blogged *by Kelly Purkey.* **Supplies** *Software:* Adobe Photoshop CS3; *Cardstock:* American Crafts; *Patterned paper:* American Crafts (wood grain) and Heidi Grace Design (green and pink); *Stickers:* Cloud 9 Designs, Fiskars Americas (epoxy), Creative Café (alphabet strip) and Heidi Grace Designs (letters); *Stamp:* Hero Arts; *Ink:* Stampin' Up!; *Circle punches, corner-rounder punch and adhesive:* Fiskars Americas; *Font:* Garamond. **ck**

create
translucent text

Translucent text adds a bit of flair to any layout. I often use it on my pages to help point the emphasis to key words. Oftentimes when we look at a scrapbook layout (or at any other design for that matter), our eye sees larger or more saturated pieces first. Using translucent text helps tell your message without overpowering the other elements on your page.

change the
opacity
of text

WE ALL HAVE those days that seem as though the storm clouds are never going to part. Then something reminds us that they will. My daughter, Rowen, often gives me that inspiration. When I took this photo of her, I saw how she took on the adventure of mastering the new balance beam in our backyard without fear or hesitation. I wanted to place my text on the photo without overpowering the image, so I made some of the text translucent and left a few key words at full saturation so they stand out on the layout.

Balance *by Jessica Sprague.* **Supplies** *Software:* Adobe Photoshop Elements 7.0; *Printer:* Epson R1900; *Photo paper:* Epson Premium Photo Paper Semi-gloss; *Patterned paper:* BasicGrey; *Letter stickers:* KitoftheMonth.com; *Photo corners:* Making Memories; *Fonts:* Impact and Myriad; *Adhesive:* Mono Adhesive, Tombow; *Other:* Ribbon.

BY JESSICA SPRAGUE

the technique

You can have fun with this technique traditionally and digitally! Here's how:

Traditional scrapbooking technique:

1. Select a text stamp and a light color of ink.

2. Stamp your text directly onto cardstock or a transparency.

3. Choose a different text treatment for the second layer of text and add it to your page.

Digital technique using Photoshop Elements:

1. Create a new blank document.

2. Select the Horizontal Type Tool, and then type your text. Click on the Move Tool to commit your text.

3. Click on the Opacity slider at the top of the Layers Palette and slide the opacity level down to the desired level.

variation 1:

Layer translucent text on a photo for your title.

Lori Anderson printed her title onto her photograph using regular and translucent text. Lori wanted the large photo of her daughter to be the focus of this layout, so she lowered the opacity of the bold font to keep it from overpowering the photo of her daughter.

Simply Stunning by Lori Anderson. **Supplies** *Software:* Adobe Photoshop Elements 7.0; *Cardstock:* Die Cuts With a View (scallop) and Wausau Paper (brown); *Patterned paper:* My Mind's Eye; *Journaling tag:* Journal Tag Freebie by Michelle Coleman; *Epoxy sticker:* Little Yellow Bicycle; *Brads:* American Crafts (red) and Little Yellow Bicycle (pink); *Rub-on:* KI Memories; *Border punch:* Fiskars Americas; *Ribbon and button:* American Crafts; *Fonts:* Franklin Gothic Heavy and LD Italic; *Adhesive:* Mono Adhesive, Tombow.

free online download

Check out this incredible set of brushes. You can download it for free, courtesy of ScrapGirls.com, at CreatingKeepsakes.com (see August 2009 issue).

One thing that has been tough on all of us is how much Mike works. He gets very little time to spend with the kids and usually that time is so rushed that it flies by. It's almost like Jackson knows that this time is precious and limited. He wants to soak up as much time with his daddy as he possibly can. You can see it when his face lights up the second Mike walks in the room. At that point no one else exists and no one else matters. He wants his daddy.

variation 2:

Place translucent text behind your journaling.

Allison Davis chose a few key words from her journaling, created a layer of translucent text, and then arranged the words behind her journaling block. She selected this placement because "it was a great way to draw attention to the journaling and the important words on my layout." Next time you want to draw the viewer's eye to your heartfelt words, try her fun take on this technique.

Daddy's Boy *by Allison Davis.* **Supplies** *Cardstock:* Bazzill Basics Paper; *Patterned paper:* BasicGrey; *Chipboard hearts:* Fancy Pants Designs and Maya Road; *Letter stickers:* American Crafts; *Transparency and paint:* Making Memories; *Glitter:* Doodlebug Design; *Fonts:* American Typewriter and LD Grunge; *Adhesive:* Memory Dots, Glue Dots International; Mono Adhesive, Tombow; Scrapbook Adhesives by 3L.

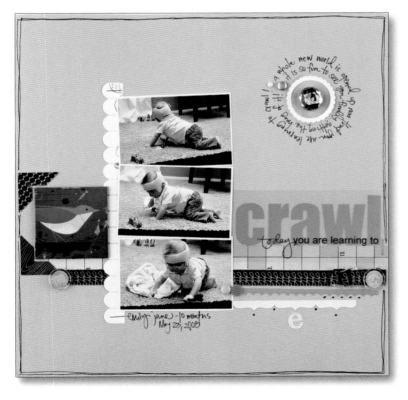

variation 3:

Print translucent text onto a transparency.

Maggie Holmes decided to use two fonts and a digital brush (layered over part of her text) to create her title. "I wanted the focus to be on the word 'crawl,' so I chose a large, bold font, and then I layered the rest of the title on top," says Maggie. Reducing the opacity of the word "crawl" helps us to see the word without it being too bold. Her use of a transparency is proof that you don't have to have a wide-format printer to get the look of text printed directly on a 12" x 12" layout.

Today You are Learning to Crawl *by Maggie Holmes.* **Supplies** *Software:* Adobe Photoshop CS3; *Patterned paper:* Making Memories (blue and white) and Sassafras (yellow); *Brush:* Everyday Hand Drawn Brushes by Ali Edwards; *Stamps:* Hero Arts and Studio Calico; *Brads:* Heidi Swapp for Advantus and Making Memories; *Ink:* Papertrey Ink; *Punches:* EK Success and Fiskars Americas; *Glass pebbles and letter stickers:* Making Memories; *Decorative tape:* Studio Calico; *Chipboard square with bird:* Old Navy; *Pen:* Zig Writer, EK Success; *Fonts:* Arial and Impact; *Adhesive:* Dot 'n' Roller, Kokuyo; Zots, Therm O Web; *Other:* Staples and transparency. **ck**

designing with *circles*

Circles are a great design element! I love adding circles, big and small, to almost every layout I make. Cutting photographs and other elements into circles in Photoshop isn't necessarily a self-evident thing, so I've created a video tutorial to walk you through the digital version of a circle cutter (watch it at *creatingkeepsakes.com/digitalcircles*). Let's get ready to design with circles!

make *cool* digital circle elements

I PURCHASED a piece of precut plywood and some inexpensive giant clothespins to create this artwork hanger, then used the circle photo technique with the scalloped edge as the focal point. Two of these (one for each of my children) hang in our front entryway, providing a versatile art display and a way to show my kids how proud I am of their creativity. I think this would be a perfect back-to-school gift for any child! If you can't find plywood, try a foam-core board for backing.

BY JESSICA SPRAGUE

Homework Hanger *by Jessica Sprague.* **Supplies** *Software:* Adobe Photoshop Elements 6.0; *Printer:* Epson R1800; *Photo paper:* PremierArt Matte Scrapbook Photo Paper, Epson; *Wooden clothespins:* Provo Craft; *Cardstock and chipboard circle:* Bazzill Basics Paper; *Patterned paper:* My Mind's Eye; *Self-adhesive die-cut felt:* Queen & Co.; *Digital patterned paper:* Everyday Inspiration—Easy Silence Paper Set by Meredith Fenwick, *www.scrapbook-graphics.com*; *Font:* Fling, Letraset; *Other:* Plywood, paint and sequins.

the technique

You can have fun with this technique traditionally and digitally! Here's how:

traditional scrapbooking method:

1. Print your photo without cropping any edges.

2. Use a circle cutter, or trace carefully around a small plate or cup, to cut your photo(s) into circles.

3. Overlap the circles, or layer them with several larger circles to create a full circular design. You can also let a large circle be the focal point of your layout or decor piece.

digital technique using Photoshop:

1. Create a new blank document. With the Elliptical Marquee Tool, draw and fill a circular shape.

2. Add your photo to the new document, with the photo layer above the circle layer.

3. Alt-click between the layers in the Layers palette to "clip" your photo onto the circular shape. Complete your image with more circles or scallops, or print as-is. Cut around the circles and adhere to your layout.

In Just 4 Months *by Nisa Fiin.* **Supplies** *Software:* Adobe Photoshop CS3; *Patterned paper:* Making Memories (ledger) and My Mind's Eye (blue); *Stamps:* Purple Onion Designs; *Ink:* StazOn, Tsukineko; *Stickers:* FontWerks; *Ribbon:* May Arts; *Pen:* Sharpie, Newell Rubbermaid; *Colored pencil:* Prismacolor, Newell Rubbermaid; *Digital scallop circle:* Jessica Sprague, www. creatingkeepsakes. com; *Digital patterned paper:* Nisa's own design; *Other:* Pencil and a blank page from an antique book.

variation 1:

line up several circle photos with scalloped mats.

Nisa sized her photos small enough to fit four across the page so she could document how Henry has grown in the four months she's known him. "I just love the idea of not losing any info with this technique," explains Nisa. "Your photo always stays intact and can be adjusted as you like—without hitting Undo and hoping you have the version you want to go back to somewhere in your history menu!"

variation 2:

layer your focal-point photo with smaller circle photos.

Kelly used the circle technique on multiple photos in different sizes and layered them together in Photoshop. Notes Kelly, "I love the masking technique because it's so easy to crop photos in a different way, but you can still manipulate the photo layer to get it cropped exactly where you'd like it."

Lady Liberty & Me *by Kelly Purkey.* **Supplies** *Software:* Adobe Photoshop Elements 6.0; *Cardstock:* Core'dinations; *Patterned paper:* K&Company (boxes) and KI Memories (blue); *Stickers:* Heidi Grace Designs; *Epoxy:* Cloud 9 Design, Fiskars; *Stamp:* Hero Arts; *Ink:* StazOn, Tsukineko, *Rub-ons and buttons:* American Crafts; *Star punch and scallop scissors:* Fiskars.

variation 3:

overlap circle photos with scalloped mats.

I wanted to celebrate some of Elliott's adventures with my camera's remote trigger. To play up the circular elements, I repeated four circles across the page and then digitally added scallops behind each one. I backed the entire thing with digital patterned paper and printed it out (not wanting to actually cut around all of those pesky scallop shapes). I then cut along the patterned paper line and adhered that paper to my background paper.

Self-Portrait *by Jessica Sprague.* **Supplies** *Software:* Adobe Photoshop Elements 6.0; *Printer:* Epson R1800; *Photo paper:* PremierArt Matte Scrapbook Photo Paper, Epson; *Patterned paper:* BasicGrey (blue and ledger) and Fancy Pants Designs (stripe); *Digital patterned paper:* Patience kit by Amanda Rockwell, *www.scrapartist.com; Title and journaling cards:* Scenic Route; *Rub-on letters ("self"):* My Mind's Eye; *Chipboard letters ("portrait"):* Heidi Swapp for Advantus; *Die-cut tags:* Fancy Pants Designs; *Buttons:* Creative Imaginations; *Font:* Myriad, Adobe Systems. **ck**

type on a
curve

Are you ready to add an eye-catching detail to your pages? Try typing in curves and swirls! Depending on the font you choose, curving type can be either fun and playful or eye-catchingly romantic. You can achieve this effect in Photoshop Elements by downloading "text paths" created in the full version of Photoshop and replacing the text with your own words. It's easy and fun, and I'll show you how to do it!

enhance your stories with this fun technique

CURVING TYPE can add a fun, playful flair to any page. For this layout, I paired my set of five text paths with a chunky, fun font and placed my journaling on a blue background before printing it. The result is a great focal element that resembles party streamers. Love it!

B-day Bot *by Jessica Sprague.* **Supplies** *Software:* Adobe Photoshop Elements 7.0; *Printer:* Epson R1900; *Photo paper:* Epson Premium Photo Paper Semi-gloss; *Patterned paper:* BasicGrey (yellow), Fancy Pants Designs (black and stripe) and Earth Wind and Sky Paper Set by Michelle Coleman; *Chipboard:* Fancy Pants Designs (star), Heidi Swapp for Advantus (letters) and KI Memories (tag); *Button:* KI Memories; *Font:* 2Peas Stop Sign; *Adhesive:* Mono Adhesive, Tombow.

BY JESSICA SPRAGUE

the technique

You can have fun with this technique traditionally and digitally! Here's how:

Traditional technique:

1. Use a pencil to either freehand or trace curves across your journaling paper.
2. Pencil in the words you'd like to write.
3. Go over your words with an ink pen; let the ink dry, and then erase the pencil lines.

Digital technique using Photoshop Elements:

1. Create a new document in Photoshop Elements. Open the text path you'd like to use. Select the Move Tool, and then click and drag the path onto your new document.

2. With the Text Tool selected, double-click the text layer in the Layers palette, and replace the placeholder type with your own words. Change the font, size and color of the text as desired.
3. Repeat steps 1–2 as desired, and then print your shaped text onto cardstock or photo paper.

variation 1:

Digitally "paint" behind the swirls for a dreamy effect.

Curved type can be strikingly romantic when paired with a close-up photo of you and your honey. In this wall art I created, I kept the font simple, and I added a watercolor Photoshop brush behind my type for some subtle color before printing out the photo and text on one page. As an alternative to digital painting, feel free to print onto watercolor paper and get out your paints for a handmade look!

Give Me a Kiss *by Jessica Sprague.* **Supplies** *Software:* Adobe Photoshop Elements 7.0; *Printer:* Epson R1900; *Photo paper:* Epson Premium Photo Paper Semi-gloss; *Watercolor brushes:* BittBox.com; *Chipboard accent:* Tattered Angels; *Font:* Myriad; *Other:* Foam core board.

variation 2:

Overlap swirled text on your photo and paper.
Cindy Tobey purchased a pre-made text path online and positioned the text so it hugged the tunnel outline in her center photo.

To create a seamless transition between the text on her photo and the text on the paper, Cindy first printed the photo and text path (they're part of the same design) onto patterned paper in blue for a tone-on-tone look. She then printed the photo and text path onto photo paper; she cut out the photo and layered it directly over the photo image on the patterned paper. This is a fun layering technique that draws your eye directly to the focal-point photo.

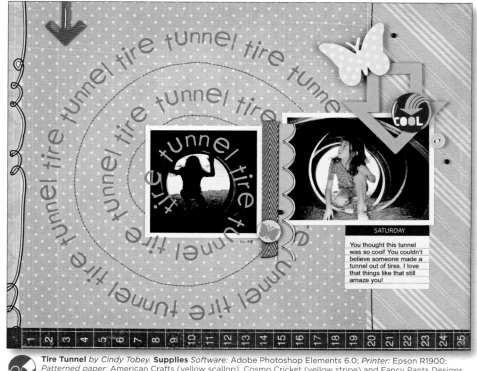

Tire Tunnel *by Cindy Tobey.* **Supplies** *Software:* Adobe Photoshop Elements 6.0; *Printer:* Epson R1900; *Patterned paper:* American Crafts (yellow scallop), Cosmo Cricket (yellow stripe) and Fancy Pants Designs (blue and black); *Journaling tag:* Heidi Swapp for Advantus; *Chipboard:* American Crafts (butterfly) and Maya Road (arrow); *Ribbon:* Cosmo Cricket; *Circle accent and acrylic arrow:* American Crafts; *Button:* Fancy Pants Designs; *Brads:* Die Cuts With a View (butterfly) and Queen & Co. (black); *Text path:* DigiKit - Follow the Path by Jen Lessinger; *Fonts:* Arial (journaling) and 2Peas Favorite Things (swirled type); *Adhesive:* 3M and Tombow; *Other:* Staple and thread.

Bubble Wishes *by Brigid Gonzalez.* **Supplies** *Software:* Adobe Photoshop CS3; *Cardstock:* Die Cuts With a View and KI Memories (purple embossed); *Patterned paper:* Wild Love by The Shabby Princess; *Epoxy stickers and corner-rounder punch:* EK Success; *Fonts:* Century Gothic Bold and Retro Rock Poster; *Adhesive:* 3M.

variation 3:

Use swirled text to convey motion or movement.
Brigid Gonzalez wanted to reinforce the circular theme throughout her layout, so she selected a fun, embossed paper with lots of circles. She used swirled text to surround the bubbles in the photo and also to show the movement of the bubbles from the bubble wand.

Product tip: Did you notice how Brigid added clear epoxy stickers on the dot paper strip? This small addition makes them look like colorful 3-D bubbles.

free text paths online

At CreatingKeepsakes.com/-issues/October_2009, you'll find 10 free text paths you can try on your next layout. **ck**

hand-color a *downloaded* element

In the past, I had tons of stamps. My drawers were overflowing. Now that I've added my computer to my scrapbooking arsenal, I can enjoy the benefits of having digital "stamps" in the form of brushes, word art and dingbat fonts without requiring lots of storage space. Join me in using these computer-based elements by printing the design onto cardstock and hand-coloring the elements.

get *creative* **with pencils, paint and your computer**

keep smiling...

PARENTAL ADVISORY FUNNY CONTENT

a day to remember · a day to remember

I absolutely love your smile! At 11, you're becoming the "too cool" pre-teen I expected you to be, but you're not too cool to still laugh and have fun with mom and dad. I hope you keep smiling and keep giggling, because it makes me giggle too.

what ever

YOU ROCK

Keep Smiling *by Lori Anderson.* **Supplies** *Software:* Adobe Photoshop Elements 7.0; *Patterned paper:* American Crafts and Bohemian Summer by Michelle Coleman; *Letter stickers and "whatever" accent:* American Crafts; *Chipboard:* Chatterbox (star) and Sandylion (circles); *Corner-rounder punch:* Marvy Uchida; *Colored pencils:* EK Success; *Fonts:* Famous Logos (altered), Seeing Stars, Tahoma and WM People; *Adhesive:* Foam Squares, Therm O Web; Mono Adhesive, Tombow; Scrapbook Adhesives by 3L.

IF YOU NEED a patterned paper to coordinate with a layout but you don't have a matching piece, create your own! In my "Keep Smiling" layout, I didn't have a star paper to match my background sheet, so I used a star dingbat to create my own.

How-To: Create patterned paper with dingbats.
To try this technique at home, download a dingbat font and open a word-processing program. Type the letter corresponding with the desired dingbat shape numerous times to create a pattern. Print the pattern onto cardstock and color in the shapes.

BY LORI ANDERSON

the technique

You can have fun with this technique traditionally and digitally! Here's how:

Traditional scrapbooking method:

❶ Select a stamp to use on your page.

❷ Stamp the image with ink onto cardstock.

❸ Hand-color the design with colored pencils, watercolor pencils, chalk or pens. Trim around the element before adding it your layout.

Digital technique using Photoshop Elements:

❶ Create a new document in Photoshop Elements; and select the brush, word art or dingbat you would like to use.

❷ Place the design on your document and resize as desired. Print the design.

❸ Hand-color the design with colored pencils, watercolor pencils, chalk or pens. Trim and place the element on your layout.

variation 1:

Use a large custom shape image to add impact to your page.

After selecting a custom-shape image from Photoshop Elements 5.0 and a digital butterfly brush, Pam Callaghan printed the elements onto cardstock and colored them with watercolor pencils for a gorgeous effect. Pam told us, "I usually don't do such artistic pages, but I am so glad I tried this technique. It's easy—if I can do it, anyone can." Pam points out, "If you cut your image while the watercolor is drying, the paper will curl up and look like real leaves." What a great tip!

 New Hairdo *by Pam Callaghan.* **Supplies** *Software and floral element:* Adobe Photoshop Elements 5.0; *Cardstock:* Bazzill Basics Paper; *Patterned paper:* Marks Paper Company (ledger) and My Mind's Eye (green); *Letter stickers:* American Crafts; *Digital butterfly stamp:* Spring Wings 'n' Things Brush Set by Cherie Mask; *Watercolor pencils:* Loew-Cornell; *Pen:* Zig Writer, EK Success; *Adhesive:* Herma, EK Success; Mono Adhesive, Tombow.

How-To: Create a custom-shape embellishment.

❶ Create a new document in Photoshop Elements.

❷ Select the Custom Shape Tool (grouped with the Rectangle Tool) and click on the desired shape in the Set Shape to Create box on the options bar (near the top of the screen).

❸ Click-and-drag the shape onto your new document. Print the shape onto cardstock, trim and color on the opposite side with watercolor pencils.

 Grin *by Paula Gilarde.* **Supplies** *Software:* Adobe Photoshop CS4; *Cardstock:* Core'dinations; *Brads:* American Crafts; *Colored pencils:* Heidi Swapp for Advantus; *Digital brushes:* DoodleDo Titles No. 02 Brushes and Stamps by Katie Pertiet; *Tearing ruler and texture template:* Fiskars Americas; *Paint pens:* Elmer's; *Font:* 1942 Report.

variation 2:

Turn digital word art into a work of art.

Paula Gilarde used a word-art brush for her title and colored in the swirls and text with a paint pen. Paula typically colors these word-art titles on her computer, but she liked using the pens. She tells us, "This was a fun technique—it reminded me of my children using their coloring books, and it's quite relaxing!" Paula plans to use this technique on doodled frames as well.

How-To: Create a word-art title.

❶ Create a new document in Photoshop Elements.

❷ Open the word-art .png file, select the Move Tool and click-and-drag the word-art image down on your new document; position as desired.

❸ Print the word-art image onto cardstock, and color with watercolor pencils.

 Our Favorite Getaway *by Lori Anderson.* **Supplies** *Software:* Adobe Photoshop Elements 7.0; *Cardstock:* Making Memories and Wausau Paper; *Leather paper:* Sizzix, Ellison; *Rub-ons and epoxy elements:* SEI; *Word stickers:* Fiskars Americas; *Watercolor pencils:* Close To My Heart; *Fonts:* Calibri and LD Aloha (altered); *Adhesive:* Scrapbook Adhesives by 3L.

variation 3:

Digitally outline a font to create a title.

To create my title for this layout, I "outlined" a font using my computer and printed it onto cardstock along with my journaling. I then colored the letters of the title using watercolor pencils to create a graduated color effect that resembled the different colors of the red rocks in my photos. I love how the effect turned out!

How-To: Outline a font.

❶ Create a new document in Photoshop Elements.

❷ Select the Horizontal Type Tool and select the desired font and font size in the options bar near the top of the screen. Click on your document and type your title; select the Move Tool and position your title in the desired location.

❸ Make sure the Move Tool is still selected. In the Layer drop-down menu, select Simplify Layer.

❹ Hold down the Ctrl key and click on your title layer in the Layers Palette; from the Layer drop-down menu, select New, and then select Layer and click OK.

❺ From the Edit drop-down menu, select Stroke (Outline) Selection. In the stroke box, select your desired width (I chose 2 pixels) and select the color of your line (click OK) and click OK.

❻ Press Ctrl+D to deselect, and then hide the original title layer by clicking on the eyeball icon next to the title layer thumbnail in the Layers Palette so it is no longer visible.

❼ Print the outlined title onto cardstock, and color it in with pencils. **ck**

handmade touches using *custom shapes*

It's easy to add custom shaped elements to your pages with the Custom Shape Tool in Photoshop Elements. Shaped die-cut papers, journaling spots and layered embellishments are all the rage lately, and you can create your own at home using your computer and printer. Check out the following pages and be inspired to create your own accents. There's no better way to save time and money!

use your *computer* to create shaped elements

MY DAUGHTER ELLIE is quite the chatterbox. She constantly talks, asks questions and shares loving sentiments that make our whole family smile. To highlight some of the phrases she repeats often, I selected a talk-bubble shape in Photoshop Elements and printed multiple sizes onto white cardstock. Repeating the shape provides a quick way to add inexpensive, instant impact to any page.

She Says *by Lori Anderson.* **Supplies** *Software:* Adobe Photoshop Elements 7.0; *Cardstock:* Bazzill Basics Paper (white) and SEI (blue); *Patterned paper and rub-on:* Heidi Grace Designs and Fiskars Americas; *Chipboard:* Anna Griffin (letters) and Fiskars Americas (label); *Ribbon, circle lips accent and pen:* American Crafts; *Clip:* KI Memories; *Font:* Tahoma; *Adhesive:* Mono Adhesive, Tombow; Scrapbook Adhesives by 3L; Foam Squares, Therm O Web.

BY LORI ANDERSON

the technique

You can have fun with this technique traditionally and digitally! Here's how:

Traditional technique:

1. Select a shaped stencil.
2. Trace around the stencil with a pencil on the reverse side of your paper.
3. With scissors or a craft knife, trim around the shape and place the shape on your layout.

Digital technique using Photoshop Elements:

1. Create a new document in Photoshop Elements and select the Custom Shape Tool (grouped behind the Rectangle Tool).
2. Click and drag the custom shape onto the new document, holding down the Shift key while you drag to keep the shape proportionate.
3. Print the document on the reverse side of your paper, trim the shape with scissors and place the cutout element on your layout.

variation 1:

Use a custom shape as a background element.

For my son Josh's tenth birthday, I created a layout listing 10 things I love about him. Josh is our easygoing, carefree child, so I selected a custom wave shape for the background of my layout to give the pages the same relaxed feel. To create the shape, I created a new 12″ x 12″ document in Photoshop Elements and drew my custom shape to span the width of the page. Once the shape was drawn, I printed it on the reverse side of a coordinating patterned paper and added it to my layout. This technique is cool and quick!

10 Things I Love about You by Lori Anderson. **Supplies** *Software:* Adobe Photoshop Elements 7.0; *Cardstock:* Bazzill Basics Paper (white), Die Cuts With a View (scallop) and Stampin' Up! (blue); *Patterned paper:* K&Company; *Chipboard:* American Crafts (heart), Maya Road (numbers) and Sandylion (circle elements); *Rub-ons:* American Crafts ("totally awesome" and circles) and Doodlebug Design (numbers); *Label:* FontWerks; *Paint:* Making Memories; *Buttons:* BasicGrey; *Corner-rounder punch:* Marvy Uchida; *Font:* Century Gothic; *Adhesive:* Mono Adhesive, Tombow; Scrapbook Adhesives by 3L; Foam Squares, Therm O Web; *Other:* Thread.

variation 2:

Create and layer handmade embellishments of any size.

When you make your own embellishments, you can use any patterned paper and create a size perfect for your layout. Cindy Tobey selected three different snowflake shapes and sizes to make the adorable patterned-paper snowflakes on her "So Much Snow" layout. To give the snowflakes a shiny finish, Cindy coated them with glossy paint for a touch of shine.

So Much Snow *by Cindy Tobey.* **Supplies** *Software:* Adobe Photoshop Elements 6.0; *Cardstock:* Bazzill Basics Paper; *Patterned paper:* Cosmo Cricket (cream), Doodlebug Design (white flocked), Fancy Pants Designs (gray and stripe), Karen Foster Design (graph), Luxe Designs (red stripe), Making Memories (red dot) and My Mind's Eye (blue dot); *Epoxy dots:* Cloud 9 Design, Fiskars Americas; *Pebble:* Prima; *Letter stickers:* American Crafts (white felt) and Doodlebug Design (white); *Snowflakes:* Making Memories (white) and Queen & Co. (blue); *Snowflake charm and paint:* Making Memories; *Ticket:* Jenni Bowlin Studio; *Border punch:* Martha Stewart Crafts; *Font:* Calibri; *Adhesive:* 3M, Glue Dots International and Tombow; *Other:* String and thread.

variation 3:

Make your own custom die-cut patterned paper.

Noel Culbertson used a custom frame shape to create one-of-a-kind die-cut patterned paper. She simply layered two frame shapes and printed them on the reverse side of her yellow patterned paper. After trimming the excess paper, Noel had a cool custom shape for her page.

Sick Day *by Noel Culbertson.* **Supplies** *Software:* Adobe Photoshop Elements 6.0; *Cardstock:* Bazzill Basics Paper; *Patterned paper:* American Crafts (yellow), Little Yellow Bicycle (gray) and Pinecone Press (yellow graphic); *Letter stickers:* American Crafts; *Chipboard circles:* Prima; *Grid sheet:* Glitz Design; *Tag:* Creative Imaginations; *Font:* Helvetica; *Adhesive:* Scotch ATG, 3M; Stampin' Up!. **ck**

15-minute layout

BY BRITTANY BEATTIE

MANY OF YOUR birthday layouts are filled with pictures of gifts, balloons, and cake. But birthdays provide a fabulous opportunity to reflect on the lives of your children as well. Find a favorite photograph from the party, and use it to express your deeper feelings about your child. It will only take 15 minutes! Then every year, let birthdays serve as a reminder to express your love for your child directly on a scrapbook page.

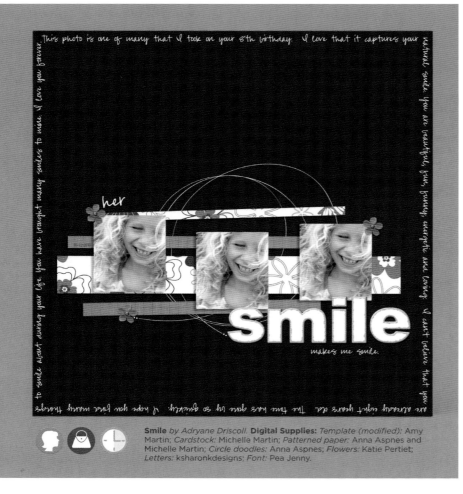

Smile *by Adryane Driscoll.* **Digital Supplies:** *Template (modified):* Amy Martin; *Cardstock:* Michelle Martin; *Patterned paper:* Anna Aspnes and Michelle Martin; *Circle doodles:* Anna Aspnes; *Flowers:* Katie Pertiet; *Letters:* ksharonkdesigns; *Font:* Pea Jenny.

EASY-TO-FOLLOW LAYOUT INSTRUCTIONS*

1. Use one sheet of 12″ x 12″ cardstock for background.
2. Use opaque pen to draw swirls on layout as shown.
3. Cut a 7½″ x ¼″ strip and a 10¼″ x 1¼″ strip from patterned paper.
4. Cut an 8½″ x ⅜″ strip and a 7″ x ½″ strip from patterned paper.
5. Crop three photos to 2⅛″ x 2⅜″.
6. Adhere strips and photos to layout as shown.
7. Adhere three flowers to page.
8. Add letter stickers below photos.
9. Use opaque pen to complete title and to journal around page edges.

* The layout was originally created digitally, but these instructions will help you re-create it with traditional scrapbooking supplies.

FUN TWISTS ON SCRAPBOOKING BIRTHDAY PHOTOS

Use your birthday photos to create more than just birthday layouts. Try these ideas as well:

- Create a layout recording the height, weight, and characteristics of your child so you can track the growth from year to year. Have your child write his or her signature on each layout.

- Keep track of childhood friends by creating a layout each birthday with photos and names of each friend. If a friend couldn't attend the party, use a photo from another day to make sure all friends are included on the layout. Write about favorite activities they enjoy together. **ck**

8 inspiring challenges

Try a
fresh idea for
your pages!

by Elizabeth
Kartchner

One of the best things about being human is the
continual chance for improvement. I'm such a work in
progress, and I'm constantly looking for ways to be a better cook,
a better wife, a better mom—a better everything! When I reach beyond my
comfort zone and try something new, I am able to learn.

So you can imagine how excited I was to be able to write a book full of scrapbooking
challenges. My own skills grew in the process of creating the projects for the book,
and I can't wait to share them with you! Start stretching yourself today with eight fun
challenges inspired by the chapters in my book, *52 More Scrapbooking Challenges*.

Cute & Silly Monsters by Elizabeth Kartchner. **Supplies** Patterned paper: Crate Paper; Letter stickers: American Crafts (black) and Making Memories (white); Buttons: Sassafras; Brads and pen: American Crafts; Other: Tags and thread.

stash challenge:
feature brads on your layout in an innovative way

We've all got certain go-to supplies that we tend to collect in abundance. Brads are definitely one of my stash stars, and since I'm always looking to find new uses for supplies, I jumped at this challenge. My solution is a cinch to create and makes a big impact: **cluster brads in a variety of colors and sizes** on a punched cardstock shape for a really cool page accent. Feel free to experiment with brads, eyelets or buttons to whip up easy and effective embellishments.

MAY 28 09

FIRST DAY BRACES FREE

Julie *by Amanda Johnson.* **Supplies** *Patterned paper:* Hambly Screen Prints; *Spray ink:* Maya Road; *Label maker:* Dymo; *Other:* Buttons, masking tape, stencils and thread.

HOW-TO: CREATE A TITLE WITH STENCILS AND SPRAY INK.

❶ Arrange letter stencils as desired on transparency.

❷ Spritz stencils and transparency with spray ink; remove stencils when the spray ink is dry.

design challenge:
allow for white space using a patterned background

White space, as you know, isn't necessarily white. The term is actually another way of referring to negative space or the space surrounding the elements on your design. The eye requires a resting spot, so when you're creating your layout, resist the urge to cover every inch of your page—in fact, why not experiment with a large, open space?

When using a lot of white space, keep the blank area interesting. Amanda Johnson chose a **patterned background with only two tones and a small, simple pattern** so that it wouldn't be too overwhelming.

Crank It Up by Beth Opel.
Supplies *Cardstock:* Bazzill Basics Paper; *Patterned paper:* Die Cuts With a View; *Rhinestones:* Doodlebug Design; *Eyelets:* Making Memories; *Ribbon:* American Crafts; *Fonts:* Arial (journaling), CAC One Seventy ("Mmm Bop"), CBX Street (title), Cheapskate Fill ("Bawitaba"), CK Chemistry ("We Didn't Start the Fire"), CK Puppy Love ("Hollaback Girl"), Desyrel ("New York, New York"), Fanciful ("Don't Go Breakin' My Heart"), Futura MdCn BT ("School's Out"), Glamour Girl ("Glamorous"), Ludovicos ("Black Dog"), Rockwell Condensed ("Glory Days") and Tagettes ("Hallelujah Chorus"); *Adhesive:* Scotch Double-Sided Tape, 3M; Zip Dry Paper Glue, Beacon Adhesives.

inspiration challenge: find a layout concept from a billboard

Beth Opel saw the title treatment for her "Crank It Up" layout on a highway billboard and quickly sketched it. (Another idea is to snap a picture with your camera phone.) She drew her entire **theme inspiration from the ad slogan.** Since she didn't have photos for the theme, she set up a camera and a backdrop and took the photos at home. Don't be afraid to set up your own photo shoot if you've got a cool layout idea but no photos.

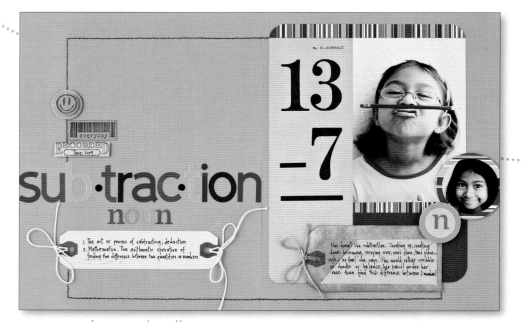

Sub•trac•tion by Mou Saha.
Supplies *Cardstock:* Die Cuts With a View; *Patterned paper:* Piggy Tales; *Letter stickers:* Luxe Designs (large) and Piggy Tales (small); *Stamps:* Autumn Leaves ("everyday" and "recorded") and Rubber Stampede, Delta Creative (smiley face); *Ink:* Tsukineko; *Tags:* Rusty Pickle; *Vintage flash card:* Cocoa Daisy; *Embroidery floss:* DMC; *Punches:* EK Success (corner rounder) and Marvy Uchida (circle); *Pen:* American Crafts; *Adhesive:* Scotch, 3M.

journaling challenge: base a layout on a definition

For a creative title and journaling approach, **choose a word and center your layout around its meaning.** Mou Saha used the word "subtraction" (complete with the part of speech and meaning) for her title. To further strengthen the theme, she used a vintage subtraction flash card in place of a patterned paper block. How will you let this journaling challenge define your next page?

That's a lot of candles!

11.26.08

Papa turned 80 years young on the 26th! He celebrated with friends and family at his surprise party. He seemed surprised, but we later found out that he thought something was up because of Grandma's excessive cleaning that week, and of course, we all found that hilarious!

11.26.08 *by Cindy Tobey.* **Supplies** *Cardstock:* Bazzill Basics Paper; *Patterned paper, chipboard, felt, ribbon and rub-ons:* Fancy Pants Designs; *Stickers:* Fancy Pants Designs (letters and scallop border) and Making Memories (candle); *Paint:* Making Memories; *Ink:* Clearsnap; *Font:* Century; *Adhesive:* Dot Roller, Tombow; Glue Dots International; Mounting Tape, 3M; *Other:* String and thread.

numeral challenge:
use a date as your page title

Cindy Tobey wanted to choose a significant date, and when she came across these photos of her father-in-law's 80th birthday party, she knew they were perfect for this challenge! **Using a date as the title for any birthday or milestone layout** is a great option and a way to change things up from your typical page titles.

HOW-TO: ADD SOME EDGE TO YOUR PAGES.

Part of the charm of Cindy's layout is her variety of edge treatments. Consider one of these options:

- **Fringe.** Cindy tore her fringed paper out of a ready-made notebook, but you could use a notebook border punch for the same effect.

- **Inking.** Inking the outer edges of the layout with multiple colors from elements on the layout relates the white background with the rest of the design.

- **Stitching.** A small, blue-thread border around the photo block helps convey a finished look.

- **Decorative-edge scissors.** Scallops and zigzags create more interest than a straight edge.

- **Bracket shape.** Cindy traced the outline of a chipboard shape onto the diamond paper and cut out the shape to draw attention to the journaling.

American Gothic *by Kelly Purkey.* **Supplies** *Cardstock and rub-ons:* American Crafts; *Patterned paper:* Crate Paper; *Stickers:* American Crafts (glitter letters) and Scenic Route (scallop border); *Stamps:* Hero Arts; *Ink:* StazOn, Tsukineko; *Rhinestones:* Queen & Co.; *Punches and adhesive:* Fiskars Americas.

photography challenge:
take pictures of something from several different angles

Admit it: you have plenty of vacation photos in front of statues and landmarks sporting a similar orientation—straight on from the front, perhaps with a waving friend or family member posed beside it. No matter what you're photographing, take a cue from Kelly Purkey and try **shooting from several new angles for a fresh viewpoint.** When you combine photos from multiple angles on a layout, it adds incredible context and meaning.

4 UNIQUE ANGLES TO TRY

Kelly Purkey's layout uses four 4" x 6" photos taken of the same statue. Normally, four shots of the same subject could look boring, but since she took her photographs from different angles, her page is full of energy. Try these ideas to make your own pictures livelier:

- Get behind the subject and see the area from its point of view.

- Crouch down and shoot upward for a great perspective.

- Use a zoom lens to get in nice and tight for great detail shots.

- Remember to take a photo from afar to capture the subject's environment and give your photo context.

Outside *by Shelley Aldrich.* **Supplies** *Cardstock:* EK Success; *Patterned paper:* 7gypsies (words), Pink Paislee (grid), Sassafras (green) and Scenic Route (blue); *Transparency:* Hambly Screen Prints; *Tiles:* Fragments, Tim Holtz; *Ink:* VersaMagic, Tsukineko; *Paint:* Liquitex; *Letters:* Die Cuts With a View and Scenic Route; *Stamp:* Stampendous!; *Punch:* Fiskars Americas; *Colored pencils:* Prismacolor, Newell Rubbermaid; *Pen:* Zig Writer, EK Success; *Adhesive:* Glossy Accents, Ranger Industries; Zots, Therm O Web.

technique challenge:
incorporate a mosaic technique on your page

Shelley Aldrich's entire layout is a loose **interpretation of a mosaic**, with her various elements working together to create a unified whole. Unlike a traditional mosaic, though, she allowed her punched shapes, photographs and accents to overlap. Try using a variety of mosaic "pieces" laid down in a deliberate manner on your next scrapbook page.

HOW-TO: CREATE CUSTOM TILE EMBELLISHMENTS WITH PUNCHES AND INK.

For maximum versatility, Shelley used clear acrylic tiles that could be glued on top of any paper or material. This technique has thousands of possibilities and takes just a minute to create. Here's how:

❶ Select your patterned paper and punch out the shape several times. Ink the edges of the punched shapes.

❷ Glue the inked shapes onto another piece of the same patterned paper.

❸ Adhere a clear acrylic tile on top of your layered papers.

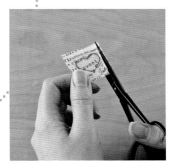

❹ Let dry and trim excess with scissors.

household challenge:
use a fortune from a cookie or a candy wrapper on a layout

Now, I'm not particularly superstitious, but I have occasionally opened a fortune cookie or a piece of candy to find a message that really hit home with me. Well, one day it hit me: why not incorporate a fortune as a ready-made theme for a page? I used my **candy-wrapper message as a flower center.**

Adore by Elizabeth Kartchner. **Supplies** *Cardstock, tissue paper, circle accent and chipboard:* American Crafts; *Patterned paper, brads and word stickers:* K&Company; *Spray ink and stencil:* Tattered Angels; *Paper flowers:* Evalicious.Etsy.com; *Tickets:* Tim Holtz for Advantus; *Other:* Adhesive, candy wrapper, buttons, sequins, trim, thread and decorative-edge scissors.

FIND MORE INSPIRATION IN *52 MORE SCRAPBOOKING CHALLENGES*!

Kick your creativity into high gear and learn new scrapbooking tricks in my book, *52 More Scrapbooking Challenges*. These challenges will inspire you with fun, imaginative ways to help you preserve your memories in style, including:

- Maximizing less-than-perfect photos
- Gaining inspiration from the world around you
- Including children's artwork on your layouts
- Sewing on your pages
- Creating pages in a limited amount of time
- Using your supply stash creatively
- Implementing new techniques and more!

With useful tips and easy step-by-step techniques throughout the book (as well as eight bonus quizzes and a worksheet to help you kick start your own scrapbooking), you'll find yourself returning to this exciting book again and again for top-notch inspiration. Order your copy today at *shopscrapandpapercorner.com*. **ck**

ILLUSTRATION BY CELESTE ROCKWOOD-JONES; FLOWER ACCENTS BY NICOLE LARUE

Fabulous
flower techniques

•

*Make your pages bloom
with colorful handmade flowers.*
by
JENNIFER McGUIRE

SPRING is such a beautiful season—gorgeous flowers are blooming everywhere and filling our world with happiness. I find this time of year so inspiring: the colors alone are enough to kick my imagination into high gear. Rich indigo irises, vibrant white daisies, darling yellow daffodils—all have me reaching for my inks and cardstock. And then there are the textures! From velvety rose petals to eye-catching sunflower centers, I can't help but want to touch and feel every flower in my yard. This, of course, compels me to search out different textures to use on my pages. It didn't take much searching to make me realize that there's no better way to add the colors and textures of spring to my pages than by creating handmade flower accents. Today, I'd like to share with you a garden of ideas for creating flowers to help your pages bloom, too!

Her by Maggie Holmes. **Supplies:** *Cardstock:* Bazzill Basics Paper; *Patterned paper:* Making Memories and Studio Calico; *Stickers:* Studio Calico; *Buttons:* Jenni Bowlin Studio and Making Memories; *Rhinestones and trim:* K&Company; *Fabric:* Heather Bailey; *Corrugated letters:* Jillibean Soup; *Pen:* EK Success; *Adhesive:* Glue Arts; *Other:* Fabric.

Maggie Holmes created a whimsical floral banner to bring attention to several adorable photos of her daughter. To create each flower, Maggie simply layered a variety of fabrics, lace, and tulle. And since fabric flattens nicely, these flowers add lots of texture with little bulk.

How-To: *Create Fabric Layered Flowers*

1 Cut fabric, tulle, and lace into circles of varying sizes.

2 Make a little fold in one piece of fabric and pinch.

3 Make another fold in the center in the opposite direction and pinch.

4 Staple folds in place at the center. Repeat with lace and tulle, layering for a fabulous flower.

10 candles

BL★OW

12	1	22	14	5
17	23	7	16	10
6	21	★	2	18
15	9	24	13	4
3	11	19	8	2

Ten years old, one whole decade! To celebrate, you selected cupcakes. No more cutesy, character birthday cakes for you. You are growing up so incredibly fast! Love you sweet girl!

10 Candles *by Cindy Tobey.* **Supplies:** *Cardstock:* Bazzill Basics Paper and Doodlebug Design; *Patterned paper:* BasicGrey, Colorbök, and Sassafras; *Journal tag:* Adornit-Carolee's Creations; *Bingo card:* Jenni Bowlin Studio; *Chipboard:* American Crafts; *Markers:* Stampin' Up!; *Ribbon:* Karen Foster Design; *Gems, glitter, and stickers:* Doodlebug Design; *Punches:* EK Success and Fiskars Americas; *Adhesive:* Glue Dots International, Scrapbook Adhesives by 3L, Tombow, USArtQuest, and Zip Dry; *Font:* CK Kelly; *Other:* Candles, cupcake liners, and twine.

Could there be anything more delicious than using baking supplies on a scrapbook page? Check out Cindy Tobey's flowers created from cupcake liners. These fun flowers add a splash of color and sparkle while also being a subtle memento of the cupcakes her family shared for her daughter's birthday. What other mementos could you make into flowers?

How-To: *Create Cupcake-Liner Flowers*

1 Flatten a cupcake liner with hand; cut liner into spiral using scissors.

2 Color along outside edge of spiral using marker.

3 Punch 2″ circle from cardstock. Adhere cupcake liner spiral to cardstock circle starting at outside. Gather liner as you go, creating ruffles.

4 Add liquid glue to top edge of rosette. Sprinkle with glitter.

Scallop Border Flower *by Jennifer McGuire.* **Supplies:** *Cardstock:* American Crafts; *Patterned paper:* Making Memories; *Button:* BasicGrey; *Punches:* EK Success and Stampin' Up!; *Adhesive:* Ranger Industries and Tombow; *Other:* String.

Border punches are an easy way to add eye-catching accents to your page. But did you know they can also be used to create dimensional flowers? This is a simple and economical way to add a flower to your layout while making the most of your leftover paper.

How-To: *Create Scallop Border Flowers*

1 Create a 12" strip, scallop one edge. Accordion-fold strip.

2 Adhere one end of folded strip to the other to make ring.

3 Press the ring down to create a flower. Apply liquid glue, hold in place until dry. Add button.

Alphabet Flower *by Jennifer McGuire.* **Supplies:** *Patterned paper:* Hambly Screen Prints; *Stamps:* Hero Arts; *Button:* Buttons Galore; *Ink:* Ranger Industries; *Other:* String.

Stamps are perfect for making flowers. Here, I repeatedly stamped an "O" image to create a daisy.

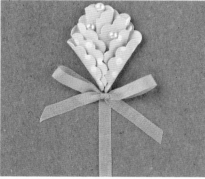

Scallop Flower *by Jennifer McGuire.* **Supplies:** *Patterned paper:* Bo-Bunny Press; *Punch:* Fiskars Americas; *Pearls:* Hero Arts; *Adhesive:* Glue Dots International; *Other:* Silk ribbon.

Paper flowers seem to come alive when you layer them for dimension. Try folding several scallop circles together to create a simple blossom.

Fabric Flower *by Jennifer McGuire.* **Supplies:** *Fabric:* Heather Bailey; *Button:* American Crafts; *Die:* Stampin' Up!; *Die-cutting machine:* Ellison; *Other:* String and needle.

Go for a whimsical look by layering frayed, fabric die-cut flowers.

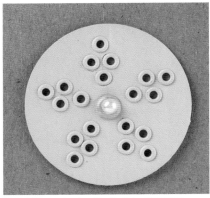

Eyelet Flower *by Jennifer McGuire.* **Supplies:** *Cardstock and eyelets:* American Crafts; *Pearl:* Hero Arts; *Punch:* EK Success.

You can create flowers from just about any small embellishment: gems, pearls, buttons, or eyelets.

Looped Flower *by Jennifer McGuire.* **Supplies:** *Patterned paper:* SEI; *Ribbon:* Maya Road; *Button:* BasicGrey; *Other:* String and needle.

Creating a flower with loopy ribbon petals is a great way to use up scraps. Just create three ribbon loops and stitch them together.

Punched Flower *by Jennifer McGuire.* **Supplies:** *Patterned paper:* Bo-Bunny Press and Prima; *Pearls:* Hero Arts; *Adhesive and punches:* EK Success.

Use a circle punch to cut ovals and arrange them in layers for a flower that'll burst into bloom on your page.

Tissue Paper Flower *by Jennifer McGuire.* **Supplies:** *Pearls:* Hero Arts; *Ink and stapler:* Advantus; *Other:* Tissue Paper.

When I was little, I used to make huge carnival flowers from tissue paper. I thought it would be fun to make a smaller version for a scrapbook page. If you can't find tissue paper in the color you need, just ink it first.

How-To: *Create Tissue Paper Flowers*

1 Cut 4-5 squares of tissue paper, all the same size. Rub with ink for desired color.

2 Accordion-fold all layers together; staple at center.

3 Fan edges and separate layers, fluffing to add dimension. **ck**

finishing *trims*

I remember visiting my grandma when I was a little girl. I would spend hours sorting through her sewing goodies. She always had the most gorgeous decorative trims—I loved the colors and textures. Now that I'm grown up, I love to use the same trims on my pages. Here are some ideas.

try these ribbon and *trim* looks

ADD trim to the edges of a photo mat for a decorative frame.

JenniferMcGuireInk.com *by Jennifer McGuire.* **Supplies** *Decorative trims:* Doodlebug Design (green, brown and blue) and Making Memories (yellow and red); *Cardstock:* Bazzill Basics Paper; *Patterned paper:* Bo-Bunny Press; *Buttons:* Hero Arts; *Fonts:* Arial Narrow and CK Higgins Handprint; *Adhesive:* Tombow; *Other:* Thread.

BY JENNIFER McGUIRE

ACCENT trims with pearls, stitching or other embellishments.

Summer Memories by Jennifer McGuire. **Supplies** *Decorative trim:* Making Memories (pink and green); *Patterned paper:* Making Memories; *Stamp and pearls:* Hero Arts; *Rub-on:* Melissa Frances; *Ink:* Memories, Stewart Superior Corporation; *Adhesive:* EK Success (dimensional) and Scrapbook Adhesives by 3L; *Other:* String and wire.

CREATE a pocket with trims and sewing. Simply layer trims over your background, and then secure them in place by sewing them on three edges.

Photos for Grandma by Jennifer McGuire. **Supplies** *Decorative trims:* Anna Griffin, Making Memories and Stampin' Up!; *Buttons:* Autumn Leaves; *Corner-rounder punch:* Fiskars Americas; *Other:* String and thread.

ADD rub-ons onto trims. For this design, I used rub-on phrases.

It's Time to Celebrate by Jennifer McGuire. **Supplies** *Decorative trim:* K&Company; *Cardstock:* Bazzill Basics Paper; *Patterned paper:* Making Memories; *Rub-ons:* Stampin' Up!; *Stamps and ink:* Hero Arts; *Adhesive:* EK Success (dimensional) and Dot 'n' Roller, Kokuyo; *Other:* String.

GATHER or pleat trim and stitch it down the center for a whole new look.

Kay by Jennifer McGuire. **Supplies** *Decorative trim:* Making Memories; *Cardstock:* Prism Papers; *Patterned paper:* Imaginisce; *Die cut:* Stampin' Up!; *Letter stamps:* Close To My Heart; *Embellishment:* October Afternoon; *Adhesive:* Dot 'n' Roller, Kokuyo; *Other:* Thread.

LINE up trims to create a decorative background.

Kindred Spirits by Jennifer McGuire. **Supplies** Decorative trims: 7gypsies (floral), Anna Griffin (white and green) and Making Memories; Cardstock: Bazzill Basics Paper; Stamp: Hero Arts; Heart brads: Doodlebug Design; Adhesive: Wonder Tape, Suze Weinberg; Other: Black pen and thread.

COVER punched shapes with trims, and then use scissors to cut away the trims hanging over the edges.

I Love You! by Jennifer McGuire. **Supplies** Decorative trims: Anna Griffin, K&Company and Making Memories; Punch: Fiskars Americas; Rub-on: Pebbles Inc.; Note card: Hero Arts; Adhesive: Dot 'n' Roller, Kokuyo.

Try it yourself!

Want to check out some decorative trims? Consider:

FELT TRIMS FLOWER PATCH
Making Memories
MakingMemories.com

FRENCH RIBBON
7gypsies
SevenGypsies.com

CAROLINA COLLECTION
Anna Griffin
AnnaGriffin.com

DESIGNER RIC-RAC COLLECTION
Close To My Heart
CloseToMyHeart.com **ck**

fabric *frenzy*

While I've always wanted to be good at sewing, I've never taken the time to learn. That doesn't mean I don't buy fabric, however! Instead, I've found great ways to use it with my scrapbooking. Fabric adds such a homemade feel to my pages, and it introduces fun texture without any bulk.

7 fabulous *textured* **looks**

ADHERE fabric to cardstock and cut it with a die-cutting machine to create fabric shapes. Scratch the edges of the shapes for a fun, frayed look.

Jana *by Jennifer McGuire.* **Supplies** *Fabric:* Amy Butler, *www.etsy.com*; *Felt letters:* Making Memories; *Die-cutting machine:* Cuttlebug, Provo Craft; *Font:* VIP, *www.myfonts.com*; *Adhesive:* Mod Podge, Plaid Enterprises; *Other:* Thread and string.

BY JENNIFER McGUIRE

USE iron-on transfer paper to add a personal message to a fabric tag.

Hoot *by Jennifer McGuire.* **Supplies** *Fabric tag:* K&Company; *Stamp:* Hero Arts; *Ink:* Close To My Heart; *T-shirt transfer paper:* Office Depot; *Circle punch:* EK Success; *Foam dots:* 3-D Dots, EK Success; *Colored pencils:* Prismacolor, Newell Rubbermaid; *Fonts:* Arial Narrow and Cocktail Shaker, *myfonts.com*; *Other:* Googly eyes and twine.

COVER chipboard with fabric and scratch the edges to fray them.

Star *by Jennifer McGuire.* **Supplies** *Fabric:* Amy Butler, *etsy.com* (dot) and Jo-Ann Stores (corduroy); *Chipboard star:* Bo-Bunny Press; *Stamp and ink:* Stampin' Up!; *Other:* String and tag.

CREATE your own ribbon from fabric. To tear fabric perfectly straight, cut a 1" notch in the edge of the fabric and tear.

Thanks *by Jennifer McGuire.* **Supplies** *Fabric:* Amy Butler, *etsy.com* (stripe), Hobby Lobby (sheer dot) and vintage (orange); *Decorative trim:* Doodlebug Design; *Flower and button:* Hero Arts; *Rub-on:* Melissa Frances; *Silk ribbon:* Creative Impressions.

COVER a tag with liquid adhesive (such as Mod Podge) and add your fabric. Run it through an embossing machine to add an embossed design. I added a dot pattern, then covered the raised dots with ink to help them stand out.

Blessed *by Jennifer McGuire.* **Supplies** *Fabric-covered tags:* papermachinations.etsy.com; *Embossing tool:* Cuttlebug, Provo Craft; *Distress ink and tool:* Tim Holtz, Ranger Industries; *Felt word:* Creative Café, Creative Imaginations; *Other:* Ribbon and twine.

STAMP directly onto fabric to transform solid colors into patterns.

Hi *by Jennifer McGuire.* **Supplies** *Fabric:* Hobby Lobby; *Stamps and gems:* Hero Arts; *Ink:* ColorBox Fluid Chalk, Clearsnap; *Die cut, felt stickers and ribbon:* Making Memories.

COVER a scrapbook organizer with fabric using Mod Podge.

Paper Holder *by Jennifer McGuire.* **Supplies** *Fabric:* Hobby Lobby; *Paper holder:* Cropper Hopper; *Clear tag:* Hero Arts; *Font:* Dreambog, www.myfonts.com; *Adhesive:* Mod Podge, Plaid Enterprises.

Try it yourself!

Want to check out some fabric? Try these:

HOBBY LOBBY,
www.hobbylobby.com

JO-ANN STORES,
www.joanns.com

VARIOUS SHOPS,
INCLUDING AMY BUTLER,
www.etsy.com

K&COMPANY,
www.kandcompany.com

attached to *staples*

Staples? Yes, staples! Staples are an unexpected way to add fun to your page. Not only can they be used to hold things in place, you can use them as part of your design. Here are some ideas to get you started with staples!

Add easy *emphasis* with a little metal

CREATE fun border designs with staples. They can even look like blades of grass!

Family *by Jennifer McGuire.* **Supplies** *Stapler, staples and acrylic stamp:* Close To My Heart; *Patterned paper:* Cloud 9 Design, Fiskars (green); My Mind's Eye (brown and gold) and Making Memories (all others); *Chipboard letters:* American Crafts; *Embroidered flower:* Fancy Pants Designs; *Buttons:* Autumn Leaves; *Corner rounder:* Fiskars; *Font:* Splendid 66, Internet; *Other:* Thread.

BY JENNIFER McGUIRE

ADD quick emphasis with staples as photo corners.

You by Jennifer McGuire. **Supplies** Patterned paper: Bo-Bunny Press; Stamp: Autumn Leaves; Staples and stapler: Office Depot; Rub-ons: BasicGrey; Ink: Close To My Heart.

STAPLE upside down for a distinctive look.

Big Sis by Jennifer McGuire. **Supplies** Staples: Making Memories; Stapler: Office Depot; Patterned paper: Anna Griffin (orange) and Scenic Route (blue and yellow); Die cuts: Spellbinders; Letters: Creative Café, Creative Imaginations; Heart punch: EK Success; Other: Ribbon and vintage text paper.

HANG a tag from a staple.

Sweet by Jennifer McGuire. **Supplies** White pen: Uni-Ball Signo, Newell Rubbermaid (distributed by Stampin' Up!); Patterned paper: Doodlebug Design and K&Company; Font: Dreambog, www. myfonts.com; Other: Thread.

USE STAPLES to hold ribbon in place.

Stuck with You by Jennifer McGuire. **Supplies** Staples: Making Memories; Stapler: Office Depot; Acetate quote: K&Company; Ribbon: Fancy Pants Designs; Sticker: Stampin' Up!; Photo corner: Heidi Swapp for Advantus; Button: Doodlebug Design.

INSTEAD of folding paper in half, staple two pieces of paper together to form a card.

Hugs *by Jennifer McGuire.* **Supplies** *Staples and stapler:* Close To My Heart; *Notebook paper:* Making Memories; *Felt shapes:* Fancy Pants Designs (heart) and Creative Café, Creative Imaginations ("hugs"); *Die-cut circle:* K&Company; *Pearls:* Hero Arts.

ATTACH acetate to anything—including paper and ribbons—with staples.

Happy Easter Jar *by Jennifer McGuire.* **Supplies** *Staples and stapler:* Close To My Heart; *Acetate:* Hambly Studios (tag) and Heidi Swapp for Advantus (butterfly); *Patterned paper:* Bo-Bunny Press (red) and *Creating Keepsakes* by Craftworks, Ltd. (other); *Ribbon:* C.M. Offray & Son; *Letter stickers:* Doodlebug Design; *Jar:* Prima.

try it yourself!

Want to check out some staples? Try these:

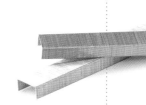

BO-BUNNY PRESS
www.bobunny.com

CLOSE TO MY HEART
www.closetomyheart.com

MAKING MEMORIES
www.makingmemories.com

SWINGLINE
www.swingline.com

a *touch* of glitter

Glitter seems to be an enduring trend in scrapbooking and card making. It never gets old! With new products on the market, glitter can be used without a mess just to add a bit of pizzazz to a project. Here are a few of the ideas I have for using glitter of all sorts.

Sprinkle on a little *sparkle* today!

GIVE photos a magical feel by adding a bit of glitter to the edges.

Very Soon by Jennifer McGuire. **Supplies** *Liquid glitter:* Stickles, Ranger Industries; *Patterned paper:* Anna Griffin (dot), Autumn Leaves (flourish), My Mind's Eye (floral), Doodlebug Design (stripe) and KI Memories (below journaling); *Letters:* Making Memories; *Buttons:* Autumn Leaves; *Pen:* American Crafts; *Other:* String and thread.

BY JENNIFER McGUIRE

COAT the back of a transparency sheet or clear tag with glitter. A sheet of double-sided adhesive works best.

I Miss You *by Jennifer McGuire.* **Supplies** *Glitter and chipboard letter:* Doodlebug Design; *Cardstock:* Bazzill Basics Paper; *Ribbon and chipboard heart:* Making Memories; *Transparent tag:* Autumn Leaves; *Double-sided adhesive sheet:* Gary Burlin; *Pen:* American Crafts; *Font:* 2Peas A Beautiful Mess, www.twopeasinabucket.com; *Other:* Staples.

ACCENTUATE stamped images or stickers by adding glitter to the design.

Let It Snow *by Jennifer McGuire.* **Supplies** *Liquid glitter:* Stickles, Ranger Industries; *Scalloped cardstock:* Bazzill Basics Paper; *Patterned paper:* My Mind's Eye; *Rubber stamps:* Hero Arts; *Chalk ink:* ColorBox, Clearsnap; *Other:* Staples.

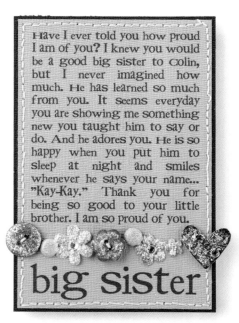

GIVE any accent a new look by covering the top with glitter. A whole row of glittered accents makes a great design!

Big Sister *by Jennifer McGuire.* **Supplies** *Glitter and gems:* Hero Arts; *Cardstock:* Bazzill Basics Paper; *Liquid glue:* Diamond Glaze, JudiKins; *Buttons:* SEI; *Chipboard heart:* Making Memories; *Flowers:* Prima Marketing; *Brads and sequins:* Doodlebug Design; *Font:* Frat Boy, downloaded from the Internet; *Other:* Thread.

ADD glitter to ribbon.

XOXO *by Jennifer McGuire.* **Supplies** *Glitter and tag:* Making Memories; *Ribbon and buttons:* Doodlebug Design; *Liquid glue:* Diamond Glaze, JudiKins; *Stamps:* My Sentiments Exactly; *Chalk ink:* ColorBox, Clearsnap; *Other:* Thread.

APPLY dots of glitter without the drying-time wait—use mini adhesive dots! Just apply the dots to the card and sprinkle glitter on.

Thanks by Jennifer McGuire. **Supplies** *Glitter:* Making Memories; *Note card and stamp:* Hero Arts; *Dimensional adhesive dots:* Glue Dots International; *Butterfly template:* Wings 'n' Things Element set, www.twopeasinabucket.com; *Punches:* Marvy Uchida; *Other:* Vintage text paper.

PUNCH OR DIE CUT shapes from double-sided adhesive sheets, then add glitter.

Audrey by Jennifer McGuire. **Supplies** *Glitter:* Doodlebug Design; *Notebook:* Target; *Double-sided adhesive sheet:* Gary Burlin; *Rub-ons:* BasicGrey; *Punches:* EK Success.

try it yourself!

Want to check out some cool glitter options? Try these, along with two great adhesives that work well for your glitter play:

DOODLEBUG DESIGN

MARTHA STEWART CRAFTS *for EK Success*

MAKING MEMORIES

DIAMOND GLAZE, JUDIKINS

SUPER TAPE, THERM O WEB

write it in *white*

I remember the first time I saw a white pen that could actually write vividly on colored paper. I instantly felt happy, and my mind starting spinning with ideas! Today, you can find white pens of all kinds. Here are some ideas for using them on your projects.

Fun tricks with *white* pens

TO GET A NICE, hand-drawn look, use a white pen to trace over a lightly stamped image.

Explore *by Jennifer McGuire.* **Supplies** *White pen:* Uni-Ball Signo, Newell Rubbermaid (distributed by Stampin' Up!); *Patterned paper and brads:* Autumn Leaves; *Stamps:* Hero Arts; *Rub-ons:* Kit of the Month, LisaBearnson.com; *Buttons:* American Crafts (large) and SEI (other); *Font:* Dreambog, *www. myfonts.com; Other:* Thread.

BY JENNIFER McGUIRE

For "perfect handwriting," print text in light gray and **TRACE** over it with a white pen.

Adore *by Jennifer McGuire.* **Supplies** *White pen:* Uni-Ball Signo, Newell Rubbermaid (distributed by Stampin' Up!); *Patterned paper:* Doodlebug Design and K&Company; *Font:* Dreambog, www.myfonts.com; *Other:* Thread.

CREATE a unique frame around or on a photo.

Original *by Jennifer McGuire.* **Supplies** *White pen:* Soufflé, Sakura; *Buttons:* American Crafts and Autumn Leaves; *Other:* String.

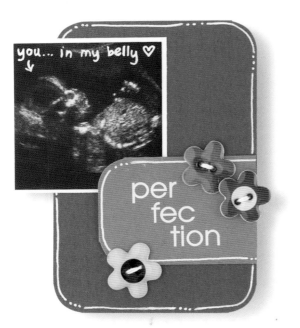

DEFINE or outline the edges of simple cardstock with white doodling.

Perfection *by Jennifer McGuire.* **Supplies** *White pen:* Uni-Ball Signo, Newell Rubbermaid (distributed by Stampin' Up!); *Rub-on:* Kit of the Month, LisaBearnson.com; *Buttons:* Making Memories; *Other:* String.

CREATE faux stitching with white pen. I made a zigzag and two straight "stitches."

Friendship Bird *by Jennifer McGuire.* **Supplies** *White pen:* Soufflé, Sakura; *Patterned paper:* Scenic Route; *Stamp:* Autumn Leaves; *Rub-on:* Déjà Views by The C-Thru Ruler Co.; *Colored pencils:* Prismacolor, Newell Rubbermaid; *Other:* Ribbon.

USE white pens on acetate or other clear surfaces for a unique and crafty look.

Our Family Home *by Jennifer McGuire.* **Supplies** *White pen:* Newell Rubbermaid, Newell Rubbermaid; *Clear album:* Pageframe Designs; *Rub-ons:* Déjà Views, by The C-Thru Ruler Co.; *Stamps:* Hero Arts; *Ink:* VersaMark, Tsukineko; *Gel embellishment:* Imagination Crafts and O'Scrap!; *Ribbon:* Strano Designs.

DOODLE on various embellishments, such as flowers, felt, buttons and more. Just be sure to give the ink time to dry.

Enjoy Card *by Jennifer McGuire.* **Supplies** *White pen:* Sharpie, Newell Rubbermaid; *Buttons and rub-on:* American Crafts; *Clear tag, gems, flower and note card:* Hero Arts; *Felt shape:* KI Memories; *Other:* String.

try it yourself!

Want to check out some white pens? Try these:

SOUFFLÉ ....
Sakura
www.gellyroll.com

UNI-BALL SIGNO ....
Newell Rubbermaid (distributed by
Stampin' Up!), www.stampinup.com

SHARPIE ....
Newell Rubbermaid
www.sharpie.com

GALAXY MARKERS ....
American Crafts
www.americancrafts.com

puttin' on the *glitz*

For years, stampers have enhanced their handmade cards and projects with pigment powders. They're wonderful for scrapbooking, too! Just use a brush to apply the ultra-fine, metallic-like powder to "sticky ink" like a glue pad, VersaMark from Tsukineko, or Perfect Medium from Ranger Industries. You can also shake the powder over liquid glue. Want to make sure the shine stays put? Spray the powder with a simple fixative.

7 fashionable looks with pigment powder

GIVE punched or die-cut shapes added shine by covering their surface with pigment powders.

Drummin' *by Jennifer McGuire.* **Supplies** *Pigment powder:* Perfect Pearls, Ranger Industries; *Ink:* Perfect Medium, Ranger Industries; *Patterned paper:* Bo-Bunny Press (dark-green dot), Doodlebug Design (blue dot) and Scenic Route (green dot); *Punches:* Fiskars; *Die-cut paper:* KI Memories; *Die-cut letters:* Cricut, Provo Craft; *Gems:* Prima.

drummin'

All Samuel wanted from Santa was a drum set. Once he got it, there was no stoppin' him! 2007

BY JENNIFER McGUIRE

RUB VersaMark over embossed images and add pigment powders to enhance.

Happy Birthday by Jennifer McGuire. **Supplies** *Pigment powder:* Perfect Pearls, Ranger Industries; *Ink:* VersaMark, Tsukineko; *Embossing template:* Cuttlebug, Provo Craft; *Rub-on:* American Crafts; *Gems:* Hero Arts; *Chipboard star:* Making Memories; *Staples:* Close To My Heart; *Other:* Thread.

BRUSH various colors of pigment powder over an image stamped with VersaMark.

Wedding Wishes by Jennifer McGuire. **Supplies** *Pigment powder:* Pearl Ex, Jacquard Products; *Ink:* VersaMark, Tsukineko; *Stamps:* Autumn Leaves (butterflies) and Stampin' Up! (greeting); *Patterned paper:* Autumn Leaves (blue) and Making Memories (scallop); *Ribbon:* C.M. Offray & Son; *Gems:* Hero Arts; *Punch:* EK Success.

COVER chipboard with liquid glue and shake pigment powders on top.

Kay by Jennifer McGuire. **Supplies** *Pigment powder:* Perfect Pearls, Ranger Industries; *Liquid glue:* Diamond Glaze, JudiKins; *Tag die cut:* Scenic Route; *Chipboard letters:* Fancy Pants Designs.

First, **STAMP** and apply pigment powders. Then, stamp over it with VersaMark, removing some powder.

Angelic by Jennifer McGuire. **Supplies** *Pigment powder:* Pearl Ex, Jacquard Products; *Ink:* VersaMark, Tsukineko; *Stamps and gems:* Hero Arts; *Patterned paper:* Making Memories; *Letter stickers:* BasicGrey; *Other:* Thread.

ADD sticker shapes and letters to your background. Apply pigment powders over stickers and background, then remove stickers (they act as masks).

I Love You Frame *by Jennifer McGuire.* **Supplies** *Pigment powder:* Pearl Ex, Jacquard Products; *Ink:* Perfect Medium, Ranger Industries; *Stickers:* Fiskars; *Frame:* Target.

ALTER cardstock blocks by rubbing with VersaMark ink and adding pigment powders, creating a background of shine.

Happy Anniversary *by Jennifer McGuire.* **Supplies** *Pigment powder:* Perfect Pearls, Ranger Industries; *Ink:* VersaMark, Tsukineko; *Rub-ons:* American Crafts (greeting) and BasicGrey (flourish); *Flower stickers:* K&Company; *Pearls:* Hero Arts.

try it yourself!

Want to discover pigment powders and inks that work well with them? Try these:

PEARL EX,
Jacquard Products
www.jacquardproducts.com/ products/pearlex

PERFECT MEDIUM,
Ranger Industries
www.rangerink.com

PERFECT PEARLS,
Ranger Industries
www.rangerink.com

VERSAMARK,
Tsukineko
www.tsukineko.com

a *clear* advantage

I've discovered something that's just as addictive as scrapbooking: stamping! I started years ago, but now I've fallen head over heels in love with stamping thanks to the recent popularity of clear stamps. They offer many great advantages over rubber stamps, with the biggest being the ease of perfect placement. I'll share several fun ideas for clear stamps that you can try today. Enjoy!

Get *creative* with clear stamps

Lego Boy *by Jennifer McGuire.*
Supplies *Clear stamps:* Autumn Leaves ("08" and "perfect play-date"), gel-à-tins ("Jan 2008"), Hot Off The Press (dot border and small alphabet), Sandylion ("create" and "play") and Hero Arts (all others); *Cardstock:* Bazzill Basics Paper; *Patterned paper:* Autumn Leaves; *Ink:* StazOn, Tsukineko (on buttons and tags) and Close To My Heart (all others); *Buttons and clear tags:* Hero Arts.

BY JENNIFER McGUIRE

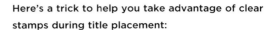

Here's a trick to help you take advantage of clear stamps during title placement:

1 Lay the clear release paper from the stamps over your layout exactly where you want the title to be. (You can achieve the placement correct without getting ink on the page until you're ready to stamp your image.)

2 Lay the letters on it exactly how you want to stamp your words—you'll be able to see through the letters and read the title.

3 Once all the letters are in place, press the acrylic mount onto them, transferring the letters to the stamping block.

You're now ready to stamp with the letters in the perfect position!

Want to position words of a clear stamp in a different way? Simply cut the image! You can then mount the words as desired, including in the original way. Notice how I cut the long greeting below into individual words.

I Care by Jennifer McGuire. **Supplies** *Clear stamps:* gel-à-tins (damask), Hero Arts (greeting) and Hot Off The Press (wings); *Patterned paper:* Bo-Bunny Press; *Ink:* ColorBox Fluid Chalk, Clearsnap; *Gems and buttons:* Hero Arts; *Other:* String and thread.

Want the look of colored embossing powder but don't have any?

1 First stamp an image with any colored ink, such as dye or chalk ink.

2 Stamp directly over the first image with a clear embossing ink, such as VersaMark by Tsukineko.

3 Finally, sprinkle on clear embossing powder and heat!

Adorable *by Jennifer McGuire.* **Supplies** *Clear stamps:* Close To My Heart; *Ink:* ColorBox Fluid Chalk, Clearsnap; VersaMark, Tsukineko; *Embossing powder:* Hero Arts; *Scallop chipboard:* Technique Tuesday; *Letter sticker:* American Crafts; *Rub-on:* K&Company; *Brad:* Stampin' Up!; *Ribbon:* C.M. Offray & Son.

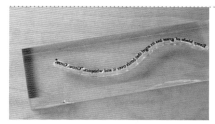

Friends *by Jennifer McGuire.* **Supplies** *Clear stamps:* Doodlebug Design; *Ink:* ColorBox Fluid Chalk, Clearsnap; *Rub-on:* Die Cuts With a View; *Pearls:* Hero Arts; *Embossing machine and die:* Cuttlebug, Provo Craft.

Looking for the perfect shape for a shadow stamp? Try this:

❶ Mount an image upside down (so the part you normally ink is positioned against the mount).

❷ Ink the back of the stamp with a light ink and stamp.

❸ Clean the back of the stamp and mount it correctly, then stamp with a dark ink. *Note:* The stamp should stick upside down if you cleaned it after your last use. If it isn't sticking, wash the stamp with soapy water and it will stick again.

Mount long, straight images at a curve to create unique results!

Grow, Grow *by Jennifer McGuire.* **Supplies** *Clear stamps:* Autumn Leaves (background), Close To My Heart (greeting) and Hot Off The Press (dots); *Patterned paper:* Autumn Leaves; *Ink:* Memories, Stewart Superior Corporation; *Flower:* Hero Arts; *Gem brad:* Stampin' Up!; *Other:* Thread.

try it yourself!

Want to check out some clear stamps? Try these:

AUTUMN LEAVES
www.creativityinc.com

CLOSE TO MY HEART
www.closetomyheart.com

HERO ARTS
www.heroarts.com

OCTOBER AFTERNOON
www.octoberafternoon.com

..... { *clearly* fun } .....

I just love using clear elements on my projects—they add unexpected interest! Here are some simple yet fun ideas to get you started with transparencies.

7 hip looks with transparencies

Run a transparency through an embossing machine for a lovely, unique look.

Heart *by Jennifer McGuire. Photos by Angela Talentino of Essenza Studio.* **Supplies** *Transparency note card and gemstones:* Hero Arts; *Embossing tools and die cuts:* Cuttlebug, Provo Craft; *Patterned paper:* Doodlebug Design (blue) and October Afternoon (aqua); *Letter stickers and button:* Doodlebug Design; *Punch (for making scallop border):* Stampin' Up!; *Clear stamp:* Hot Off The Press; *Ink:* VersaMark, Tsukineko.

BY JENNIFER McGUIRE

CUT personalized, transparent, die-cut shapes and define the edges with glitter.

Wonderful Memories by Jennifer McGuire. **Supplies** *Transparency:* Autumn Leaves; *Bird die cut (for tracing shape):* Jenni Bowlin Studio; *Glitter:* Stickles, Ranger Industries; *Stamps and hardware:* Close To My Heart; *Gem:* Hero Arts; *Other:* Ribbon and vintage text paper.

CREATE your own printed transparency with stamping.

A Note of Thanks by Jennifer McGuire. **Supplies** *Acetate*

ENHANCE printed transparencies by painting on the back.

Beauty by Jennifer McGuire. **Supplies** *Printed transparency:* Fancy Pants Designs; *Paint:* Paint Dabbers, Ranger Industries; *Patterned paper:* Anna Griffin; *Brads:* Doodlebug Design; *Other:* Thread.

To provide a raised, shadowed look, ADHERE a printed transparency shape to accents with dimensional adhesive dots.

Time to Celebrate by Jennifer McGuire. **Supplies** *Transparent die cut:* Making Memories; *Stamp:* Stampin' Up!; *Ink:* Close To My Heart; *Scallop die:* Spellbinders; *Punch:* Fiskars; *Other:* Star accents and adhesive dots..

FOLD a printed transparency to make an unexpected card!

Thank You Very Much *by Jennifer McGuire.* **Supplies** *Printed transparency:* Hambly Studios; *Patterned paper:* Bo-Bunny Press; *Rub-on:* Scenic Route; *Glitter chipboard:* Making Memories; *Felt flowers:* Stampin' Up!; *Gems:* Hero Arts.

LAYER small transparency blocks to create a clear mini book, punching holes in the side and tying the layers together with ribbon.

Seize the Day Mini Book *by Jennifer McGuire.* **Supplies** *Transparency:* Hambly Studios; *Printed message:* The Living Room Floor, www.etsy.com; *Stamps:* Hero Arts; *Ink:* StazOn, Tsukineko; *Transparent ribbon:* Maya Road.

try it yourself!

Want to check out some transparencies? Try these:

MAYA ROAD
mayaroad.com

HAMBLY SCREEN PRINTS
hamblyscreenprints.com

FANCY PANTS DESIGNS
fancypantsdesigns.com

MAKING MEMORIES
makingmemories.com

{ label *love* }

As a scrapbooker, I'm always looking for products with a timeless feel—something I know I will still like 20 years down the road. And one of the best products for this is artisan labels. Check out how I used them this month.

Use *artisan labels* for great looks

USE folded labels as tabs on a mini book.

Kay's Ideas *by Jennifer McGuire.* **Supplies** *Artisan labels:* Collage Press; *Patterned paper:* K&Company (floral) and October Afternoon (grid and stripes); *Stamps and gems:* Hero Arts; *Chipboard:* Making Memories (letters) and Scenic Route (butterfly); *Rub-ons:* American Crafts ("my ideas"); *Ribbon:* Bo-Bunny Press; *Other:* Composition notebook.

BY JENNIFER McGUIRE

CUT out the center of the label to create a frame.

Love by Jennifer McGuire. **Supplies** Artisan label: Making Memories; Printed tag: The Living Room Floor, www.livingroomfloor.etsy.com; Other: Twine.

CUT a label in half and cut the edges apart to create a unique set of parentheses.

Happy Bear by Jennifer McGuire. **Supplies** Artisan label: FontWerks; Foam bear and text rub-on: American Crafts; Tag: Creative Café, Creative Imaginations; Ribbon: C.M. Offray & Son.

TAPE a label to copy paper and run it through a printer to add computer journaling.

Serve the Lord by Jennifer McGuire. **Supplies** Artisan label: Sassafras; Patterned paper: Anna Griffin; Epoxy sticker: Love, Elsie for KI Memories; Font: American Typewriter, Internet.

LAYER labels with adhesive dots for added dimension and a cute accent.

Love You by Jennifer McGuire. **Supplies** Artisan labels: KI Memories; Glitter flower and brad: Making Memories; Rub-on: Pebbles Inc ; Other: Velvet (for petals).

{Photos taken while vacationing in Anagada and Virgin Gorda, 2008.}

it's really ME

Is this really me? Seems like a different person – relaxed, without a care in the world. Doesn't seem real. But it IS me. Just a different *part* of me that comes out when there are no work or worries.

I love that this relaxed person comes alive when in the Caribbean. It is the only time I truly like who I am deep down... care-free, fun and extremely happy. It really is me. What a good thing.

CUT the edges from labels and use them to create a unique border.

Me *by Jennifer McGuire.* **Supplies** *Artisan stamp and patterned paper:* Making Memories; *Cardstock:* Bazzill Basics Paper; *Die-cut letters:* Cricut, Provo Craft; *Ribbon:* Bo-Bunny Press; *Ink:* Close To My Heart; *Buttons:* Autumn Leaves; *Font:* American Typewriter Light, Internet; *Other:* Thread.

TURN two pieces of cardstock into a note card by joining them together with a label.

Hello *by Jennifer McGuire.* **Supplies** *Artisan label:* Autumn Leaves; *Cardstock:* Bazzill Basics Paper; *Stamps:* Stampin' Up!; *Punches:* Martha Stewart Crafts.

...hello to my absolutely delightful friend...

try it yourself!

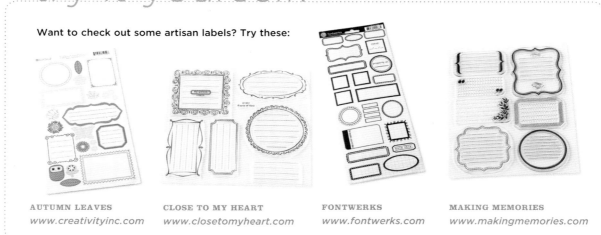

Want to check out some artisan labels? Try these:

AUTUMN LEAVES
www.creativityinc.com

CLOSE TO MY HEART
www.closetomyheart.com

FONTWERKS
www.fontwerks.com

MAKING MEMORIES
www.makingmemories.com

on-the-spot *journaling*

Journaling blocks, also known as "journaling spots," are all the craze right now! But I often find myself stumped on how to incorporate them into my pages. To help, I challenged myself to come up with fun ideas for journaling blocks. Let's see what *you* can create.

use fun *journaling* blocks for great looks

CUT journaling blocks in half and use them to frame a photo.

Two by Jennifer McGuire. **Supplies** *Journaling blocks:* Maya Road; *Die-cut number:* Cricut, Provo Craft; *Patterned paper:* Bo-Bunny Press; *Buttons:* Autumn Leaves; *Other:* Cardstock, thread, adhesive dots and string.

BY JENNIFER McGUIRE

SEW three sides of a journaling block to a cardstock block of the same size to create a pocket for photos.

Big Day *by Jennifer McGuire.* **Supplies** *Journaling block:* Scenic Route; *Star punches:* Fiskars; *Rub-ons:* American Crafts; *Gems:* Hero Arts; *Other:* Cardstock and thread.

TURN a journaling block sideways and use the lines as stems for flowers.

First Day *by Jennifer McGuire.* **Supplies** *Journaling block:* Maya Road; *Flowers:* Doodlebug Design; *Scallop-edge paper:* Bazzill Basics Paper; *Font:* CK Jessica, www.scrapnfonts.com; *Other:* Cardstock, string, thread and permanent pen.

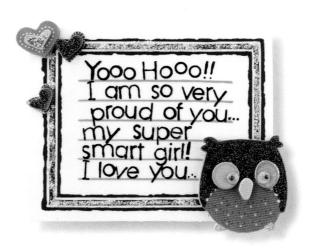

ENHANCE lines on a journaling block with stitching.

Kay *by Jennifer McGuire.* **Supplies** *Journaling block stamp:* Close To My Heart; *Tag:* K&Company; *Flourish stamp and mini buttons:* Hero Arts; *Ink:* ColorBox Fluid Chalk, Clearsnap; *Other:* Cardstock, thread and beaded chain.

EMBELLISH a journaling block frame with glitter and stickers for added fun.

Yooo Hooo!! *by Jennifer McGuire.* **Supplies** *Journaling block:* American Crafts; *Glitter:* Doodlebug Design; *Dimensional stickers:* K&Company; *Stamps:* Hero Arts; *Ink:* StazOn, Tsukineko; *Other:* Cardstock.

USE a journaling block for the address block on an envelope.

Envelope by Jennifer McGuire. **Supplies** *Journaling block rub-on:* Hambly Studios; *Stamps, note cards and gems:* Hero Arts; *White pen:* Ranger Industries; *Other:* Ribbon and googly eyes.

USE a journaling block as a tag for a gift.

Gift Bag Tag by Jennifer McGuire. **Supplies** *Journaling block:* SEI; *Stamps:* Stampin' Up!; *Buttons:* Doodlebug Design; *Bag:* Jolee's Boutique, EK Success; *Other:* Gift bag, ribbon and string.

try it yourself!

Want to check out journaling spots for your own use? Try these:

AMERICAN CRAFTS
www.americancrafts.com

MAYA ROAD
www.mayaroad.com

SANDYLION
www.sandylion.com

UPSY DAISY DESIGNS
www.upsydaisydesigns.com

{ chip *away!* }

Chipboard has been a scrapbooking staple for many years now. I just can't get enough of it! Since I've got a lot of chipboard in my stash, I decided to challenge myself to come up with new ways to use it. I hope these ideas inspire you to get creative with your chipboard as well.

get more from your *chipboard*

COVER a background paper with chipboard pieces and coat with layers of acrylic paint.

Roxie *by Jennifer McGuire.* **Supplies** *Chipboard:* American Crafts (dog), Bo-Bunny Press (arrows, buttons, circles and hearts), Boxer Scrapbook Productions (large bones), Close To My Heart (top "rox"), Die Cuts With a View, Inque Boutique (scallop edge), me & my BIG ideas (large circle), Piggy Tales (bottom "rox") and Oriental Trading Company, Inc.; *Foam letters:* American Crafts; *Paint:* Heidi Swapp for Advantus; *Other:* String.

BY JENNIFER McGUIRE

USE chipboard as a mask. Here, I used a star as a mask for spraying glitter onto my tag background, then I used the "mask" piece as an accent as well, adhering it to my tag with dimensional adhesive for extra pop.

Proud by Jennifer McGuire. **Supplies** *Chipboard:* Rusty Pickle; *Tag:* Creative Café, Creative Imaginations; *Ribbon:* Creative Impressions; *Gems:* Hero Arts; *Other:* Glitter spray.

COVER chipboard with paper, and sand the edges for a smooth, finished look.

Happiest Boy by Jennifer McGuire. **Supplies** *Chipboard tag and quote balloon:* Inque Boutique; *Silver stickers:* Jo-Ann Stores; *Ribbon:* Creative Impressions; *Patterned paper:* Scenic Route; *Sanding block:* Boxer Scrapbook Productions; *Font:* CK Footnote, www.scrapnfonts.com.

PEEL chipboard into thin layers so you can die cut it into shapes. Then, adhere the pieces back together into thick chipboard shapes. I peeled my hearts into three layers for this project.

Happy Birthday by Jennifer McGuire. **Supplies** *Chipboard:* K&Company; *Die cut:* Cuttlebug, Provo Craft; *Crackle paint:* Tim Holtz, Ranger Industries; *Letter stamps:* Hero Arts; *Rub-ons:* Imaginisce ("happy birthday") and Stampin' Up!; *Ink:* StazOn, Tsukineko; *Other:* Beaded chain, library card and string.

PIECE shapes together, and ink them to create your own themed embellishment.

Boo! by Jennifer McGuire. **Supplies** *Chipboard:* EK Success (nesting circles), Making Memories (letters) and me & my BIG ideas (glittered scrolls); *Ink:* ColorBcx, Clearsnap; *Other:* Google eyes, tag, walnut ink, string and trim.

SEPARATE chipboard into thin layers to emboss.

Hey There! *by Jennifer McGuire.* **Supplies** *Chipboard:* FontWerks (circles) and K&Company (scroll used for the tree trunk); *Patterned paper:* Imaginisce; *Stamps and note card:* Hero Arts; *Embossing machine:* Cuttlebug, Provo Craft; *Ink and inking tool:* Tim Holtz, Ranger Industries; *Other:* String.

See the rest of this album online at *www.creating-keepsakes.com.* >>

USE a craft knife to scratch and distress the edges of your chipboard. Ink with Distress Ink as well.

10 Reasons *by Jennifer McGuire.* **Supplies** *Chipboard and acrylic album:* Tinkering Ink; *Ink and inking tool:* Tim Holtz, Ranger Industries; *Stamps:* Hero Arts; *Ink:* StazOn, Tsukineko; *Rub-ons:* Stampin' Up!; *Button brads:* Imaginisce; *Other:* Beaded chain and ribbon.

try it yourself!

Want to check out some chipboard? Try these:

BO-BUNNY PRESS
www.bobunny.com

INQUE BOUTIQUE
www.goinque.com

K&COMPANY
www.kandcompany.com

SCENIC ROUTE
www.scenicroutepaper.com

sparkling gemstones

I'm always looking for inexpensive accents that add a bit of interest to my lay-outs without a ton of bulk. At first I didn't think I would like gemstones, but once I used them I was addicted. It's amazing the fun pizzazz they add to a project! Check out these ideas.

add extra *shimmer* to your pages this season

EASILY form a gemstone title by adding gems over stamped letters.

Capture by Jennifer McGuire. **Supplies** *Gemstones:* Hero Arts; *Letter stamps and ink:* Stampin' Up!; *Patterned paper:* Bo-Bunny Press (dot), Making Memories (text) and Scenic Route (green); *Scallop border:* Bazzill Basics Paper; *Punch:* Fiskars; *Ribbon:* Creative Impressions.

BY JENNIFER McGUIRE

INCORPORATE gemstones into a patterned-paper design.

Good Day *by Jennifer McGuire.* **Supplies** *Pearls:* K&Company; *Patterned paper:* Anna Griffin (orange) and Making Memories (other); *Stamp:* Stampin' Up!; *Ink:* Close To My Heart; *Chipboard accent:* Chatterbox; *Other:* String.

ADD a gem to the center of an eyelet.

December *by Jennifer McGuire.* **Supplies** *Gemstones:* Prima; *Patterned paper:* Bo-Bunny Press; *Eyelets:* American Crafts; *Clear tag and felt snowflakes:* Hero Arts; *Rub-on:* Melissa Frances; *Ribbon:* Creative Impressions.

CHANGE the color of your gemstones and pearls with permanent markers.

Making Spirits Bright *by Jennifer McGuire.* **Supplies** *Gems:* Buttons Galore (star) and Hero Arts (circles); *Stamps:* Hero Arts (tree and greeting) and Papertrey Ink (dots); *Ink:* ColorBox, Clearsnap; *Pens:* Sharpie, Newell Rubbermaid; *Other:* Twine, vintage text paper and thread; *Technique idea:* Tami Hartley.

ENHANCE rub-on images with gemstones.

Happiness *by Jennifer McGuire.* **Supplies** *Gems:* me & my BIG ideas; *Rub-ons:* Stampin' Up!; *Distress ink and tool:* Tim Holtz, Ranger Industries; *Other:* Fabric tag and jute.

SET OFF a scalloped border with gemstones.

Home by Jennifer McGuire. **Supplies** Gems: me & my BIG ideas (heart) and Hero Arts (other); Patterned paper: Chatterbox (green), Scenic Route (brown dot), Stampin' Up! (blue) and www.twopeasina-bucket.com (digital); Stamps and ink: Hero Arts; Chipboard house: Maya Road; Scallop border: Fiskars; Other: Thread.

ADD a gemstone frame around a photo or a journaling block.

Moment by Jennifer McGuire. **Supplies** Gemstones: Hero Arts; Notebook: Target; Ticket: Jenni Bowlin Studio; Button: Doodlebug Design; Other: String.

Try it yourself!

Want to check out some gemstones? Try these:

ANNA GRIFFIN
www.annagriffin.com

BUTTONS GALORE
www.morebuttons.com

CLOSE TO MY HEART
www.closetomyheart.com

HERO ARTS
www.heroarts.com

ORIENTAL TRADING COMPANY
www.orientaltrading.com

{ sheer *elegance* }

hen I first started scrapbooking years ago, I remember how vellum was all the rage. Even today, it still offers elegance and a classy feel that is hard to beat. Here are some ideas that will get you reaching for your vellum once again.

Add *vellum* for instant class

DIE CUT letters from vellum for a title look that won't distract. **>>**

Going Places *by Jennifer McGuire.* **Supplies** *Vellum:* Autumn Leaves; *Cardstock:* Bazzill Basics Paper; *Patterned paper:* Doodlebug Design; *Die-cut letters and shapes:* Cricut, Provo Craft; *Vellum adhesive:* Scrapbook Adhesives by 3L; *Font:* American Typewriter.

BY JENNIFER McGUIRE

CREATE a vellum frame.

Together by Jennifer McGuire. **Supplies** *Vellum:* Hobby Lobby; *Patterned paper:* Bo-Bunny Press; *Vellum adhesive:* Scrapbook Adhesives by 3L; *Rub-on:* Melissa Frances; *Button:* Doodlebug Design; *Ribbon:* American Crafts.

STAMP and emboss with white on vellum for a "floating" look.

You're One of a Kind by Jennifer McGuire. **Supplies** *Vellum and flower stamp:* Autumn Leaves; *Vellum adhesive:* Scrapbook Adhesives by 3L; *Message stamp:* Close To My Heart; *Background stamp:* Studio Calico; *Ink:* VersaMark, Tsukineko; *Label die cut:* Spellbinders; *Gems and embossing powder:* Hero Arts; *Other:* String.

SCORE lines on vellum to create your own pattern.

Marvelous You by Jennifer McGuire. **Supplies** *Vellum:* Papertrey Ink; *Patterned paper:* October Afternoon; *Vellum adhesive:* Scrapbook Adhesives by 3L; *Letter stickers:* Making Memories; *Stamp and scallop border punch:* Stampin' Up!; *Mini brads:* Close To My Heart; *Embellishment:* KI Memories; *Other:* String and bone folder.

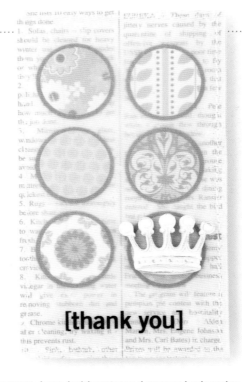

TONE down bold patterned papers by layering vellum on top.

Thank You by Jennifer McGuire. **Supplies** *Vellum:* Papertrey Ink; *Patterned paper:* October Afternoon and Scenic Route; *Vellum adhesive:* Scrapbook Adhesives by 3L; *Rub-ons:* Scenic Route; *Crown embellishment:* Melissa Frances; *Other:* Thread.

EMBOSS a pattern on vellum.

For You *by Jennifer McGuire.* **Supplies** *Vellum:* Papertrey Ink; *Vellum adhesive:* Scrapbook Adhesives by 3L; *Scallop circle punch:* EK Success; *Ribbon:* Creative Impressions; *Rub-ons:* Close To My Heart; *Ink:* Tim Holtz Distress Ink, Ranger Industries; *Pearls:* Hero Arts.

Delicious *by Jennifer McGuire.* **Supplies** *Vellum:* Autumn Leaves; *Stamps, note cards and ink:* Hero Arts; *Vellum adhesive:* Scrapbook Adhesives by 3L; *Font:* Splendid; *Mini brads:* Close To My Heart; *Other:* Color pencils, photo corners and glitter.

try it yourself!

Want to explore the latest in vellum? Consider these:

PAPERTREY INK
PapertreyInk.com

HOBBY LOBBY
HobbyLobby.com

GRAFIX
GrafixArts.com

E-Z RUNNER FOR VELLUM
Scrapbook-Adhesives.com

lovely lace cardstock

I always get excited when something brand-new and different hits the market. I remember the first time I saw lace cardstock and its lovely die-cut patterns—I couldn't help but smile. My mind was instantly flooded with new ways to use this cool product. Enjoy a few of my favorites!

use these 7
fun
and fresh
ideas

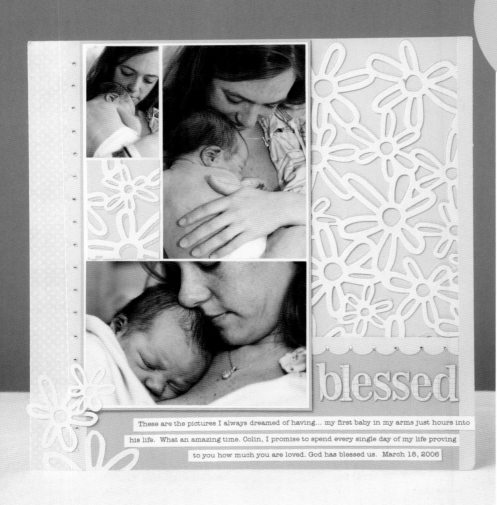

These are the pictures I always dreamed of having... my first baby in my arms just hours into his life. What an amazing time. Colin, I promise to spend every single day of my life proving to you how much you are loved. God has blessed us. March 18, 2006

LAYER and slightly offset two lace papers for a fun look. **>>**

Blessed *by Jennifer McGuire.* **Supplies** *Lace paper:* KI Memories; *Cardstock:* Bazzill Basics Paper; *Patterned paper:* Bo-Bunny Press; *Chipboard letters:* Making Memories; *Gems:* Hero Arts; *Font:* American Typewriter.

BY JENNIFER McGUIRE

ADD glitter to lace paper, then back the lace design with a monochromatic color of cardstock.

T by Jennifer McGuire. **Supplies** *Lace paper:* KI Memories; *Liquid glitter:* Stickles, Ranger Industries; *Chipboard letter:* BasicGrey; *Silk ribbon:* Creative Impressions; *Brad:* Making Memories; *Punches:* Paper Shapers, EK Success.

USE lace paper as a mask for inking.

Be Mine by Jennifer McGuire. **Supplies** *Lace paper:* KI Memories; *Ink:* Memories, Stewart Superior Corporation (white) and StazOn, Tsukineko; *Kraft paper and stamp:* Hero Arts; *Chipboard heart:* Gin-X, Imagination Project; *Clear charm:* Tim Holtz; *Embossing machine:* Cuttlebug, Provo Craft; *Punches:* Marvy Uchida; *Other:* String.

STAMP on lace paper before adding the specialty paper to your project.

Warm Wishes by Jennifer McGuire. **Supplies** *Lace cardstock:* Creative Imaginations; *Patterned paper:* KI Memories; *Stamps:* Hero Arts (greeting and text) and Studio Calico (butterfly); *Ink:* ColorBox, Clearsnap; *Gems:* Hero Arts; *Other:* Photo corners.

ADD stitching inside the die-cut designs to enhance the pattern.

XOXOXO by Jennifer McGuire. **Supplies** *Lace paper:* Midnight Oil Scrapbook Designs; *Patterned paper:* Bo-Bunny Press (pink) and KI Memories (yellow); *Stamps:* Hero Arts; *Ribbon:* Strano Designs; *Other:* Thread.

ADHERE lace paper to your project, then paint over it to create an embossed look.

KME *by Jennifer McGuire.* **Supplies** *Lace paper:* Sandylion; *Album:* Tinkering Ink; *Stamp:* Justrite Rubber Stamps; *Ribbon:* Creative Impressions; *Paint:* Paint Dabbers, Ranger Industries; *Pearls:* Hero Arts; *Punches:* Paper Shapers, EK Success.

RAISE lace papers with foam adhesive to add dimension, then tuck accents into the raised areas.

Have a Beautiful Birthday *by Jennifer McGuire.* **Supplies** *Lace paper:* Creative Impressions; *Flowers, button, ink, gems and note card:* Hero Arts; *Stamps:* Stampendous!; *Ribbon:* Making Memories; *Foam dots:* EK Success; *Other:* String.

try it yourself!

Want to check out some lace papers (or good adhesive for them)? Try these:

KI MEMORIES

KIMemories.com

MIDNIGHT OIL SCRAPBOOK DESIGNS

MOSDInc.com

SANDYLION

Sandylion.com

ZOTS BY THERM O WEB

ThermoWeb.com

simply *scallops*

I'll admit it: I'm addicted to scallops. Scallop borders, scallop punches . . . I love anything scalloped! It's just a fun and simple way to add a dimensional look to your layouts. Here are seven new ways to use scallops on your projects.

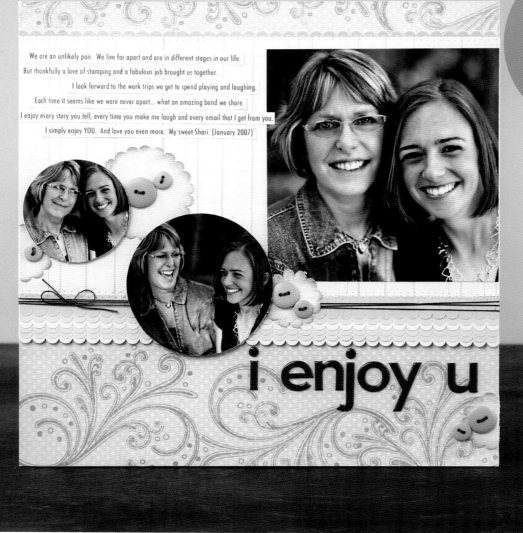

get *creative* **with scallops**

LAYER multiple scallop borders for a one-of-a-kind dimensional look.

I Enjoy You by Jennifer McGuire. *Photography by Jamie Waters.* **Supplies** *Scallop borders:* Doodlebug Design; *Scallop fabric circles:* Technique Tuesday; *Patterned paper:* Bo-Bunny Press (dot) and Making Memories (ledger); *Letter stickers:* Making Memories; *Stamps, buttons and ink:* Hero Arts; *Font:* Futura Condensed; *Other:* String and thread.

BY JENNIFER McGUIRE

ENHANCE scallop borders with small stamped images, like the flowers I used here.

Kay *by Jennifer McGuire.* **Supplies** *Scallop border sticker and glitter letter stickers:* Making Memories; *Patterned paper:* Scenic Route (dot) and Making Memories (stripe); *Stamps:* BasicGrey (butterfly) and Hero Arts (flower); *Glitter paint:* Stickles, Ranger Industries; *Ink:* ColorBox, Clearsnap; *Other:* Colored pencils and thread.

TRACE scallop borders to create your own patterned paper. (See my block of green cardstock.)

Cute as a Bug *by Jennifer McGuire.* **Supplies** *Scallop border punch (for tracing), cardstock and pen:* Stampin' Up!; *Patterned paper:* My Mind's Eye; *Ladybug accent and ribbon:* American Crafts; *Letter stamps:* Papertrey Ink; *Ink:* Memories, Stewart Superior Corporation; *Punches:* Paper Shaper, EK Success; *Other:* Vintage textbook paper.

CUT notches into your scallop for a whole new look.

Missing You *by Jennifer McGuire.* **Supplies** *Scallop punch:* Paper Shaper, EK Success; *Patterned paper:* BasicGrey; *Stamps:* My Sentiments Exactly; *Ink:* Stampin' Up!; *Pearls and flowers:* Hero Arts; *Other:* Silk ribbon.

PUNCH holes in a scallop pattern for a fancy look.

Thank You Very Much *by Jennifer McGuire.* **Supplies** *Scallop circle die cut:* Spellbinders; *Patterned paper:* Bo-Bunny Press; *Hole punch:* Crop-A-Dile, We R Memory Keepers; *Flower accent:* me & my BIG ideas; *Rub-on:* American Crafts.

FOLD scallop borders over for added dimension.

Leslie by Jennifer McGuire. **Supplies** *Scallop borders:* Bazzill Basics Paper; *Patterned paper:* Heidi Swapp for Advantus; *Bag:* Target; *Stamp and ink:* Stampin' Up!; *Rub-ons:* American Crafts; *Gems:* Hero Arts.

CUT a thin scallop from a larger border. (See the blue strip.)

You're a Star by Jennifer McGuire. **Supplies** *Felt scallop border and stars:* Fancy Pants Designs; *Patterned paper:* My Mind's Eye; *Stamps, note card, gems and embossing powder:* Hero Arts; *Embossing ink:* VersaMark, Tsukineko.

try it yourself!

Want to check out some scallop accents? Try these:

PAPER FRILLS
Doodlebug Design,
Doodlebug.ws

2" CIRCLE SCALLOP
EK Success,
EKSuccess.com

FELT SHAPES, SASSY
Fancy Pants Designs,
FancyPantsDesigns.com

TEXTILE SCALLOPS
Technique Tuesday,
TechniqueTuesday.com

SCALLOP-EDGE PUNCH
Stampin' Up!,
StampinUp.com

border
rub-ons

Admit it: you are as addicted to rub-ons as I am, aren't you? They're a wonderful way to add pizzazz to any project, and I find the border rub-on the most useful. Here are some ideas for using them on your projects!

7 great
ideas
for rub-ons

ADD border rub-ons to plain ribbon for a new look.

Travel Buddies by Jennifer McGuire. **Supplies** *Rub-on borders:* 7gypsies (multicolor) and Luxe Designs (white); *Word rub-ons:* 7gypsies ("together"); *Patterned paper:* Autumn Leaves (blue) and Stampin' Up! (green); *Ribbon:* Doodlebug Design and May Arts; *Stamps:* Studio Calico ("travel") and Hero Arts (letters and globe); *Ink:* Memories, Stewart Superior Corporation; *Other:* Thread.

BY JENNIFER McGUIRE

APPLY border rub-ons repeatedly to create your own patterned paper (see my green block).

A by Jennifer McGuire. **Supplies** Border rub-ons: Imaginisce; Rub-on letter: me & my BIG ideas; Patterned paper: Doodlebug Design; Punches: Stampin' Up!; Gems: Hero Arts.

USE border rub-ons to create journaling lines.

Friends by Jennifer McGuire. **Supplies** Border rub-ons: Heidi Grace Designs; Word rub-on: Close To My Heart; Patterned paper: Doodlebug Design; Letter stamps: Hero Arts; Ribbon: American Crafts; Button: Autumn Leaves; Other: String.

DECORATE a die-cut outline shape with border rub-ons.

Smile by Jennifer McGuire. **Supplies** Border rub-ons: American Crafts; Star die cut: QuicKutz; "Smile" embellishment: October Afternoon; Other: String.

APPLY a border rub-on along the curve of a photo or paper.

Let's Cuddle by Jennifer McGuire. **Supplies** Border rub-on: Close To My Heart; Icon rub-on: Cosmo Cricket; Patterned paper: Bo-Bunny Press.

ACCENTUATE border rub-ons with gems between or on the designs.

You Always Know *by Jennifer McGuire.* **Supplies** *Border rub-ons:* Luxe Designs; *Greeting rub-on:* Little Yellow Bicycle; *Felt flowers:* Stampin' Up!; *Gems:* Hero Arts; *Other:* String.

DECORATE your craft supplies with rub-ons. I added them to pencils.

Pencils *by Jennifer McGuire.* **Supplies** *Border rub-ons:* Imaginisce.

Try it yourself!

Want to check out some border rub-ons? Try these:

BELLA JOURNEE
Bo-Bunny Press *BoBunny.com*

ON EDGE
Hambly Screen Prints
HamblyScreenPrints.com

FLORAL BORDERS III
Luxe Designs *LuxeDesigns.com*

**IT'S RAINING,
IT'S PORING**
Piggy Tales
PiggyTales.com

circle *punches*

If all the tools I have, I seem to reach for my circle punches the most. Why? When creating a page with so many straight lines, it's fun to break it up with circles. Here are some fun ideas to get you started.

seven *great* new looks

CREATE rings by first punching a small circle and then punching a large circle from the negative.

Sunny by Jennifer McGuire. **Supplies** *Circle punches:* Paper Shapers, EK Success; *Patterned paper:* Anna Griffin (orange), Autumn Leaves (blue floral), Doodlebug Design (white flocked dot), Heidi Swapp for Advantus (large big dot), Scenic Route (small blue dot) and Stampin' Up! (green); *Glitter chipboard letters:* Die Cuts With a View; *Gems:* Hero Arts; *Font:* AL Hightlight.

BY JENNIFER McGUIRE

CUT small slits into punched circles to create a flower.

Blessings by Jennifer McGuire. **Supplies** *Circle punch:* Stampin' Up!; *Patterned paper:* BasicGrey (pink), Bo-Bunny Press (dot) and Making Memories (ledger); *Stamps:* Hero Arts (leaves) and Maya Road (words); *Ink:* ColorBox Fluid Chalk, Clearsnap; *Pearls and button:* Hero Arts; *Other:* String.

TUCK small punched circles under paper to create a faux scallop border.

Hi, Owl by Jennifer McGuire. **Supplies** *Circle punch:* EK Success; *Patterned paper:* BasicGrey; *Rub-ons:* Stampin' Up!; *Gems:* Hero Arts; *Other:* String.

USE Use a small circle punch to create a decorative "wave" or "reverse scallop" border.

Bonus idea: Use the negative of a small circle punch as a mask to create stamped clouds. (Just move the mask around several times to create a complete cloud look.)

Thinking of You by Jennifer McGuire. **Supplies** *Punch:* EK Success; *Stamps:* Close To My Heart (sentiment) and Papertrey Ink (boat and dots); *Ink:* ColorBox Fluid Chalk, Clearsnap; *Other:* Ribbon.

FOLD 11 small circles in thirds and combine/arrange them in a large circle shape for a dimensional flower.

"Hi" Flower by Jennifer McGuire. **Supplies** *Circle punches:* Marvy Uchida; *Patterned paper:* Bo-Bunny Press; *Chipboard:* BasicGrey; *Other:* Plastic letters and vintage text paper.

TO CREATE a circle card, punch two large circles of the same size. Score at the top of one of them, making a small flap. Put adhesive on the flap and adhere it to the back of the other circle.

You're a Star *by Jennifer McGuire.* **Supplies** *Punches:* Marvy Uchida; *Patterned paper:* Scenic Route; *Stamps and ink:* Close To My Heart; *Gems:* Hero Arts.

CREATE dimension by punching many circles, folding them in half and adhering the backs together.

Five Ways *by Jennifer McGuire.* **Supplies** *Circle punch:* EK Success; *Patterned paper:* Making Memories (blue) and Stampin' Up! (green); *Clipboard:* Stampin' Up!; *Paint:* Paint Dabbers, Ranger Industries; *Number sticker:* Doodlebug Design; *Gems:* Hero Arts; *Font:* American Typewriter.

Try it yourself!

Want to purchase some circle punches? Try these surefire finds:

EK SUCCESS
EKSuccess.com

MARVY UCHIDA
Marvy.com

STAMPIN' UP!
StampinUp.com

FISKARS AMERICAS
FiskarsCrafts.com

chipboard *letter* makeovers

Chipboard has been a staple in scrapbooking for a few years now, and chipboard letters are perfect for titles. The added dimension is great for drawing attention, but there are more things you can do with chipboard letters besides simply adhering them directly to a layout. Here are a few fun ideas for new looks!

7 new takes for *chipboard* **letters**

DRY emboss or heat emboss chipboard letters for added dimension. I used a combination of both techniques on this layout.

Spoil You *by Jennifer McGuire.* **Supplies** *Chipboard letters:* Maya Road ("because," "spoil" and "us") and Stampin' Up! ("we," "spoil," "you" and "You"); *Decorative cardstock:* Bazzill Basics Paper; *Patterned paper:* Bo-Bunny Press; *Ink:* ColorBox, Clearsnap; *Embossing machine:* Cuttlebug, Provo Craft; *Black gems and embossing powder:* Hero Arts; *Adhesive:* Mini Glue Dots, Glue Dots International.

BY JENNIFER McGUIRE

CAREFULLY peel chipboard letters in half and adhere the bottom layer slightly offset from the top layer for a shadow look.

 Right at Home *by Jennifer McGuire.* **Supplies** *Chipboard letters:* **American Crafts** ("right at") *and* **Anna Griffin** ("home"); *Cardstock:* **Bazzill Basics Paper;** *Patterned paper:* **Cosmo Cricket** (fish), **Doodlebug Design** (stripe) *and* **October Afternoon** (house); *Decorative border punch:* **Fiskars Americas;** *Adhesive:* **EK Success.**

KEEP the negatives of your chipboard letters and carefully cut an outline of them for unique monograms.

K *by Jennifer McGuire.* **Supplies** *Chipboard letter, stickers, label and patterned paper:* **Stampin' Up!;** *Button:* **Buttons Galore;** *Other:* **String** *and* **pen.**

COVER a chipboard letter with patterned paper and file or sand the edges for a finished look.

A *by Jennifer McGuire.* **Supplies** *Chipboard letter:* **Maya Road;** *Patterned paper:* **Doodlebug Design;** *Flower punch:* **EK Success;** *Ribbon:* **Creative Impressions;** *Adhesive:* **Dot 'n' Roller, Kokuyo.**

SCRATCH the edges of chipboard letters for a distressed look.

Luv You Lots by Jennifer McGuire. **Supplies** *Chipboard letters:* Maya Road; *Ink and ticket:* Tim Holtz; *Rub-on letters:* American Crafts; *Brad:* Making Memories; *Adhesive:* Kokuyo.

ADD stitching to secure letters in place.

You by Jennifer McGuire. **Supplies** *Chipboard letters:* Die Cuts With a View; *Patterned paper:* Cosmo Cricket; *Word stickers:* October Afternoon; *Button and flower:* Hero Arts; *Other:* Thread.

CREATE your own patterned paper by tracing chipboard letters onto cardstock.

You Are My Angel by Jennifer McGuire. **Supplies** *Chipboard letters and patterned paper:* BasicGrey; *Heart punch:* Fiskars Americas; *Embossing machine:* Cuttlebug, Provo Craft; *Pearls:* Hero Arts; *Pen:* American Crafts; *Other:* Thread.

Try It Yourself!

Want to check out some chipboard letters? Try these:

BLOSSOMS & BUTTERFLIES FOILED ALPHABET
Die Cuts With a View
DCWV.com

FASHION DISTRICT ALPHA
me & my BIG ideas
MeandMyBigIdeas.com

TYPO
American Crafts
AmericanCrafts.com

ON BOARD TIMELESS TYPE
Stampin' Up!
StampinUp.com

.....{ *die-cut* designs }.....

Die-cutting machines have been a staple in the scrapbooking industry for years. However, new and improved machines have recently come out, opening the door for more uses and creative applications. Here are some ideas for your creativity!

do more
with your dies

COVER die-cut letters and shapes with Glossy Accents to make them shiny and give them an epoxy-like finish.

Dream Job *by Jennifer McGuire. Photos by Jamie Waters.* **Supplies** *Die-cutting machine:* Silhouette, QuicKutz; *Cardstock:* Die Cuts With a View; *Patterned paper:* Bo-Bunny Press (tan and green), My Little Shoebox (pink) and Sassafras (yellow and green dot); *Rubber stamps and pearls:* Hero Arts; *Ink and glossy medium:* Ranger Industries; *Font:* American Typewriter; *Adhesive:* EK Success (dimensional adhesive) and Elmer's (glue stick).

BY JENNIFER McGUIRE

ADHERE fabric to cardstock with a glue stick. Let the glue dry, and then die cut the shape. Fray the edges for a homespun feel.

It's a Girl *by Jennifer McGuire.* **Supplies** *Die-cutting machine:* Sizzix Big Shot for Stampin' Up!; *Dies:* Nestabilities, Spellbinder (circle), Sizzix (leaves) and Stampin' Up! (flowers); *Patterned paper and button:* Doodlebug Design; *Stamp and ink:* Hero Arts; *Adhesive:* Elmer's; *Other:* Fabric.

LAYER many die cuts of the same size to create faux chipboard. I used four or five layers.

Faithful *by Jennifer McGuire.* **Supplies** *Dies and die-cutting machine:* Sizzix Big Shot for Stampin' Up!; *Cardstock:* Bazzill Basics Paper; *Rub-on letters:* American Crafts; *Pearls:* Hero Arts; *Ink and inking tool:* Ranger Industries; *Adhesive:* EK Success.

CUT many die-cut shapes, and adhere them to a background of the same color for a tone-on-tone look.

Kay *by Jennifer McGuire.* **Supplies** *Die and die-cutting machine:* Revolution, QuicKutz; *Cardstock:* Core'dinations; *Letter stickers:* American Crafts; *Ribbon:* May Arts; *Pearls:* Hero Arts; *Adhesive:* EK Success.

LAY vellum over die and press down around the shape to leave an embossed impression.

Happy Everything *by Jennifer McGuire.* **Supplies** *Dies:* QuicKutz (flower) and Nestabilities, Spellbinders (circle and scallop); *Patterned paper:* KI Memories (blue) and Making Memories (ledger); *Vellum and greeting stamp:* Papertrey Ink; *Leaf stamps, ink and pearls:* Hero Arts; *Adhesives:* Scrapbook Adhesives by 3L.

LAYER die-cut shapes of different sizes, like my stars, for added dimension.

To You *by Jennifer McGuire.* **Supplies** *Die-cutting machine and star and box dies:* **Sizzix Big Shot for Stampin' Up!**; *Cardstock, patterned paper, stamp, ink and adhesive:* **Stampin' Up!**; *Ribbon:* **Creative Impressions**.

CREATE a card background from a large die-cut shape. To turn two shapes into a card, I adhered together the top ¼"–½" of the shapes.

Feel Better Soon *by Jennifer McGuire.* **Supplies** *Die and die-cutting machine:* **Sizzix Big Shot for Stampin' Up!**; *Cardstock:* **Bazzill Basics Paper**; *Patterned paper:* **October Afternoon**; *Stamps, felt flower, ink and rhinestones:* **Hero Arts**.

Try It Yourself!

Are you in the market for a die-cutting machine? Try one of these great options.

BIG SHOT	**SLICE**	**SILHOUETTE SD**	**CRICUT EXPRESSION**
Sizzix	Making Memories	Silhoette America	Provo Craft
Sizzix.com	*MakingMemories.com*	*SilhoetteAmerica.com*	*Cricut.com*

tools & techniques

BY JENNIFER McGUIRE

ONE OF THE BEST things about using chalk on your scrapbook pages is that it offers a softness that no other product can. And there are so many fantastic ways to use chalk, from changing the color of a paper flower to coloring a stamped image. Here are ten ideas to get you inspired to use chalk today.

chalk techniques you'll want to try!

TECHNIQUE: Apply metallic chalk over an embossed image for a soft background.

It is the simple moments like these that remind me how great our life is. (10/09)

Life Is Great *by Jennifer McGuire.* **Supplies:** *Metallic chalk:* Pebbles; *Cardstock:* American Crafts; *Patterned paper:* 7gypsies, Anna Griffin, BoBunny Press, and My Mind's Eye; *Punch:* EK Success; *Dies and die-cutting machine:* QuicKutz; *Stamps, embossing powder, and pearls:* Hero Arts; *Adhesive:* American Crafts; *Other:* Thread.

ADD CHALK to textured cardstock.

Fern *by Jennifer McGuire.* **Supplies:** *Chalk:* EK Success and Hampton Arts; *Cardstock:* American Crafts; *Die-cutting machine:* Silhouette America; *Pearls:* Hero Arts; *Twine:* Creative Impressions; *Punch:* EK Success; *Other:* Adhesive.

USE CHALK on kraft cardstock to create a muted look on accents.

Mother *by Jennifer McGuire.* **Supplies:** *Chalk:* Craft-T Products and EK Success; *Cardstock:* Bazzill Basics Paper; *Stamps:* Hero Arts and Waltzing Mouse; *Trim:* Ellen Hutson; *Ink:* Tsukineko; *Adhesive:* Glue-Arts; *Other:* String.

APPLY CHALK over cardstock and use an eraser to create a pattern.

Kindness *by Jennifer McGuire.* **Supplies:** *Chalk:* Stampin' Up!; *Cardstock:* Bazzill Basics Paper; *Stamps and pearls:* Hero Arts; *Ink:* Ranger Industries and Tsukineko; *Punch:* EK Success; *Adhesive:* GlueArts.

COLOR stamped images with chalk for colorful accents.

Butterfly *by Jennifer McGuire.* **Supplies:** *Chalk:* EK Success, Hampton Arts, and Stampin' Up!; *Patterned paper:* October Afternoon; *Stamp and ink:* Hero Arts; *Punch:* EK Success; *Adhesive:* American Crafts; *Other:* String.

COLOR white flowers with chalk to complement your layout's color scheme.

Simply the Best *by Jennifer McGuire.* **Supplies:** *Chalk:* Pebbles and Stampin' Up!; *Cardstock:* American Crafts; *Patterned paper:* Making Memories and My Mind's Eye; *Flowers and trim:* Prima; *Stamps:* Hero Arts and Stampin' Up!; *Stickers:* October Afternoon; *Punches:* EK Success; *Adhesive:* American Crafts.

1 Ink flower using water-mark inkpad.

2 Chalk over flower.

not your average chipboard

I just love the many types of chipboard out on the market—everything from fabric-covered to shiny. There are even unique products like "grungeboard," which is a chipboard-like material that's flexible. With all these products, the possibilities for making chipboard products your own are endless. Here are a few ideas!

10 creative takes on chipboard

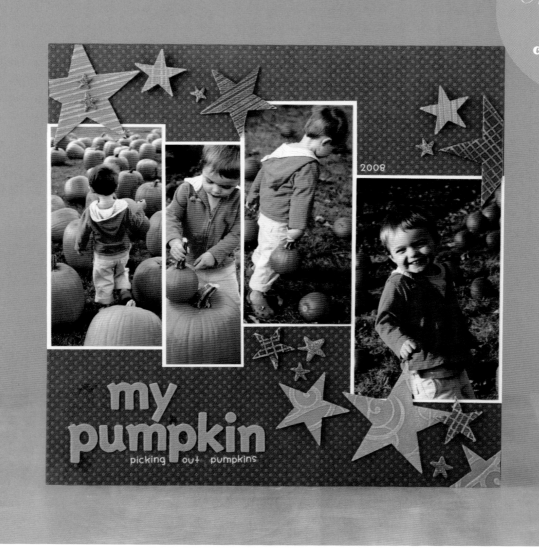

❶ DIE CUT, paint, dry emboss and then sand chipboard for added texture on your page.

My Pumpkin *by Jennifer McGuire.* **Supplies** *Chipboard:* Grungeboard, Tim Holtz for Advantus; *Cardstock:* Bazzill Basics Paper; *Embossing tools:* QuicKutz and Sizzix for Stampin' Up!; *Star die cuts:* Sizzix for Stampin' Up!; *Felt letters and glitter stars:* American Crafts; *Mini rub-ons:* Doodlebug Design; *Adhesive:* EK Success; *Other:* Pen and thread.

BY JENNIFER McGUIRE

❷ **SECURE** glitter on chipboard with a layer of Glossy Accents—this liquid adhesive will seal in the glitter leaving no mess.

Bird *by Jennifer McGuire.* **Supplies** *Chipboard:* Grungeboard, Tim Holtz for Advantus; *Die cut:* Jillibean Soup; *Glitter:* Ranger Industries; *Ink:* Distress Ink, Ranger Industries; *Adhesive:* Glossy Accents, Ranger industries (liquid); Scrapbook Adhesives by 3L; *Other:* Textbook paper.

❸ **CRUMPLE** shiny chipboard accents and then distress them with a sanding block to remove the sheen. Distress the chipboard with ink for a new look.

All Boy *by Jennifer McGuire.* **Supplies** *Glossy chipboard:* Cosmo Cricket; *Ink:* Distress Inks, Ranger Industries; *Cork paper:* QuicKutz; *Punches:* EK Success (corner rounder) and Stampin' Up! (notebook edge); *Rub-ons:* Doodlebug Design; *Adhesive:* 3D-Dots, EK Success; Dot 'n' Roller, Kokuyo; *Other:* String.

❹ **DRY** emboss chipboard, and then lightly rub the surface with ink to enhance the embossed texture.

Home *by Jennifer McGuire.* **Supplies** *Chipboard:* Grungeboard, Tim Holtz for Ranger Industries; *Die cut:* QuicKutz; *Embossing tools:* Sizzix for Stampin' Up!; *Rub-on letters:* American Crafts; *Stamps:* Hero Arts; *Ink:* Distress Inks, Ranger Industries; *Felt branch:* Prima; *Adhesive:* Dot 'n' Roller, Kokuyo; *Other:* String.

❺ **USE** a chipboard shape as a stamp. Just add ink to the top and then press it onto paper. That's how I created the flourish shape on this tag.

Congratulations *by Jennifer McGuire.* **Supplies** *Fabric-covered chipboard and brads:* American Crafts; *Decorative brad:* Chatterbox; *Stamp and patterned paper:* Papertrey Ink; *Ink:* Distress Ink, Ranger Industries; VersaMark, Tsukineko; *Tag:* Making Memories; *Embossing powder and flower:* Hero Arts; *Adhesive:* Dot 'n' Roller, Kokuyo; *Other:* Thread.

❻ WRAP string around chipboard shapes to add a textured look.

Family of 5 *by Jennifer McGuire.* **Supplies** *Chipboard:* Grungeboard, Tim Holtz for Advantus; *Tag:* Office Depot; *Stamp:* Tim Holtz for Stampers Anonymous; *Ink:* Distress Ink, Ranger Industries; *Twine:* Papertrey Ink; *Adhesive:* 3D-Dots, EK Success.

❼ USE a bone folder to press lined creases into raw chipboard. Experiment with different designs, like my diamond pattern.

Family *by Jennifer McGuire.* **Supplies** *Raw chipboard:* Die Cuts With a View; *Printed chipboard:* me & my BIG ideas; *Stamps:* Hero Arts; *Ink:* ColorBox, Clearsnap; *Adhesive:* Dot 'n' Roller, Kokuyo; *Other:* Button, ribbon and string.

❽ PAINT, score and fold a large piece of grunge-board to form a thick, one-of-a-kind card.

True Friendship *by Jennifer McGuire.* **Supplies** *Chipboard:* Grungeboard, Tim Holtz for Advantus; *Patterned paper:* Making Memories; *Punch and die cut:* Stampin' Up!; *Stamps:* Papertrey Ink (damask) and Tim Holtz for Stampers Anonymous (greeting); *Paint:* Paint Dabbers, Ranger Industries; *Pearls and embossing powder:* Hero Arts; *Ink:* VersaMark, Tsukineko; *Adhesive:* Dot 'n' Roller, Kokuyo.

❾ STAMP a design onto glossy white chipboard using a clear embossing ink. Rub colored ink over the image; the colored ink will resist the clear-stamped image, leaving some white color from the glossy chipboard.

Flower Pencils *by Jennifer McGuire.* **Supplies** *Glossy chipboard flowers:* Doodlebug Design; *Stamps, pearls and embossing powder:* Hero Arts; *Ink:* Adirondack Alcohol Ink, Ranger Industries; VersaMark, Tsukineko; *Ribbon:* Creative Impressions; *Liquid adhesive:* Glossy Accents, Ranger Industries; *Other:* Pencils.

10 DO YOU WANT raw chipboard instead of a specialty type? Just tear off the top layer and ink the core as desired. The chipboard letters on this layout originally had a fabric finish.

Melt Me *by Jennifer McGuire.* **Supplies** *Fabric-covered chipboard and brads:* American Crafts; *Cardstock:* Bazzill Basics Paper; *Patterned paper:* Doodlebug Design; *Decorative die-cut trim:* Silhouette, QuicKutz; *Stamp:* Tim Holtz for Stampers Anonymous; *Ink:* Distress Ink, Ranger Industries; *Heart punch:* Stampin' Up!; *Adhesive:* Dot 'n' Roller, Kokuyo; *Other:* Thread.

Try It Yourself!

If you want to check out some great chipboard products, try these:

My Edgy Album: Cascading
Bo-Bunny Press
BoBunny.com

Ripe Berry Flocked Chipboard Accents
Colorbök
Colorbok.com

Plain & Simple Chipboard Flower Bouquet
Doodlebug Design,
Doodlebug.ws

Mélange Chipboard Border Stickers
Creative Imaginations,
CreativeImaginations.us **ck**

border stickers and beyond

I bet most of us started our scrapbooking journey with an enormous amount of stickers. They are still a favorite product of mine. Border stickers are my favorite type because they can be used to span an entire page. There are many other unique techniques you can try with them. Here are a few ideas to get you started.

7 new *ideas* **to try**

DRAW attention to a favorite photo by adding border stickers around it to create a one-of-a-kind frame.

Our Little Mister *by Jennifer McGuire.* **Supplies** *Border stickers:* Doodlebug Design; *Cardstock:* Bazzill Basics Paper; *Patterned paper:* Anna Griffin (orange), KI Memories (green) and Making Memories (stripe); *Stamps and ink:* Hero Arts; *Letter stickers:* American Crafts; *Twine:* Papertrey Ink; *Border punches:* EK Success; *Adhesive:* Dot 'n' Roller, Kokuyo; *Other:* Thread.

BY JENNIFER McGUIRE

PLEAT a border sticker for added fun.

So Sweet *by Jennifer McGuire.* **Supplies** *Border sticker:* ColorBox, Clearsnap; *Tag:* Elle's Studio; *Stamps and ink:* Hero Arts; *Markers:* Copic; *Adhesive:* EK Success.

WEAVE border stickers together for a unique background design.

Your Friendship *by Jennifer McGuire.* **Supplies** *Border stickers:* Doodlebug Design; *Stamp and ink:* Stampin' Up!; *Die cut:* Silhouette, QuicKutz; *Adhesive:* Dot 'n' Roller, Kokuyo.

COVER border stickers with Glossy Accents for extra shine—it creates an epoxy-like finish.

Today, Tomorrow, Always *by Jennifer McGuire.* **Supplies** *Border sticker:* Hambly Screen Prints; *Tag:* Making Memories; *Stamp and ink:* Hero Arts; *Bird brad:* Creative Imaginations; *Liquid adhesive:* Glossy Accents, Ranger Industries; *Adhesive:* Dot 'n' Roller, Kokuyo.

ADD stitching to a border sticker for more interest.

I Simply Enjoy You *by Jennifer McGuire.* **Supplies** *Border stickers:* BasicGrey; *Die cut:* QuicKutz; *Stamps and patterned paper:* Stampin' Up!; *Buttons and pearl:* Hero Arts; *Ink:* Distress Ink, Ranger Industries; *Adhesive:* Scrapbook Adhesives by 3L; *Other:* Thread.

EVEN though stickers are already self-adhesive, add foam dots for dimension when adhering your border to your project.

Thank You by Jennifer McGuire. **Supplies** Border sticker: Reminisce; Background stamp, inks, pearls and note card: Hero Arts; Letter stamps: Maya Road; Die cut: Silhouette, QuicKutz; Adhesive: 3D-Dots, EK Success; Dot 'n' Roller, Kokuyo; Other: Button, ribbon, twine and thread.

DECORATE a plain gift bag with stripes of border stickers.

Sending You Birthday Wishes by Jennifer McGuire. **Supplies** Border stickers: Hambly Screen Prints; Stamp and ink: Stampin' Up!; Other: Flower, twine and brown bag.

Try It Yourself!

Are you looking for some beautiful border stickers? Try these:

Paper Ribbon: Delightful
Creative Memories
CreativeMemories.com

Fancy Frills: Key Lime
Doodlebug Design
Doodlebug.ws

Kraft Cardstock Stickers
Hambly Screen Prints
HamblyScreenPrints.com

Border & Tag
Stickers: Passport
Making Memories
MakingMemories.com ck

a touch of *felt*

I am always looking for ways to add texture to my scrapbook pages without adding too much bulk. One of my favorite textures comes from felt—a product I remember crafting with as a child! Here are some fresh technique takes for incorporating felt into your upcoming projects.

7 new *twists* for using felt

Merry Christmas, Little Dude

Christmas 2006

happy

FANCY up felt accents with sewing and gemstones.

Happy *by Jennifer McGuire.* **Supplies** *Felt:* Close To My Heart (snowflakes and scallop circle frame) and Martha Stewart Crafts (letters); *Cardstock:* Bazzill Basics Paper; *Patterned paper:* KI Memories; *Stamps and rhinestones:* Hero Arts; *Ink:* Distress Ink, Ranger Industries; *Twine:* Papertrey Ink; *Circle punches:* EK Success; *Adhesive:* 3D-Dots, EK Success; Dot 'n' Roller, Kokuyo; *Other:* Thread.

BY JENNIFER McGUIRE

ADD lines of faux stitching to felt using Liquid Pearls or another dimensional paint.

Wishing You Peace by Jennifer McGuire. Supplies *Felt:* Close To My Heart (scallop) and EK Success (flower); *Patterned paper:* Bo-Bunny Press (dot) and Making Memories (ledger); *Stamps and ink:* Hero Arts; *Dimensional paint:* Liquid Pearls, Ranger Industries; *Corner-rounder punch:* Corner Chomper, We R Memory Keepers; *Adhesive:* Glue Dots International.

LAYER felt for added dimension.

Joy, Joy, Joy by Jennifer McGuire. Supplies *Felt:* Close To My Heart; *Stamps, ink and rhinestones:* Hero Arts; *Ink and glitter glue:* Ranger Industries; *Other:* Thread and string.

TEMPORARILY ADHERE felt to an acrylic mounting block and use it to stamp with paint.

Merry Christmas by Jennifer McGuire. Supplies *Felt:* BasicGrey (flower) and Close To My Heart (flourishes used for stamping); *Stamp, ink, rhinestones and note card:* Hero Arts; *Paint:* Paint Dabbers, Ranger Industries; *Corner-rounder punch:* Corner Chomper, We R Memory Keepers.

PAINT felt for a new look.

Joy by Jennifer McGuire. Supplies *Felt:* Kaisercraft (border), Making Memories (letters) and Martha Stewart Crafts (white stars); *Patterned paper:* Studio Calico; *Paint:* Dimensional Pearls, Ranger Industries; *Rhinestones:* Hero Arts; *Adhesive:* Dot 'n' Roller, Kokuyo.

MAKE an ornament with felt, pins and a foam ball.

Ornament *by Jennifer McGuire.* **Supplies** *Felt:* Hero Arts; *Ribbon and string:* Creative Impressions; *Other:* Foam ball and pins.

COVER felt with glitter for extra shine.

A Happy New Year *by Jennifer McGuire.* **Supplies** *Felt:* American Crafts; *Patterned paper:* Making Memories; *Stamp and ink:* Hero Arts; *Glitter glue:* Stickles, Ranger Industries; *Corner-rounder punch:* Corner Chomper, We R Memory Keepers; *Adhesive:* Dot 'n' Roller, Kokuyo; *Other:* Ribbon.

fabulous felt finds

Check out these great felt products you're sure to enjoy.

Woolies: Eskimo Kisses
BasicGrey
BasicGrey.com

Fozz Fontz
Kaisercraft
Kaisercraft.net

Classic Scroll Black
Queen & Co.
QueenandCompany.com

Feltalicious
Blueye Dezines
BluEyeDezines.com.au **ck**

⸙ in a *punch* ⸙

Punches of basic shapes are staples for scrapbookers, but they become a creative goldmine when you think about using them in clever ways. Just by clipping an edge or folding a corner, you can change the look of a simple punched shape instantly! Check out a few of my favorite ways to get creative with punches.

8 new *techniques* using everyday punches

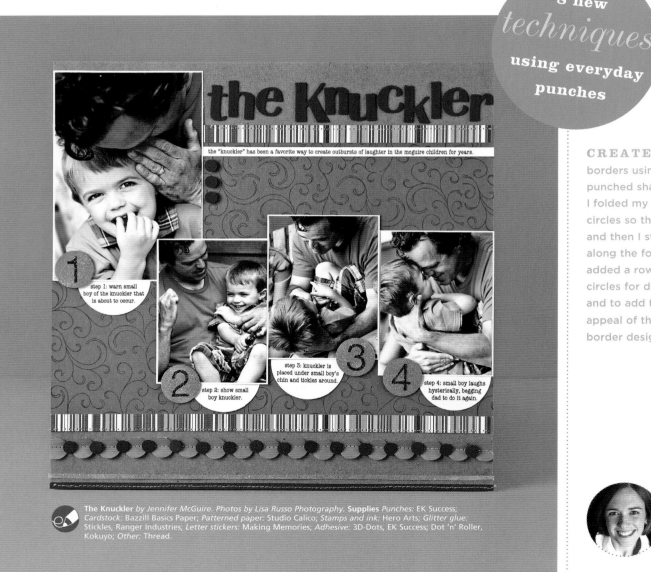

The Knuckler *by Jennifer McGuire. Photos by Lisa Russo Photography.* **Supplies** *Punches:* EK Success; *Cardstock:* Bazzill Basics Paper; *Patterned paper:* Studio Calico; *Stamps and ink:* Hero Arts; *Glitter glue:* Stickles, Ranger Industries; *Letter stickers:* Making Memories; *Adhesive:* 3D-Dots, EK Success; Dot 'n' Roller, Kokuyo; *Other:* Thread.

CREATE unique borders using punched shapes. I folded my green circles so they lift up, and then I stitched along the fold. I added a row of red circles for dimension and to add to the appeal of the border design.

BY JENNIFER McGUIR

CREATE a ticket shape from a rectangle block by punching a quarter circle from each outside corner of the rectangle.

Kay *by Jennifer McGuire.* **Supplies** *Punches:* EK Success; *Stamps:* Studio Calico; *Rub-on:* Melissa Frances; *Embossing folder and machine:* Cuttlebug, Provo Craft; *Ribbon and twine:* Creative Impressions; *Adhesive:* 3D-Dots, EK Success.

PUNCH vellum circles in several sizes, distress the edges and then layer them to create a flower.

Baby Girl *by Jennifer McGuire.* **Supplies** *Circle punches:* McGill; *Patterned paper:* Papertrey Ink; *Stamp and ink:* Hero Arts; *Tag die cut:* Silhouette, Quickutz; *Fabric brad:* K&Company; *Markers:* Copic; *Adhesive:* 3D-Dots, EK Success; *Other:* Vellum.

CREATE an owl (or any shape) by mixing and matching your punched shapes. This owl was created with square, circle, heart and leaf punches.

Owl Always Love You *by Jennifer McGuire.* **Supplies** *Punches:* EK Success (circles), McGill (squares) and Stampin' Up! (heart); *Patterned paper:* Hero Arts and Papertrey Ink; *Stamps:* Hero Arts; *Ink:* Distress Ink, Ranger Industries; *Embossing folder and machine:* Cuttlebug, Provo Craft; *Font:* American Typewriter; *Adhesive:* Dot 'n' Roller, Kokuyo; *Other:* Googly eyes and vintage text paper.

HOW-TO: CREATE AN OWL FROM PUNCHED SHAPES

1. Punch a square for the owl body. Round the two bottom corners. Punch a large rounded edge from the top using part of a large circle punch.

2. Create eyes with a circle punch.

3. Punch two leaves for the arms.

4. Finish the look with a punched heart and a punched or hand-cut triangle for the beak.

TRANSFORM two punched hearts and a few rhinestones into a butterfly shape.

Live *by Jennifer McGuire.* **Supplies** *Punches:* Fiskars Americas; *Patterned paper:* Bo-Bunny Press; *Rhinestones, stamps and ink:* Hero Arts; *Tag:* Studio Calico; *Adhesive:* Dot 'n' Roller, Kokuyo.

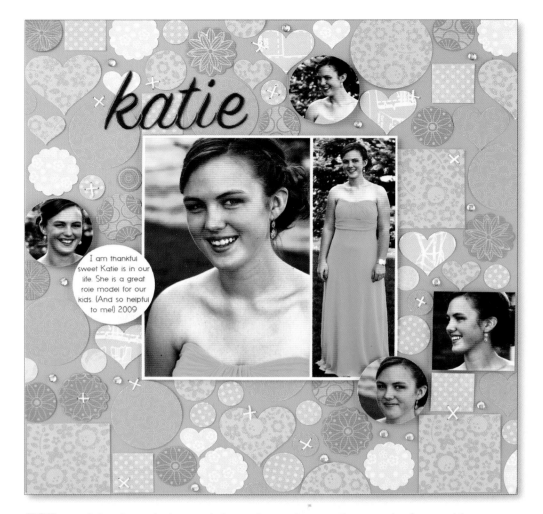

I am thankful sweet Katie is in our life. She is a great role model for our kids. (And so helpful to me!) 2009

USE a variety of punch sizes and shapes to create an entire page background from paper scraps. You can even punch some photos in the shapes to add unity to your page design.

Katie *by Jennifer McGuire.* **Supplies** *Punches:* Creative Memories (square), Fiskars Americas (hearts), McGill (scallops) and Oriental Trading Company (circles); *Cardstock:* Bazzill Basics Paper; *Patterned paper:* Autumn Leaves (small flower), Bo-Bunny Press (dot), Doodlebug Design (flower and flourish) and Studio Calico (sewing pattern); *Stamps, ink and rhinestones:* Hero Arts; *Letter stickers:* American Crafts; *Font:* Dreambog; *Adhesive:* 3D-Dots, EK Success, Dot 'n' Roller, Kokuyo; *Other:* String.

try it yourself

Once you're ready to experiment with punches, try one of these fabulous finds.

Square Maker
Creative Memories
CreativeMemories.com

Diamond
EK Success
EKSuccess.com

Oval 'n Oval Again
Fiskars Americas
FiskarsCrafts.com

Circle
McGill
McGillInc.com

pedal to the *metal*

When I first started scrapbooking six years ago, metal embellishments were the new craze. Scrapbook companies were just introducing them to the market—the products were so innovative and fun! Metal is just as popular today. Here are some ideas for using this great product on your pages.

8 new *looks* **for metal**

Kindness *by Jennifer McGuire.* **Supplies** *Metal accents:* American Art Clay Company (border sticker), Close To My Heart (photo corners), Making Memories (butterflies) and Stampin' Up! (brads); *Textured cardstock and letter stickers:* American Crafts; *Patterned paper:* Close To My Heart; *Punches:* Fiskars Americas (border) and The Punch Bunch (label); *Paint:* Paint Dabbers, Ranger Industries; *Adhesive:* 3D-Dots Foam Adhesive, EK Success; Dot 'n' Roller, Kokuyo.

PAINT metal embellishment and then sand the top to reveal portions of the metal below.

BY JENNIFER McGUIRE

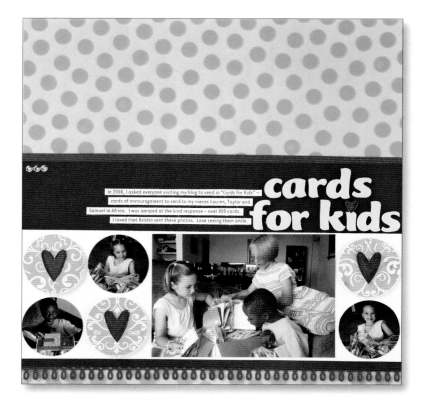

In 2008, I asked everyone visiting my blog to send in "Cards for Kids" — cards of encouragement to send to my nieces Lauren, Taylor and Samuel in Africa. I was amazed at the kind response – over 800 cards. I loved that Kristin sent these photos. Love seeing them smile.

cards for kids

ADD rub-ons to metal for a new look. I added flourish rub-ons to silver paper and punched three circles from the sheet.

Cards for Kids by Jennifer McGuire. **Supplies** Metal sheet: Funky Film, Graphix; Cardstock and letter stickers: American Crafts; Patterned paper: Bo-Bunny Press; Textured paper: Doodlebug Design; Rub-ons: Maya Road; Punches: Fiskars Americas (circle), Martha Stewart Crafts (border) and Stampin' Up! (heart); Flat metal gems: Hero Arts; Adhesive: 3D-Dots Foam Adhesive, EK Success, Dot 'n' Roller, Kokuyo; Glossy Accents, Ranger Industries.

STAMP on metal with black ink. *Note:* Be sure to use a solvent-based ink, such as StazOn from Tsukineko, for best results on the metal surface.

Sky's the Limit by Jennifer McGuire. **Supplies** Metal sheet: Funky Film, Graphix; Patterned paper: SEI; Brads: Stampin' Up!; Airplane stamp and tape: Studio Calico; Ink: StazOn, Tsukineko; Message stamp: Hero Arts; Corner-rounder tool: Corner Chomper, We R Memory Keepers; Other: Fabric.

SAND shiny metal for a textured finish, like I did with the flower accent.

Bonus Tip: Cut a metal sheet to tag size and round the corners—it provides a fun alternative to patterned paper or regular tags.

Thinking of You by Jennifer McGuire. **Supplies** Metal sheet: Funky Film, Grafix; Metal accent: Making Memories; Patterned paper: October Afternoon; Rub-ons: Melissa Frances; Sanding block: Tim Holtz for Advantus; Ribbon: Creative Impressions; Pearl: Hero Arts; Corner-rounder tool: Corner Chomper, We R Memory Keepers.

DIE cut shapes from thin sheets of metal.

Together *by Jennifer McGuire.* **Supplies** *Metal sheet:* Funky Film, Graphix; *Cardstock:* American Crafts; *Stamp and ink:* Hero Arts (background) and Stampin' Up! ("together"); *Embossing folder:* QuicKutz; *Die-cut shape:* Sizzix, Ellison (flower) and Spellbinders (label); *Ink:* Distress Ink, Ranger Industries; *Other:* Gems.

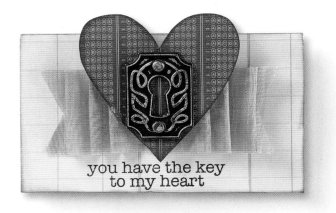

PLEAT a strip of metal mesh like you would a piece of ribbon.

Bonus Tip: Combine metal accents with punched cardstock for a paper-pieced design.

You Have the Key *by Jennifer McGuire.* **Supplies** *Metal mesh:* American Art Clay Company; *Patterned paper:* Cosmo Cricket (red) and Making Memories (ledger); *Metal keyhole charm:* Tim Holtz for Advantus; *Stamps and ink:* Hero Arts; *Embossing powder:* Ranger Industries.

Beautiful *by Jennifer McGuire.* **Supplies** *Metal sheet:* American Art Clay Company; *Stamps:* Close To My Heart ("beautiful") and Hero Arts (swirl); *Ink:* Distress Ink, Ranger Industries; *Flowers:* Sassafras; *Ribbon:* Anna Griffin.

TURN A STAMP IMAGE INTO AN EMBOSSED DESIGN IN METAL SHEETS. HERE'S HOW:

❶ Stamp an image on the back of a metal sheet.

❷ Place the stamped image on a foam pad and trace the image with a dry-embossing tool. Flip the metal over to show the embossed pattern.

USE TEXTURED METAL AS A STAMP, HERE'S HOW:

Be Mine *by Jennifer McGuire.* **Supplies** *Metal border:* American Art Clay Company; *Stamps:* Papertrey Ink; *Ink:* ColorBox Chalk Ink, Clearsnap; *Punch:* Fiskars Americas; *Other:* String and kraft paper.

try it yourself

Want to check out some metals? Try these:

Metal Accent Sheets
American Art
Clay Company
Amaco.com

**Jolee's Jewels:
Heart Lock & Key**
EK Success
EKSuccess.com

Funky Film
Graphix Funky Film
GrafixArts.com

Hodgepodge Hardware
Stampin' Up!
StampinUp.com **ck**

Scrapbook a YEAR

of memories in one night

What an exciting (and exhausting) year it's been. You've probably had a busy year participating in sporting activities, attending celebrations, traveling and taking care of your home and family. But do you sometimes find that after you've photographed all the fun throughout the year that it's harder than you expected to scrapbook each of the many pages on your to-do list? Me, too! My suggestion is to create a year-in-review design to showcase your fun-filled year on one layout. Place this must-create layout at the top of your to-do list today for instant scrapping satisfaction.

By Lori Anderson

it was a great year 2008...

Create a Photo Collage of Highlights

How great would it feel to scrapbook an entire year's worth of memories in one evening? That's exactly what I did in my "It Was a Great Year" layout. To create the layout, I selected 12 photos that had special meaning to me and wrote a small paragraph about each photo. In one quick glance, you can see what my family has been up to this year, and I can rest easy knowing that if I get the chance to scrapbook only once in awhile, this important layout is finished and in my album.

It Was a Great Year *by Lori Anderson.* **Supplies** *Cardstock:* Bazzill Basics Paper; *Letter stickers:* Anna Griffin (red) and Making Memories (black); *Rub-ons:* American Crafts ("you rock"), Glitz Design (dot) and KI Memories (white letters); *Flowers:* Sandylion; *Brad:* Die Cuts With a View; *Fonts:* Calibri, Pupcat and You Are Loved; *Adhesive:* Mono Adhesive, Tombow; Scrapbook Adhesives by 3L; Foam Squares, Therm O Web.

Focus on the "Bests" of 2009

Have you seen the "Best of" articles highlighted on magazine and newspaper headlines this month? Try creating a "Best of" list of your own and turn it into a layout. Here, Brigid Gonzalez created her "Best of 2009" layout by including photos of some favorite books, movies and family moments of 2009. To mimic the high-contrast, vintage look of the photos she found on the Internet, Brigid added a Hue/Saturation adjustment layer in Photoshop to give her personal photos the same feel.

PHOTO HOW-TO: The photos on this layout are all 2½" squares.

Best of 2009 *by Brigid Gonzalez.* **Supplies** *Cardstock:* Die Cuts With a View (gray) and The Paper Company (orange); *Software:* Adobe Photoshop CS3; *Fonts:* Calibri and Impact; *Adhesive:* Scrapbook Adhesives by 3L; *Square punch:* Marvy Uchida.

Destination 2009 *by Summer Fullerton.* **Supplies**
Cardstock: Bazzill Basics Paper (white and black)
and Jillibean Soup (kraft); *Patterned paper:* Jillibean
Soup (kraft, red, green and blue) and October
Afternoon (map); *Die cut and vacation sticker:*
October Afternoon; *Felt:* Creative Imaginations;
Chipboard accent: Maya Road; *Corrugated numbers
and twine:* Jillibean Soup; *Paint:* Making Memories;
Buttons: Autumn Leaves (black) and Jillibean
Soup (green); *Brads:* BasicGrey; *Scallop punch:*
Stampin' Up!; *Embroidery floss:* DMC; *Fonts:* Arial
and Typenoksidi; *Adhesive:* Kokuyo and Scrapbook
Adhesives by 3L; *Other:* Staples.

Follow a Page-Protector Design

If you're one of those people always off on an adventure, why not scrapbook
your journeys from an entire year on one layout, just as Summer Fullerton did
here? Summer created this layout in record time by mimicking a six-up photo
page protector design. She placed her 4" x 6" photos on her pages and filled
the open areas with patterned paper to serve as a background for her ticket
stubs and title. It's so cute and so easy!

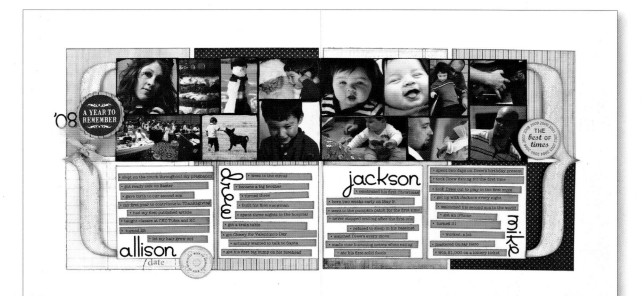

A Year to Remember *by Allison Davis.*
Supplies *Cardstock:* Bazzill Basics Paper;
Patterned paper: Creative Imaginations
(notebook) and Pink Paislee (blue, black
dot and green stripe); *Chipboard:*
Imagination Project (circles) and Making
Memories (brackets); *Stickers:* Creative
Imaginations ("Best of Times" circle) and
Doodlebug Design (letters); *Ink:* Making
Memories; *Ink:* ColorBox Fluid Chalk,
Clearsnap; *Ribbon:* May Arts; *Font:* American
Typewriter; *Adhesive:* Glue Dots International;
Pop Dots, All Night Media, Plaid Enterprises;
Scrapbook Adhesives by 3L.

Include the Journaling of Family Members

Why not ask family members about *their* favorite memories from the year and
incorporate their words in columns on your project? On this layout, Allison
Davis created a section for each family member, recorded the favorite memories onto journaling strips and placed a few photos of each family member
above the respective journaling sections. If you don't have photos that cor-
respond with each event mentioned in the journaling, it's okay. Just add any
favorite photos of your family members taken in 2009.

Utilize Pockets

One of Maggie Holmes's favorite aspects about creating a year-in-review layout is that she can use her meaningful photos that she wouldn't normally create an entire layout for. In her "2008 Review" layout, Maggie placed photos in baseball-card page protectors (trimmed to fit on her layout) and stapled them onto her pages. These pockets hold multiple photos and a journaling card about the month corresponding to the number on the front. By placing photos in the pockets, Maggie created a clean, crisp design and a fun, interactive layout.

2008 Review *by Maggie Holmes.* **Supplies** *Cardstock:* Prism Papers; *Patterned paper:* Lily Bee (red), Sassafras (yellow circle) and Studio Calico; *Number stickers:* American Crafts and Heidi Swapp for Advantus; *Stickers:* October Afternoon and Sassafras; *Journaling spot and felt star:* Making Memories; *Transparency and rub-on:* Hambly Screen Prints; *Stamps:* Studio Calico; *Ink:* Papertrey Ink; *Brads:* Making Memories and Sassafras; *Pen:* Slick Writers, American Crafts; *Scallop scissors:* Fiskars Americas; *Other:* Baseball-card page protectors and staples.

Perfect Pocket and Envelope Options

Maggie Holmes utilized baseball-card page protectors for her layout, but you could also try one of these options:

❶ **Bigz Scallop Envelope die**
Sizzix for Stampin' Up!
StampinUp.com

❷ **Glassine Envelope Findings**
Making Memories
MakingMemories.com

❸ **Memorabilia Pockets**
Creative Memories
CreativeMemories.com

❹ **Memorabilia Pockets**
Therm O Web
ThermOWeb.com

❺ **Keepsake Envelopes**
Scrapbook Adhesives by 3L
Scrapbook-Adhesives.com

❻ **BW Madeline Journal Pockets**
K&Company
KandCompany.com

january
01 new year's day
07 emma turns 6
february
14 stan sends gifties for valentine's day
23 great grandma rusk in art show
march
14 torrey's knocked out tooth came in
19 emma's kangaroo farm field trip
20 up to laconner to see the daffodil fields
25 torrey at young authors conference
april
09-11 surprise trip to seattle with girls for spring break
17, 30 up to roozengaarde to see tulips
may
09 torrey's state park field trip
11 mother's day & silly pictures
24 made homecoming signs for stan
june
06 stan comes home from 5th six month deployment
19 last day of school
24-30 vacation to yellowstone & the ranch
july
02 torrey turns 8 & we close on our new house
19-21 noel at c.h.a.
august
01-06 grandpa gene & grandma linn visit
15 emma lost her 2 front teeth
september
02 first day of school
5-7 camping at camano island state park with fuentes
25 stan turns 33
october
11 pumpkin patch with the family
23 torrey's rock quarry field trip
november
10 stan speaks at the veteran's day assembly
14 our 9 year anniversary
27 family thanksgiving at our house
december
09 torrey gets glasses, lots of snow & sledding
23 noel turns 32
25 family christmas at our house
30 stan hit by drunk driver

i heart this

life 2008

I Heart This Life *by Noel Culbertson.*
Supplies *Software:* Adobe Photoshop Elements 6.0; *Patterned paper:* Hoopla: Oh Happy Day by Paislee Press Designs; *Stamps and elements:* Hoopla: Oh Happy Day, Happy as a Lark Kit and Sociologie Kit by Paislee Press Designs; *Frame:* Labeled Frames + Clipping Masks by Paislee Press Designs; *Fonts:* Decker and You Are Loved.

Make a Chronological List of Dates

Every family has important events and traditions that occur throughout the year. Record the important dates from the past year in chronological order. On this page, Noel Culbertson recorded multiple events for each month. She then selected a photo that represented one of the big moments or traditions that her family holds dear.

Even More Year-in-Review Ideas

Try some of these year-in-review layout ideas and you'll be on your way to completed albums in no time!

• Vacations
• School highlights
• Baby's first year
• Sporting activities
• Birthdays and holidays
• Family traditions **ck**

january *to-do list*

A new year means opportunity—a chance to plan, to create, to try something new. Don't be overwhelmed by the entire year, though. Let's take it month by month. Consider January . . .

plan now to accomplish *more* this month

toast

Toast *by Amanda Probst.* **Supplies** *Cardstock:* Prism Papers; *Letter stickers:* American Crafts; *Brad:* Déjà Views by The C-Thru Ruler Co.; *Pens:* Precision Pens, American Crafts (black); Mark-It, Bic (yellow); Zig Writer, EK Success (brown); *Other:* Fiber.

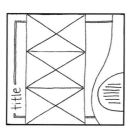

☐ **CELEBRATE POOH BEAR.** A.A. Milne's birthday is January 18. Document a favorite childhood book or stuffed animal.

☐ **MAKE AN ORNAMENT ALBUM.** When taking down decorations, snap a photo of your ornaments. Make a mini album or a layout telling the stories behind the ornaments.

☐ **CHEERS!** Scrapbook a New Year's toast or your own New Year's tradition.

☐ **BREAK IT DOWN BY MONTH.** In making your resolutions this year, assign projects to specific months to make your list more manageable.

☐ **PLAN AHEAD.** If your January is slow like mine, use the time to create a stash of cards for the year in advance.

☐ **WRITE IT DOWN.** The fourth week of January is National Handwriting Analysis Week. Handwrite your journaling on at least one layout this month. **ck**

BY AMANDA PROBST

february

Ah, February. Love is in the air. Beyond the hearts and flowers, though, what's your passion? This February, think outside the (chocolate) box as you share your love.

accomplish **more** *this month*

From the Bottom of My Heart *by Amanda Probst.*
Supplies *Cardstock:* Prism Papers; *Glitter letters:* Making Memories; *Journaling card:* October Afternoon; *Vinyl letters and pen:* American Crafts.

☐ **SEND YOUR OWN VALENTINES.** They don't have to come from boxes or be just for kids. Make your own this year and bring smiles to those you love.

☐ **PASS IT ON.** The second week of February is Random Acts of Kindness Week. Celebrate by sending a "RAK" to a friend or colleague.

☐ **CAPTURE BEAUTY.** With winter in full force, February isn't always the prettiest of months. Take time to photograph samples of beauty when you find them.

☐ **SOMETHING OLD AND SOMETHING NEW.** Take up an old hobby or try a new one this month (or incorporate a favorite into your next layout). Find something you love!

☐ **MARK THE PLACE.** Scrapbook a place (or places) you really love and explain why. **ck**

BY AMANDA PROBST

a *plan* for march

March didn't turn out very well for Julius Caesar ("Et tu, Brute?"). For the rest of us, though, March may well conjure "lucky" images of little green leprechauns, the beginnings of spring and pots of gold. Given that, let's concentrate on the fortunate things in our lives, shall we?

enjoy 5 **lively** *activities together*

Today Was Good *by Amanda Probst.* **Supplies** *Cardstock:* Prism Papers; *Fonts:* Century Gothic and Stop Sign.

□ **UNCOVER YOUR OWN POT OF GOLD.**
Beyond friends and family, what is it that you treasure or collect?

□ **WISH DR. SEUSS A HAPPY BIRTHDAY!**
March 2 is *Read Across America Day* in honor of Dr. Seuss's birthday. Use a Seussian quote on a layout this month like I did.

□ **FRESHEN UP YOUR SCRAP SPACE.**
Spring cleaning is in order! Purge your stash and give the extras to a local charity or school.

□ **VISIT THE ZOO.**
March supposedly comes in like a lion, right? When was the last time you went to the zoo? Bet that picture of you near the lion exhibit will make a great layout!

□ **EAT CHOCOLATE.** Yes, it's true. The third week of March is American Chocolate Week. Celebrate by hosting a crop and providing chocolate for your scrapbooking friends! ck

BY AMANDA PROBST

april
activities

As we move from winter into the full force of
spring, what says "spring" to you?

The Bubble Recipe *by Amanda Probst.* **Supplies** *Cardstock:* Prism Papers; *Pens:* Precision Pens,
American Crafts; Mark It, BIC; *Fonts:* Century Gothic and CK Taliatype.

☐ **BUY A NEW UMBRELLA.**
Be protected from those April
showers—alter an umbrella with
your scrapbooking supplies to
make it a bit more personal.

☐ **ENCOURAGE GREEN
COMPANIES.**
More and more scrapbooking com-
panies are going green. Support
these pioneers as you celebrate
Earth Day on April 22.

☐ **GO WITH A THEME.**
Easter baskets needn't be just
about candy. Try a theme such as
sand toys, sidewalk chalk, bath fun,
pirates, games . . . the list goes on.

☐ **MAKE BUBBLES.**
It's hard to beat the sheer delight
of a child with bubbles. Mix up
some of your own (and photograph it!).

☐ **REMEMBER NUMBERS.**
April is Mathematics Education
Month. What kinds of numbers did
you deal with this month? How can
you include numbers on a layout?

☐ **EXPERIENCE
METAMORPHOSIS.**
Everyone should raise caterpillars
to butterflies at least once. Take a
picture a day and I promise you'll
be in awe. **ck**

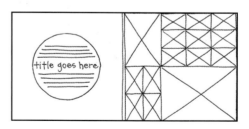

BY AMANDA PROBST

your May *plan*

Now that spring has fully sprung, get outside! May has always seemed extra busy with the school year ending and summer preparations starting, but the sunshine and warm temperatures always remind me to take some time for myself, preferably outdoors.

11 Wheels & Counting *by Amanda Probst.* **Supplies** *Cardstock:* Prism Papers; *Patterned paper:* Teresa Collins; *Pen:* Precision Pens, American Crafts; *Acetate star:* Fancy Pants Designs; *Iconoclasp:* Fred; *Fonts:* CK Racer, Impact and Rockwell.

☐ **PREPARE YOUR TOOLS.** Just as you'll turn sprinkler systems back on and tune up that lawnmower, take time to reacquaint yourself with outdoor photography camera tips.

☐ **WRITE A LETTER.** The first full week of May is National Teacher Appreciation Week. Send a heartfelt note to a long-lost teacher to share how much you appreciated his or her time.

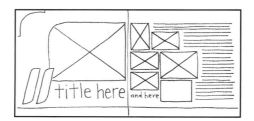

☐ **CELEBRATE FIRSTS.** Sally Ride was the first American woman in space. Her birthday is May 26, 1951. What have you been "first" at?

☐ **WALK DOWN MEMORY LANE.** It's that time of year. Prom. Have you scrapbooked your prom photographs yet?

☐ **RIDE A BIKE.** May is National Bike Month. Have you ridden yours lately? This month, I scrapbooked about how many "wheels" are in my family because of my three boys (see layout above). **ck**

BY AMANDA PROBST

june *joys*

Ah, summer. For many of us, June means a change of pace as the school year closes and summer activities commence. New schedules are adopted and sunshine reigns. What changes does summer bring to your life?

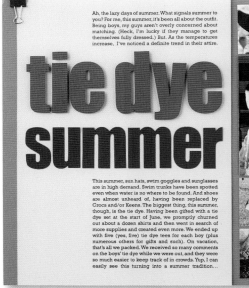

Tie Dye Summer by Amanda Probst. **Supplies** *Cardstock:* Prism Papers; *Fabric ribbon:* Imagination Project; *Die-cutting machine:* Silhouette, QuicKutz; *Fonts:* Impact and Rockwell; *Adhesive:* 3D Foam Squares and E-Z Runner, Scrapbook Adhesives by 3L; Dot n' Roller, Kokuyo; *Other:* Bracelet, staples and binder clip.

☐ **CELEBRATE THE SOLSTICE.** The longest day of the year seems a prime opportunity for a sunshine party . . . or an all-day crop, perhaps?

☐ **LOOK IN THE MIRROR.** What does your summer wardrobe consist of? Do you have a favorite outfit? Document it, like I did for my children on the layout above!

☐ **DRINK SOME ICED TEA.** June is National Iced Tea Month. How do you make yours? Is it worth recording any secret recipes?

☐ **COUNT THE GUYS.** Beyond fathers, who are the other guys in your life? Do a layout or mini album featuring them.

☐ **CREATE A FLAG.** In honor of Flag Day on June 14, why not design your own family flag with your scrapbook supplies? **ck**

BY AMANDA PROBST

july *days*

With summer in full swing, July is a perfect month for lazy days, time spent outdoors and reflections on patriotism. Beyond fireworks celebrations, July seems to find my family engaged in barbeques, water fights and explanations about our country's history. How do you spend July?

get *creative* with a July twist

 Star of the Water Fight *by Amanda Probst.* **Supplies** *Cardstock:* Prism Papers; *Patterned paper:* Fancy Pants Designs; *Glitter stars:* Prima; *Felt star:* Making Memories; *Die-cutting machine:* Silhouette, QuickKutz; *Fonts:* Century Gothic, Impact, VNI-Thufap2 and Wingdings; *Adhesive:* Dot 'n' Roller, Kokuyo; Glue Dots, Glue Dots International.

☐ **GO ALIEN.** July 2 is World UFO Day. Even if you don't believe in life on other planets, why not use some fun monster-, alien- or robot-themed products to celebrate? They're great for boy pages.

☐ **HIT A HOME RUN.** No matter which summer sports you (or your kids) participate in, quick and easy photo books are a grand-slam way to capture all those action shots.

☐ **USE THE SUNLIGHT.** It's often so much easier to take photos outdoors. Take advantage of the natural light during family reunions to get some great shots.

☐ **GIVE THE FLOWERS A REST.** July is the perfect month to switch things up with your typical page accents and use star embellishments galore instead of flowers. I used glitter, felt and hand-cut stars on my "Star of the Water Fight" layout.

☐ **CELEBRATE HALF.** July marks the halfway point of the year—a perfect opportunity to take stock and make a half-year-in-review layout. **ck**

BY AMANDA PROBST

august *to-dos*

August is always a little bittersweet to me. It usually finds my family trying to fit in any remaining vacation time while simultaneously gearing up for the coming school year. Given this, it's often a month on the move and is almost always packed with photo ops. Where are you going this August?

try these *five* creative ideas

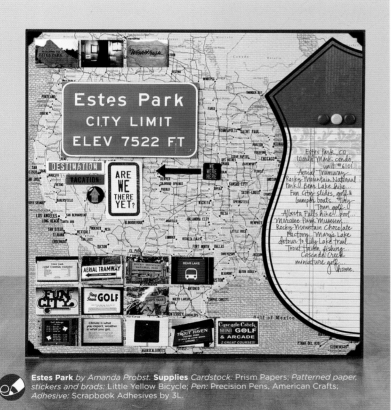

Estes Park *by Amanda Probst.* **Supplies** *Cardstock:* Prism Papers; *Patterned paper, stickers and brads:* Little Yellow Bicycle; *Pen:* Precision Pens, American Crafts; *Adhesive:* Scrapbook Adhesives by 3L.

BY AMANDA PROBST

☐ **READ THE SIGNS.** If you're going on a trip this month, a quick and easy way to document your route is to photograph the signs along the way. Use them altogether or use them individually as layout titles—I did both in my "Estes Park" layout.

☐ **CELEBRATE LEFT-HANDEDNESS.** Are you a lefty? Then August 13 is for you! It's International Left-Hander's Day. Though only about 10 percent of the population is left-handed, we can all celebrate. Try doing everything with the opposite hand that day, just for fun.

☐ **DOCUMENT TRANSPORTATION.** What gets you around? Most of us spend plenty of time in our vehicles, so why not make a layout about our car? If you're taking a trip, what modes of transportation did you use?

☐ **SHARE YOUR LIST.** What's on your back-to-school shopping list? Think of the layout opportunities it presents: the list itself, the shopping bags afterward, a fully stocked backpack and more.

☐ **BE FAIR.** August 26 is Women's Equality Day, held in honor of the passage of the 19th Amendment giving women the right to vote. What rights do you value? What rights do you take for granted? Document your thoughts on a page! **ck**

it's back
to business

5 ideas
for september

I love September. I love the way it's a new beginning of sorts, with the new school year and a new daily routine after a lazy summertime. I love the smell of newly sharpened pencils and the joy found in a new backpack. This month, I have five ideas on my list. Mostly, though, I just love getting down to business.

Apples of My Eye *by Amanda Probst.* **Supplies** *Cardstock:* Prism Papers; *Patterned paper:* October Afternoon; *Paper apple:* Jolee's by You, EK Success; *Fonts:* Century Gothic, CK Surfer and Rockwell; *Adhesive:* Scrapbook Adhesives by 3L; Ranger Industries.

☐ **MAKE BACKPACK TAGS.** Though your kids probably won't lug their baby albums to school with them, they're sure to let you use your supplies to make a fun backpack tag for them.

☐ **BE INSPIRED BY A BOOK.** Are you in need of a muse? Try browsing your bookshelf! I love borrowing design and layout titles from book covers. Try it!

☐ **MAKE YOUR OWN LIST OF RULES.** In honor of Constitution Day (September 17) and school teachers everywhere, create your own list of rules to live by. Frame your layout and hang it in your home or office.

☐ **USE APPLES.** Speaking of school teachers, bring on the apples! With so many fun apple embellishments and papers available today, be sure to use some apples this month. (You don't even have to scrapbook about a teacher!)

☐ **BE GRATEFUL.** The fourth week of September is Banned Books Week. What books could you not live without? Why? Take a moment this month to share your appreciation. **ck**

BY AMANDA PROBST

10 fun things to do in October

October is such a photo-worthy month, don't you think? Between pumpkin patches, fall leaves, soccer seasons and kids in costumes, it's no wonder that I tend to take more pictures in October than in any other month. Here are 10 things to be sure to do (and photograph) this month.

what will *your family* **do?**

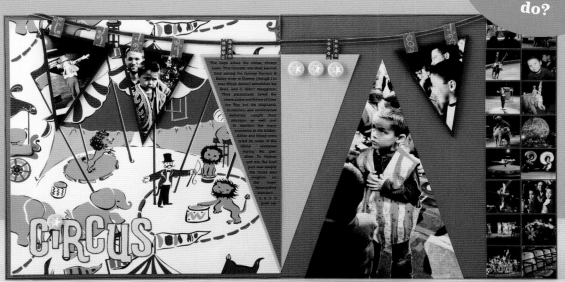

Circus *by Amanda Probst.* **Supplies** *Cardstock:* Prism Papers; *Patterned paper, brads and paper ribbon:* Anna Griffin; *Ribbon:* May Arts; *Die-cutting machine:* Silhouette, QuicKutz; *Pens:* Precision Pens, American Crafts (black) and Mark-it, Bic (green); *Fonts:* CK Surfer (title) and Rockwell; *Adhesive:* Scrapbook Adhesives by 3L; Glossy Accents, Ranger Industries; *Other:* Staples.

☐ **CLEAN UP.** Kids with rakes are pretty dang cute.

☐ **MAKE A TIMELINE.** Capture the selection and creation of the costume.

☐ **GO TO THE CIRCUS.** Speaking of costumes, have you been to the circus lately? You'll find my take on this subject in the layout above.

☐ **LET THEM ATTACK.** Have kids throw leaves at you . . . and the camera. (You may want to stand back and zoom in.)

☐ **ADMIT YOUR FEARS.** Photograph something that scares you.

☐ **SIT ON IT.** A child sitting on a pumpkin . . . you can't beat it.

☐ **MAKE AN ANGEL.** Leaf angels are cooler than snow angels.

☐ **USE THE SEEDS.** Close-up shots of pumpkin innards make great backgrounds for scrapbook pages if you enlarge the photo.

☐ **PULL OUT THE SWEATERS.** Take some macro shots of your favorite sweater.

☐ **VISIT A FARM.** Try a hayride, apple picking or a horse ride—there are so many possibilities. **ck**

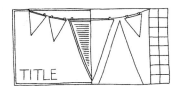

BY AMANDA PROBST

journaling ideas for november

November is my favorite month. Fall is in full swing, the holidays are approaching and soccer season is over. It's the perfect month for reflection, gratitude and family. Further, November is a month for traditions. Have you recorded yours?

try one of these 5 ideas

 My Sibs *by Amanda Probst.* **Supplies** *Cardstock:* Prism Papers; *Fabric letters:* American Crafts; *Die-cutting machine:* Silhouette, QuicKutz; *Rub-on:* Maya Road; *Monogram:* My Mind's Eye; *Rhinestones:* Kaisercraft; *Pens:* Precision Pens, American Crafts; Sketch Marker, Copic; *Fonts:* VNI-HLThuphap and Rockwell; *Adhesive:* Dot 'n' Roller, Kokuyo; E-Z Runner and 3D Foam Squares, Scrapbook Adhesives by 3L.

☐ **CELEBRATE SIBLINGS.** November 29 is Louisa May Alcott's birthday. As Jo March does in *Little Women*, record your relationship with your siblings. That's what I did for my "My Sibs" layout.

☐ **PLACE YOUR VOTE.** Although this year isn't as "big" of an election year as 2008 was, you can still scrapbook your voting activities. You can also scrapbook about last year if you haven't already.

☐ **VISIT SOME GOBBLERS.** My dad used to raise turkeys and liked to show them off to his grandkids. Live turkeys plus children equals a photo op!

☐ **PRESERVE A PRAYER.** Though many of us say them, how many of you have recorded a favorite prayer and why you like it?

☐ **ADOPT A NEW TRADITION.** November celebrates National Adoption Week. In honor of it, find something to adopt in your life; you could adopt a new tradition into your life or note one you cherish today. **ck**

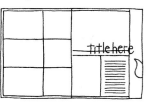

BY AMANDA PROBST

december enjoyments

Is it December already? How did that happen? Despite the best intentions, you're probably swamped this month. Amid the shopping, wrapping and getting last-minute hostess gifts, be sure to take a moment for yourself. If it's a scrappy moment, that's all the better!

5 ideas to try this month

Ornament a Day *by Amanda Probst.* **Supplies** *Cardstock:* Prism Papers; *Die-cutting machine:* Silhouette, QuicKutz; *Stamps:* Cornish Heritage Farms (dot pattern), Hero Arts (wood-grain pattern); *Ink:* VersaMark, Tsukineko; *Fonts:* CK Racer, Rockwell and Rockwell Extra Bold; *Adhesive:* E-Z Runner and 3D Foam Squares, Scrapbook Adhesives by 3L; Glossy Accents, Ranger Industries.

☐ **MAKE AN ORNAMENT A DAY.** Rather than counting down on an advent calendar, my boys and I made an ornament a day last December. It's more work than setting up an advent calendar, but it's worth it. Check out our results on my layout above.

☐ **PHOTOGRAPH THE WRAPPING PART.** I've been meaning to do this for years, but I can't seem to remember to take a picture of me actually wrapping gifts instead of just photographing the unwrapping part. I always forget. This year I'll remember. Really!

☐ **CAMP OUT BY THE TREE.** A neighbor once told me that her family has a tradition of pulling out the sleeping bags one night before Christmas. As a family, they camp out by the lights of the Christmas tree and read and just enjoy being together. I'm going to copy her.

☐ **GROW SNOWFLAKES.** This activity involves Borax and some time, but you can grow your own snowflakes this December. Trust me, kids think it's cool. For a link to directions, visit CreatingKeepsakes.com/issues/-December_2009.

☐ **USE CATALOGS.** I love browsing the scads of catalogs that arrive in the mail during December. Rather than justtossing them when I'm done, I use a portion of them on layouts. Some of those covers are truly amazing. **ck**

BY AMANDA PROBST

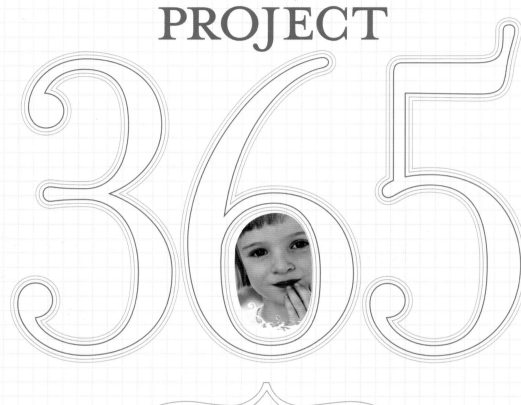

PROJECT 365

Snap a picture a day this year—then
scrap them all with this simple approach

BY BECKY HIGGINS

Like many of you, this past year I challenged myself to take a photo each day
for the entire year. While the challenge was fun and exciting, I quickly found
myself stumped when I tried to store, organize and present the pictures I'd
taken. I wanted to display a week's worth of photos at a time, but I couldn't
find any page protectors that worked with my 4" x 6" photos in this format.

To solve my dilemma (and possibly yours), I was inspired to create a kit
to kick off the new year—and you can do the same. Design your kit to present
a week's photos on a two-page layout with journaling. Following are two quick
examples I created using my kit, plus different takes by contributing editors
Jessica Sprague and Elizabeth Kartchner. You'll also find 365 ideas for photos
(see page 286). Now that you've got an easy way to present what you photograph, start snapping!

Capture 7 Days in 7 Photos

It couldn't be easier: insert your seven 4" x 6" photos (one for each day of the week) in seven of the pockets, then put a "Week of" card in the eighth pocket. Jot down notes on the journaling cards, then slip them in the bottom pockets. You've got a week of photos documented!

January 13–19 *by Becky Higgins.* **Supplies** January 2009 Kit of the Month, CreatingKeepsakes.com.

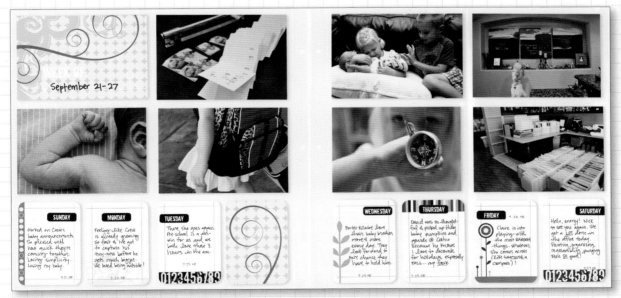

September 21–27 *by Becky Higgins.* **Supplies** January 2009 Kit of the Month, CreatingKeepsakes.com.

TIP: Put clear stickers on top of the page protector instead of directly on your photos.

Use transparent photo overlays and clear stickers (to label days of the week). Here, Jessica positioned patterned paper behind her clear stickers as a design element. To add a little variety, Jessica placed smaller photos in the journaling pockets and journaling in some larger pockets.

June 9, 2008 *by Jessica Sprague.* **Supplies** January 2009 Kit of the Month, CreatingKeepsakes.com.

September 8, 2008 *by Jessica Sprague.* **Supplies** January 2009 Kit of the Month, CreatingKeepsakes.com.

Tell the Story

At times, you may want to tell a longer story in your scrapbooks, while at other times you're fine with keeping things brief. I'm the same way—which is why I designed my kit to be as versatile as possible. You can make it "yours" at any time by simply adding a few pieces from your stash.

For the "Today" layout shown here, Elizabeth inserted all of her photos in the small pockets at the bottom of the page protectors. This gave her more journaling room in the 4" x 6" pockets at the top of the pages.

January 24 *by Elizabeth Kartchner.* **Supplies** *Patterned paper and journaling cards:* January 2009 Kit of the Month, CreatingKeepsakes.com; *Alphabet stickers:* American Crafts; *Word sticker:* KI Memories; *Stamp:* Autumn Leaves; *Ink:* StazOn, Tsukineko.

365

365 DAYS, 365 IDEAS FOR PHOTOS

1. Your backyard on a snowy day **2.** Your backyard on a rainy day **3.** Your backyard on a sunny day **4.** Your backyard on a fall day **5.** Your backyard on a spring day **6.** The view out your front door in winter **7.** The view out your front door in spring **8.** The view out your front door in summer **9.** The view out your front door in fall **10.** Your cleaning products **11.** You or a loved one at the computer **12.** Your self-portrait taken in a mirror **13.** Mittens, scarves, hats and boots **14.** Your hairstyle **15.** A close-up of icicles **16.** An elderly couple **17.** A close shot of a couple holding hands **18.** Your breakfast **19.** A child playing dress-up **20.** An outdoor ice-skating rink **21.** A hand proffering a valentine **22.** Rosy cheeks **23.** A steaming cup of hot chocolate with marshmallows **24.** Your open jewelry box **25.** A sunset **26.** A bowl of limes or lemons **27.** A frosty mug of beer or a glass of wine **28.** Family member's smiles **29.** A basketball game **30.** The first flowers of spring **31.** The first robin of spring **32.** Field trips **33.** Someone mowing the lawn **34.** Neighborhood produce or a flower stand **35.** A local flea market or a garage sale **36.** Gardening tools **37.** Your place of worship **38.** Teenagers in prom attire **39.** The grave of an ancestor **40.** Your car **41.** Someone riding a bicycle **42.** Farm animals **43.** Graduates with diplomas **44.** Someone playing with a pet **45.** A wedding party **46.** Your father's profile **47.** A child eating a Popsicle **48.** A motorboat on a lake **49.** Children playing in a fountain or sprinkler **50.** Cattails in a ditch **51.** Your car trunk packed for a vacation **52.** The main street of a small town **53.** A big-city skyline **54.** A hot-dog stand **55.** A grandmother playing with a grandchild **56.** A Ferris wheel or attractions at a local carnival **57.** Vines ripe with berries **58.** A parade **59.** People watching a fireworks display **60.** Children with sparklers **61.** Your most prized possession **62.** A cornfield **63.** A colorful patio or beach umbrella **64.** People waving flags **65.** Friends sitting on a park bench **66.** People playing catch **67.** A pitcher of lemonade or iced tea **68.** Someone getting a haircut **69.** Your workplace **70.** Your kids' schoolbooks **71.** Your grocery store **72.** A high-school football game **73.** Lunch boxes or lunch bags **74.** A school crossing guard on duty **75.** A soccer team practicing **76.** Your purse **77.** Pumpkins or gourds **78.** Birds flying south **79.** Baled hay stacked in fields **80.** A close-up of a colorful leaf in a puddle **81.** Costumed Halloween revelers **82.** A basket of apples **83.** A haunted house **84.** Someone on a cell phone **85.** Someone dressed in military apparel **86.** A leafless tree silhouetted against a twilight sky **87.** Freshly baked pies **88.** The Thanksgiving table **89.** A woman applying lipstick **90.** A wreath on a door **91.** Boxed ornaments or decorations **92.** Your family Bible **93.** A mailbox with holiday cards **94.** A face illuminated by candlelight **95.** Christmas shoppers with packages **96.** Gifts under a tree **97.** A large Christmas tree in the center of town **98.** Kids in pajamas **99.** Flowers in a garden **100.** Flowers in a pot **101.** A natural landscape **102.** Parades **103.** Events at a fair **104.** Horse shows **105.** Rodeos **106.** Auto shows **107.** Sidewalk art shows **108.** Musical instruments **109.** A statue or a fountain **110.** Stonework on an old wall **111.** Monuments **112.** Clouds **113.** A photograph for each letter of the alphabet (for example, an apple for the letter "A") **114.** Your home's decor **115.** Your favorite chair **116.** Your favorite food **117.** Cooking and baking **118.** Your favorite restaurants **119.** Your jewelry **120.** Your clothing **121.** Family eyeglasses **122.** Garden tools **123.** Your old shoes **124.** Your car **125.** Things that bother you **126.** Textures **127.** Puddles **128.** Rainstorms **129.** Umbrellas **130.** Mountains **131.** Grass **132.** A street lamp **133.** A pair of skis **134.** An old house **135.** Your house **136.** Your mailbox **137.** Your doorbell **138.** Your knocker **139.** A pile of clutter **140.** You doing your housework **141.** Volunteer work **142.** Where you work **143.** The movie theater **144.** Relatives **145.** Church activities **146.** Grocery shopping **147.** Doing laundry **148.** Painting the deck **149.** Arranging flowers **150.** Walking the dog **151.** Visiting neighbors **152.** A picnic in the living room **153.** A fort made of cushions **154.** A yard sale **155.** Cleaning out the closet **156.** High-school memorabilia **157.** You studying or reading **158.** Your breakfast **159.** Your unmade (or made) bed **160.** Your sleeping kids or husband **161.** A sunrise **162.** Your kitchen **163.** Your bathroom **164.** Your living room **165.** Your bedroom **166.** Your lunch **167.** A favorite treat, such as cupcakes **168.** A snack of cookies and milk **169.** Your car **170.** Your vegetable garden **171.** Your flower garden **172.** A street sign **173.** Your closet **174.** Your outfit **175.** Your feet **176.** Your shoes **177.** Your sports equipment **178.** A gas station with gas prices **179.** Your dinner **180.** Someone cooking dinner **181.** The people in your life—family, coworkers, roommates, friends and more **182.** A local movie theater **183.** Your computer **184.** A self-portrait **185.** Your creative space **186.** Any art or scrapbook projects in process **187.** Your favorite pillow or fabric **188.** Family coats **189.** Your iPod **190.** Running shoes **191.** Birthday parties **192.** Birthday cakes **193.** Birthday decorations **194.** Bridal/baby showers **195.** Housewarming parties **196.** A wedding ceremony **197.** A wedding reception **198.** A wedding cake **199.** Wedding presents **200.** Wedding guests **201.** Family dinners **202.** A barbecue **203.** A day at the amusement park **204.** Animals at the zoo **205.** Children visiting the zoo **206.** A day at the park **207.** An important graduation **208.** Pets **209.** Neighborhood pets (like horses or that yappy dog down the street!) **210.** Outdoor concerts **211.** Farmer's markets **212.** Drive-in movie theaters **213.** Your gym **214.** Your local bakery **215.** Your neighbors **216.** Your cell phone **217.** A favorite magazine **218.** A favorite book **219.** A favorite movie **220.** A favorite CD **221.** Your jewelry box **222.** Your child's favorite toy **223.** Your favorite place to shop **224.** Swimming pools **225.** Swimming at the lake or on the beach **226.** A camping trip **227.** The autumn leaves in the canyon **228.** Someone running under a waterfall **229.** Hiking **230.** Boating **231.** Waterskiing **232.** Snow skiing **233.** Cross-country skiing **234.** Snow-shoeing **235.** Sledding **236.** Building snowmen **237.** Making snow angels **238.** Throwing snowballs **239.** Drinking hot chocolate **240.** Decorating cookies

241. Making valentines **242.** Trick-or-treating **243.** Christmas carolers **244.** A pile of opened presents and ripped wrapping paper on Christmas **245.** Carving pumpkins **246.** Dying Easter eggs **247.** An Easter egg hunt **248.** An Easter basket with candy **249.** Dance parties **250.** A child's recital or performance **251.** A family or friends playing games **252.** Bonfires **253.** Gardening **254.** Holiday parties **255.** A family reunion **256.** A road trip **257.** Your parent's childhood home **258.** Your childhood home **259.** A school reunion **260.** A newborn baby **261.** A remodeled room **262.** An unfinished (or finished) crossword puzzle **263.** Your mother on Mother's Day **264.** Your father on Father's Day **265.** Party decorations before a party **266.** A party invitation **267.** A thank-you note you received **268.** A Thanksgiving turkey **269.** A pumpkin pie **270.** Everyone working in the kitchen on Thanksgiving **271.** A pile of dirty dishes after Thanksgiving dinner **272.** A Christmas Eve program **273.** Christmas stockings hung at the fireplace **274.** A New Year's Eve party **275.** A snowman **276.** Christmas cards you received **277.** Valentines you received **278.** A visit to an assisted-living home **279.** A visit to a museum **280.** A visit to an art gallery **281.** Spring blossoms on the trees **282.** You exercising **283.** The first snowfall **284.** What you see on an evening stroll **285.** Your child's school **286.** Your child's teacher **287.** Your child's best friend **288.** Your child learning to walk **289.** Your child learning to ride a bike **290.** A favorite Christmas decoration **291.** Christmas in stores *already* in *September*! **292.** A house decoration that's important or you just finished **293.** Sunday dinner rituals **294.** A dessert **295.** Your homemade bread **296.** Something that strikes you as important that day **297.** A quote by someone and this person's picture **298.** What you do that relaxes you **299.** A book your child is reading **300.** Your husband's profession **301.** What makes you happy **302.** A date with your husband **303.** A bucket of paint you plan to use on a room **304.** Your children in a sandbox **305.** Your children swinging on a swing **306.** Cookies straight out of the oven **307.** Interesting architecture you see **308.** Someone jumping in the air **309.** An umbrella in a rainstorm **310.** A train station **311.** People at an airport **312.** Luggage you're taking on a trip **313.** Athletes at a sporting event **314.** Spectators at a sporting event **315.** A bandstand in a park **316.** Christmas lights on a house **317.** Your child getting on a school bus **318.** Headlines on a daily newspaper **319.** A bird's nest with eggs **320.** Newly hatched birds in a nest **321.** A baby's crib **322.** A birthday present **323.** A bowl of soup on a cold day **324.** Your everyday dishes **325.** Your fine china **326.** A trip to the library **327.** A leafless tree in the winter **328.** You child's favorite outfit **329.** A cemetery on Memorial Day **330.** The view out your bedroom window **331.** Your favorite cereal **332.** Your child walking to school or catching the bus **333.** Your favorite spot to relax **334.** A local pumpkin patch **335.** A local Christmas tree farm **336.** Piles of laundry **337.** The inside of your refrigerator **338.** Your bookshelves **339.** Puddles **340.** Fog **341.** A family heirloom **342.** The place where your parents were married **343.** The place where you were married **344.** Your child's first date **345.** A recognition or award ceremony for someone in your family **346.** A new pair of shoes **347.** Where you went to school **348.** Where you went to college **349.** A weight-loss progress chart **350.** Your clothes before and after weight loss **351.** Your diet food **352.** Your favorite Halloween costume of all time **353.** Your favorite band **354.** Your favorite ice cream **355.** Your favorite recipe **356.** Your favorite piece of furniture **357.** Your favorite website **358.** People you meet **359.** Your alarm clock **360.** A full moon **361.** A new moon **362.** Your "bucket list" **363.** Your favorite vacation destination **364.** Your hair-care products **365.** Items in your favorite color

4 bonus techniques

BY LORI FAIRBANKS

FASHION TEXT-PATTERNED PAPER FLOWERS

❶ Punch a large circle from text patterned paper, newspaper or an old book. Cut triangle-shaped wedges from it to create a flower shape. *Note:* Spray old papers or newspaper with a deacidifacation spray.

❷ Punch a small circle from a dot-, stripe-, or floral-patterned paper.

❸ Layer the punched pieces, and place a button on top. Stitch all three elements together.

MAKE A PEEK-A-BOO CORNER

Show off the "B" side of your double-sided patterned paper.

❶ Fold over a corner and attach it to your page using stitches, brads, or eyelets.

❷ Adhere a scrap of patterned paper behind the folded corner to square up your layout.

❸ Attach a charm or accent to the new page corner.

STITCH A PRETTY BORDER

Next time you stitch on a page, try one of the fancy stitches on your sewing machine, like this pretty scallop. *Tip:* Pair a fancy stitch with a simple straight stitch to create a lovely border on your layout.

CREATE CANDY-WRAPPED ACCENTS

Wrap circle-shaped accents in cellophane to create cute embellishments that look like candy.

❶ Stamp and emboss a swirl shape on a white cardstock circle.

❷ Layer it on circles cut from two shades of pink cardstock.

❸ Wrap the accent with a small piece of cellophane, and adhere it to your layout. **ck**